Simon Portwain is your average guy; he was born wi[illegible]etic privileges than the average person. His upbringing in a workin[illegible]gave him the thirst to achieve more and make something of himself. In par[illegible]r, to provide his children with everything that he desired as a child but didn't have.

From a young age, Simon focused on knowledge. He wanted to learn from the great minds of the past and present and what better way than through the vast selection of books and audiobooks. He studied everything he could; business acumen, finance, management, psychology, time management, sales, motivation. His view was that if he could read, understand and apply everything he learnt then he would be far more experienced than his peers who may have decades more experience in the workplace than him.

And it paid off. After years of study and application, Simon found himself excelling in sales, his choice of profession. His thirst for knowledge wasn't the only reason for this though. Simon was very inquisitive from a young age, and over time developed great skills in pattern recognition. Moreover, he was incredibly analytical in his approach, hence in his formal education he studied mathematics in his degree.

It was early on in his sales career that he started to use pattern recognition and analytical thinking to his advantage. He started to look for commonalities in his own work and processes and that of his peers. He took note of things that worked and those that didn't. He assessed what the pitfalls were of most and ways to get around them and over time he created a formula for success.

He applied this formula to his own practices and it worked emphatically. So he started to coach more and more people, and again it worked time after time. It was then that Simon formally wrote down these disciplines to put together, those which you hold in your hands today.

For my granddad.

Simon Portwain

Sales Icon – Selling in the Shadows

Austin Macauley Publishers™
London • Cambridge • New York • Sharjah

A CIP catalogue record for this title is available from the British Library.

ISBN 9781528918923 (Paperback)
ISBN 9781528918930 (Hardback)
ISBN 9781528962506 (ePub e-book)

www.austinmacauley.com

First Published (2020)
Austin Macauley Publishers Ltd
25 Canada Square
Canary Wharf
London
E14 5LQ

I am a firm believer that I have been shaped by the protagonists in my life; if it were not for them, I wouldn't be half the man that I am, and I owe so much to so many.

First and foremost to my wife, Georgia, the biggest inspiration I have. She is the reason I wake and strive for more every day, for her, for our family and for the future that we aspire for. Without her, I would be a mere shadow of what I am.

To my mother, who taught me a level of emotional intelligence that has shaped my life and career. Her kind nature and positivity has rubbed off immeasurably so.

To my father, who has always challenged me academically and will also remain the smartest man I will ever meet. I thank him dearly for the thirst for knowledge he has instilled in me from such a young age.

To Paul Janes, a man who I admire and hold in the highest regard. His success and business acumen has inspired me since the moment I met him, and I hope one day to have a fragment of the success that he has, and would be proud to be even half of the father he has been to his children.

To Vicky Janes, one of the kindest women I have ever encountered. Her love and support will never go unnoticed; without her, our family would not have the strength that it does.

To John Harley, a man who has challenged and mentored me from the very beginning. A truly inspirational man who I will forever respect dearly.

To Paul Healey, a man who taught me a great deal about the power and the joy of teaching and coaching others. He influenced my future and without his guidance I'm certain I would not be where I am today.

To all those who rejected me in my life. Without them, I would not have been so motivated to make something of myself and prove them all wrong.

Finally, to everyone who has bought and read my book, I am ever grateful and hope that it helps you to change your life and live your dreams.

Table of Contents

Introduction

In this book I will demonstrate to you how to become a sales icon. We all know of sales icons in our business or in our industry; they are those salespeople that make everything look effortless. They're the salesperson who we all idolise, who everyone looks up to; they have the level of success we all aspire for and they reap the commissions we all envy. This is what this book will give you; it will take hard work, application and a step change in your approach, but remain true to the cause and soon you'll be regarded as a sales icon.

I've been the beneficiary of many a sales book in my time and from reading hundreds of books on the topic, I was left troubled as to how to become the best salesperson I can be. The problem I found with most sales books is that many of them focus on intangible characteristic improvements. Things like you need to be more enthusiastic or become a good listener or be persistent. Whilst these are all desirable traits, I was always left with uncertainty around how I can improve, what are the logical steps I can take to be a better salesperson. This is where the book comes in. Instead of brash statements about characteristics you need to have or improve, I focus on a clear structure of disciplines you can follow in your journey to becoming a sales icon.

Some people would call these attributes, others would call them processes; I prefer the term disciplines, as it takes great discipline to become a true sales icon. If you want to stand out from the crowd in sales, become wealthier than you can imagine and the number-one salesperson in not only your company but in your industry then this is the book for you.

"Success is processional. It's the result of a series of small disciplines that lead us into habitual patterns of success that no longer require consistent will or effort" – Tony Robbins.[1]

This book is all about small disciplines; adopt them and apply them correctly and you'll meet your full potential in sales. Irrespective of where you are in your career, the book will be of value; if you're new to sales then apply everything. If you're experienced in sales then maybe take the bits you like and apply them to your processes that you already follow. Solely reading the book is simply not enough though, application is everything; learning without application is wasted time. So apply what you learn, use the calls to action from activities and you'll get the most out of both the book but more importantly your lucrative career in sales.

So before I go any further, I should explain to you the title of the book and why it's different from that of any other sales book on the market. Well, it's known as selling in the shadows as that's where success is made. It's not in the moments of jubilation when you receive a purchase order; it's not in the moments of sheer excitement from the fun parts of sales. Success is made in the shadows. Just look at any success out there, all you're seeing is their successful state.

"It took years to be an overnight success!" – various people

Take Walmart for example, people see how this is now one of the largest corporations in the world. What they don't see is how long it took to build and how Sam Walton initially had to plead with bank after bank until one finally believed in him. How about Airbnb, it took them seven years to get to their evaluation of $10 billion. What you don't see is how initially they rented out their own air mattress in their apartment to pay their rent. You don't see the other business they had to develop selling Obama O's breakfast cereal simple to raise capital for the Airbnb business. You don't see the months of rejection and making only $200 a week, the hours sifting through red tape to simply get the business off the ground. The point I make is that when we see success we don't necessarily see what's behind that success. All the success you will ever see was made in the shadows.

How do I define selling in the shadows? Well it's those countless hours of graft, the optimistic attitude that doesn't waver, it's the laborious planning and strategising, the ability to pick ourselves up no matter how hard we fall. It's the willingness to improve ourselves, to strive for more both in ourselves and in our peers. It's the aptitude to not accept a failure as final, to hold ourselves in higher regard but most of all it's the burning desire to be the best that we can be.

Do I believe that this is the one and only sales book you'll ever need to read? Absolutely not! But if you can apply these disciplines to your approach in conjunction with some other techniques and practices discussed in some of the other great sales books then you'll be a force to be reckoned with. There are such a vast number of sales books on the market, some good and some bad. For me I have always been a firm believer that the best salespeople are chameleons, not in that they can change colour, in that they adapt to any environment. So if a chameleon salesperson meets with a pragmatic prospect they adapt, if they meet someone who is abrupt, they adapt; if they talk to someone who is personable, they adapt. They understand that no one approach will work and they flex their approach to the person or circumstance.

I'm also a believer that the best salespeople have much in common to a fine recipe. If you were to put together a mixture of poor ingredients, it would be quite rare that the result would be a fine-tasting dish. However, if you were to put together some of the finest ingredients into a recipe, then it has success written all over it. To put this in layman's terms, I believe that the best salespeople are merely small fragments of other good salespeople all comprised into one; we steal the parts that are working well for others, attach our own style and the process continues until we have the finished article. This is the art to becoming a sales icon, and my hope is that this book will provide you with some disciplines to follow, to add your approach to and add to other successful techniques.

So first let me briefly tell you about my story to add some credibility to what is to follow. From a young age I was always passionate about selling. I had a thirst for knowledge and devoted much of my time to studying theories and success stories. I read a range of subjects from business to sales, to leadership to motivation. This investment in learning enabled me to craft the disciplines which I detail in this book and have led to substantial success for both myself and the students who I have trained. The disciplines enabled me to become the number-one salesman in many organisations. Notably in one blue chip company my success led me to multiple promotions whereby I was managing a sales team who were all older and much more experienced than I (one of the members of my team was thirty years my elder who had spent his whole career in sales) and this was when I was only twenty-three years old. I've broken sales records, signed multi-million-pound deals and earned large commissions. This story could also be yours in the very near future if you but follow the disciplines. You hold the power in your hands right now, the question is whether you are willing to take the leap and become a sales icon!

Discipline 1 – Time

Time is one of the only assets in life where everyone is on a level playing field; come richer come poorer we all have the same finite amount of time and it's how we utilise that time which determines who will be successful or not.

"Time waste is in some ways worse than material waste because there can be no salvage" – Henry Ford.[2]

You should think about discipline one – time with everything that you do within your working activities. It will feature in many ways as we move forward in this book.

In this chapter time will be the underlying thought. We will begin the chapter by reviewing our time association. We will uncover how a person's time represents a value, and that value differs depending on the person in question. For some people one hour of their time equates to more value than another person's total value in a year. We'll uncover why and what that means.

We will then discuss how to use your time as effectively as possible by splitting your activities into two categories, high pay off and low pay off. With this, we will discover how we can maximise our working day and receive the highest return on investment for the time that we put in.

We'll then dive into some great techniques for saving time and improving our efficiencies. Such topics include a note-taking technique, ways to boost our meeting count, planning our drop-in calls and our route planning.

One of the real gems of this book features in this chapter and that is the flagging system. Without giving away too much it's a discipline that will ensure you never forget any follow-up actions with a prospect or customer ever again; it's simple yet profoundly effective.

We finish the chapter by identifying which hours of the day are best suited for certain activities if you want to become a sales icon. We'll digress how to best take advantage of your golden hours, those which are prime selling time. Then in closing, we'll talk about mastering our minutes, in planning our days to the finest detail to ensure that we finish every single day saying that it's been successful and we've accomplished a great deal.

So join me on the start of our journey to becoming a sales icon, to mastering our minutes and using our time as effectively as we can.

1.1 – Time Association – High Pay Off

If you were to collate the riches of the eight wealthiest people in the world, that wealth would be more than that of 3.6 billion people. This rich list includes the likes of Bill Gates and Mark Zuckerberg who have wealth totalling $426 Billion. For most, this type of wealth is unimaginable. Now with those such individuals and any top performing individual, time is precious. I can bet you that Bill Gates doesn't mow the lawn in his garden, he doesn't empty the bins in his office and most probably he doesn't even cook himself dinner anymore. Why I hear you ask? Well the reason is that his time is precious; why would he spend part of his day doing tasks that take up valuable time when he can pay someone else to do it whilst he focuses on other more important tasks such as making himself more money?

The point here is that time has a value and it differs for every person. This isn't solely for the super-rich either, take for instance households in the bracket of the top 5% earnings. They will bring home an annual salary of $214,000 plus, a bracket any sales icon aspires to get to. Again, people in this bracket like the super-rich will associate a value to their time; many tasks they will delegate off to someone else as their time isn't worth wasting on such tasks. For instance, they'll have window cleaners, housecleaners, dog walkers, baby sitters and the list goes on and on, the reason is that their time is better spent elsewhere.

The point is that there is a value associated to everyone's time; for some people it will be more and for others it will be less.

Let's take a deeper dive into this by looking at salaries for professions. In the first instance let us look at the salary of a cleaner, which is often a low paid profession. The reason for this is because it requires no expert skill, and there are almost no barriers to entry to becoming a cleaner. Pretty much anyone could become a cleaner tomorrow if they wanted to be, there are no qualifications or certifications needed, just simply the right work rate and some cleaning equipment. Now don't get me wrong, cleaners do a good job and it's as credible a job as any. But the fact remains that it's low paid because there are surplus supply of cleaners as you don't require specialist knowledge for this profession.

Juxtapose this to a doctor. Here's a professional that requires a high level of intellect. Schooling alone to qualify as a doctor can surpass seven years at university, and you must be in the top percentile to even get into the universities to study as a doctor. As a result they have a large amount of specialist knowledge. Moreover, the quantity of doctors is less than other professions as you need to be of a highly educated calibre and put in the years of study to become qualified.

Now let's compare the salary of cleaners with doctors:

Cleaners wages = £16k per annum
Doctors wage = £60k per annum

Let's break this down further, to find out what the hourly rate of pay would be:

Weekly pay (52 weeks per year)
Cleaner's weekly pay = £308
Doctor's weekly pay = £1,154

Hourly pay (assume a 40-hour workweek for simplicity)
Cleaner's hourly pay = £7.70
Doctor's hourly pay = £28.85

So what should you read from this? Well what you should notice is that some people's time is worth more than others, the reason being that their skills are more valuable and therefore return a higher yield, in this case, higher pay. In this example we've compared cleaners and doctors, with doctors being a high-paid profession because of its difficulty, high-level expertise required, high demand and low supply as well as specialist knowledge and training/qualifications necessary. Taking this into account, it's no wonder that a doctor earns almost four times more than a cleaner.

So the vital point here is that some people's time is more valuable than others, and the same applies to you!

You're a salesperson, you're a specialist. You do a job that not everyone can do, and because of that your level of reward is higher, either through basic pay or commission. This is the key, the principle of time association, where we need to gauge what your time is worth and what tasks merit your valuable time.

Before I go any further and without getting too theoretical, to explain this point I want to first focus on something known as equity theory. Equity theory is a concept developed by J. Stacy Adams who was a workplace and behavioural psychologist. It's a theory that came to light in the 1960s and is based around the motivational drivers of an employee. It addressed the concept of an individual's search for an equilibrium or balance between their efforts and outcomes. So in layman's terms, if a person at work feels that their pay, commission, praise or even holiday allowance isn't in proportion to all the work that they put in then their equitable compensation isn't sufficient. In such circumstance that a person feels there is an imbalance, the result will be that they change their behaviour to bring this into balance.[3]

Equity theory might be something that applies to you in your role currently or you've seen with a peer. If you've ever had the thought process of something like "they don't pay me enough to do that" or "why haven't they noticed all the work I've put in for this" then you have been a witness to equity theory at play.

So how does this apply to you in your role? Well what we're trying to avoid is what Adams called a negative tension state. This is where an individual feels that there is a negative imbalance so they reduce their input accordingly.

This is exactly what we don't want to happen. My wish would be that every business out there would address their equity theory to ensure that there is never a negative imbalance for its staff. In such a utopia, staff would always be striving to achieve more to reach a state of equity equilibrium and the business would reap substantial rewards for having such a stance. In reality, I can't make this happen. I can't control every business out there. The only thing I can do is influence you, then you're in control of such balance.

So what I would propose is counteracting any negative tension state. You need to be in control, you need to hold yourself in higher regard. If you don't feel that you're rewarded for everything you do then force your business to offer you the rewards you seek. Am I saying threaten your business, say you'll leave if you don't get X, hold them at gunpoint? Of course I am not.

What I am saying, is to change your ways of working to ensure that there is such a positive imbalance in your input that the business has no other choice than to reward you with that which you deserve. They simply must reward you, as you've become too valuable to overlook. So this begs the question, how can we do this? How do we ensure that we have a positive imbalance? How do we make sure that we're producing more?

Well, my recommendation for sales icons is to focus on high-pay-off activities.

On this topic we need to first determine how you differentiate where to spend your precious time and where not to. Well, this question can be answered quite simply by splitting your daily activities into two parts, those being:

High pay off
Low pay off

High pay off – these are the tasks that return a high yield for their activity. Such actions would include interactions with customers such as meetings and phone calls etc.

Low pay off – these are the tasks that return a low yield for their activity. Such actions would include admin tasks like arranging deliveries, returns or processing orders.

In an ideal world, you'd want all of your activities to be high-pay-off activities, the more of these you conduct the more pay off you'll see. Though in reality this is a hard task to achieve, nonetheless you should aspire to the goal that the majority of your activities are high pay off.

How do we achieve this?

Achieving this isn't easy; what you need to start with is looking at all of your day-to-day activities and categorising them into high-pay-off or low-pay-off activities. Then address how much time you spend on such activities, here's an example.

In this example I will use a real-life story from my past. I used to work for an IT provider, and their business model was that sales staff look after all of their processes. That being marketing, lead generation, selling, buying, returns, invoicing, basically the lot. Now being slightly naïve in my career at this time and ever the optimist I looked at this in a positive light. I thought it was a brilliant approach as the buck stops with me, I am the sole contact for everything my customer needs. I influence everything and I won't have any customer of mine dissatisfied from the service level of my peers as only I'm to blame.

Now whilst this is well and true, I found that I became overstretched and limited as to what sales I could achieve; the reason lied with time association. I'd got to a point where I was so busy, working harder and harder to try and achieve more and be the best, yet I'd hit a plateau in my sales. So in this slightly frustrated state, I decided to take a step back and analyse my activities; what I discovered was staggering. My findings were as follows:

For every customer sale I made each week, I was spending:

- 0.5 hours roughly on administration tasks such as buying, arranging delivery, invoicing, returns etc.

  For account management of current customers I was spending:
- 0.5 hours roughly a week per customer.

  For new business development I was spending:
- 5 hours a week on tasks such as developing marketing campaigns, emailing them out as well as other lead generation tasks.
- 15 hours a week cold calling.

  For selling activities I was spending:
- 10 hours a week on tasks such as new business and account meetings.

  For travelling to customers and prospects I was spending:
- 5 hours per week.

When you consider that I had twenty main accounts that would spend with me, it accounted to a 55-hour workweek!

And this was without considering other aspects like travel to the office, grabbing a bite to eat for lunch etc. Truth be told, I found that I was on a downward spiral, as the only way to become more successful was to work more and more hours and run myself into the ground. I was in a difficult position. I was ambitious therefore I wanted to achieve these greater sales, but I knew that for every customer I brought on board, the more the time taken up by other activities which didn't aid me in selling more, those being low pay off activities.

The solution? Well, this is when I analysed my activities in greater depth and categorised them into high or low pay off activities. I did this by asking myself the question, 'what activities are essential to selling more, and what activities could easily be delegated to someone else?' In asking this question I was also keen to bear in mind whether specialist knowledge (that I possess) was needed, or whether more or less anyone could undertake the activity.

My findings were astounding to me. Out of my working day, I classed only 30 hours as high-pay-off activities. That meant that 54% of my time was spent on high-pay-off activities, which was well below where it needed to be in order to meet my aspirations.

I categorised the time association per week as follows:

High-pay-off activities

- 10 hours on account management activities
- 5 hours cold calling (note – a third of time spent cold calling)
- 10 hours on selling activities
- 5 hours travelling

Low-pay-off activities

- 10 hours administration activities
- 5 hours new business development activities
- 10 hours cold calling

What I deduced was that 25 hours of my week could easily be delegated to someone else, somebody who doesn't have the specialist knowledge that I have but could carry out those activities just the same.

This is where it hit me and it all made sense. To fulfil my aspirations and make more sales, I need to increase the percentage of my time spent on high-pay-off activities. Then on a personal level my feeling of being successful would be heightened.

But looking at this from a broader angle, such as from a business perspective, this time association principle makes sense too. To prove this let's carry out our analysis once again on salaries. However, let's look closer to home. In this we'll compare a salesperson's salary to somebody who works in admin. Let's for instance say that the salaries are as follows:

Salesperson salary – £25k per annum = £12 per hour

Admin salary – £16k per annum = £7.70 per hour

Relating this to my example of my activities in my 55-hour workweek, I found that it costs the business £300 per week for a salesperson to carry out the low pay off activities, in total amounting to £15,600 per annum. Whereas, it would cost the business £192.50 per week for an admin person to carry out the low pay off activities, in total amounting to £10,010 per annum. So taking salary as a single entity, by effectively using the time association principle the business would save £5,590 per annum, but this truly is only the tip of the iceberg.

1.2 – Return on Investment

This principle of time association becomes profound when you look at return on investment. Salespeople aren't cheap, and the reason they're not cheap is that they're valuable. For every pound spent on a salesperson in salary or commission, the business will reap a return of X amount back. That's unlike any other role in the business, whilst everyone is of value whether it be admin, IT, accounts staff etc., there is no other role in the business that reaps a return on investment other than sales.

So let's revisit my previous example, and for simplicity let us say that for my 55-hour workweek I was achieving £200k gross profit per annum. We already discovered that only 54% of my time is spent on high pay off activities, therefore 54%=£200k gross profit. If I utilised 100 per cent of my time on high pay off activities that would mean my return on investment would be:

£200k / 54 = £3,703.70
1% = £3,703.70
£3,703.70 X 100 = £370,370
100% = £370,370

As I said, this is the profound part. In this simple example, I have identified that just by changing your time association you can reap substantial rewards. In my example, I could do the same amount of work in terms of hours but add an additional £170,370 gross profit to my return on investment. Commission wise if you were earning 10% of gross profit, that's the difference between taking home £20k commission and £37k commission for no additional work other than associating your time to produce the highest pay off.

Now a word of advice. If you're a business owner then try to set up your sales process in such a way as to focus on high-pay-off activities and delegate the low pay off activities to other staff who are just as able. If you're an employee and the business you work for doesn't have a business model to permit this then don't fail to act as nothing will change. Instead put together this time association plan and present this to your superiors, show them how by making such a change not only will they save more money but will incur a higher return on investment. Show them how it's a win-win for all parties. If that fails then give them my book; that may help them to help you. If all this fails then get out of that business and find one that enables you to focus on high pay off activities, otherwise your success and earning potential will always be limited.

Activity

Take some time now to work out your own time association. Look at your regular activities each day and split them into high-pay-off and low-pay-off activities. Remember if you're struggling then ask yourself the questions which I did:

- What activities are essential to selling more, and what activities could easily be delegated to someone else?
- What activities require specialist knowledge (that I possess) and therefore cannot be delegated?

From this, you should have a list of high-pay-off activities and low pay off activities.

Now deduce how much time you spend each week on these activities. This task sounds more difficult than it is, but really you just need to be disciplined. Start this at the beginning of the week, and for every task you do, note down roughly how long it took you. For example, if you start the day by spending an hour replying to emails then denote that as replying the emails – 1 hour – low pay off

Do this for all your tasks for the day, and then for that week and you'll probably notice some patterns occurring. For instance, that one hour replying to emails may occur every day, meaning that five hours a week are spent replying to emails. Remember to try and take your average week, if you take a week which is extraordinary, such as a week when you have three times as many meetings as a normal week then your findings will be misleading.

Now with your high and low pay off activities listed in hours, you then need to total all the hours for that week, this is to discover your average working hours per week. From this we will be able to deduce what's your time association split. For clarity it's useful to work this out as a percentage, to find the percentage of your time that you spend on high pay off activities just divide the number of hours spent on high pay off activities by the total number of hours per week.

Now you'll have your time association percentage. Now for fun, let's compare your current performance with what it would be if you completely adopted the time association principle. We do this as before by looking at your current return on investment and what it could be through adopting the principle.

So take your time association percentage, i.e. the percentage of time that you currently spend on high pay off activities. This percentage is equal to your current total sales, for example if your total sales for the year were £500k, and your time association percentage was 65%, then this would equate to:

65% = £500k

Now work out what 1% would equal to, this can be accomplished by dividing your total sales by your time association percentage. For this example it is equal to:

1%= £500k/65
1% = £7,692.30

Then multiple this 1% by 100, this will work out what 100% is:

100% = £7,692.30 X 100
100% = £769,230

This 100% is based on staying exactly the same as you did now in terms of work rate but making the change of delegating your low pay off activities. This is so that you could focus 100% of your time on high pay off activities. Therefore this 100% figure outlines what sales you could achieve with the time that's been opened up to you just by adopting this principle.

So great job if you've undertaken this activity as now you can see what your time association is and how you can maximise your working day. But just noting down your time association isn't enough, we need to act upon it, and to truly maximise our working day we need to ask ourselves a few questions.

What can I cut? – look at your analysis again and ask yourself this question. Is there any activity that I don't need to do, can I delegate it to someone else to deal with or could I scrap the task completely? Is there a process I'm following that's not aiding me? Am I simply going through the motions because that's what I have always done?

I can remember attending a talk once. I forget who the speaker was but one of the messages really hit home with me. The focal point of his speech was all about Kaizen also known as continuous improvement, in particular he was focusing on cutting down on processes that we use. He used a great analogy which I'll share with you now.

The story went like this, a lady was sharing her famous recipe with her daughter for cooking a joint of meat. This such recipe had been passed down the family from the daughter's great grandmother. The lady went into streams of detail as to how the recipe should be followed and prepared, how the meat should be rested, marinated in certain herbs, and how additional ingredients be added only at certain times. It all made sense up until the final point before putting the meat into the oven, as the step before this stage was to cut the two ends off.

The young daughter found this bemusing; she asked her mother why this is so. She replied by saying "It's what we've always done, I think that this helps it cook faster." Still bemused the young daughter didn't accept this as gospel, so she asked her grandmother, the grandmother again gave the same answer as her mother. Still not satisfied the daughter went to the source and asked her great grandmother why the recipe asked for the meats ends to be cut off before cooking? The daughter explained to the great grandmother what her mother and grandmother had answered with and questioned as to whether this was so?

The great grandmother laughed in amusement. With smile she turned to her great granddaughter and explained, "When we were young we only had a small oven, we had to cut the two ends off just to fit it in!"

Now this sounds like a silly story, it's probably not even true but the point of it is excellent. The point being is that just because you've always done something a certain way doesn't mean that it's correct. It's this principle of being ruthless with your processes that will help you to cut out those activities that add no value.

Where can I save time? – This is another great question to ask yourself once you have reviewed your analysis of time association. You may find that all the processes you follow are integral therefore you can't scrap them, but you could refine them so that they don't take up so much time. A clear sign that your processes are too time consuming will come from your time association analysis. If you see that in one area, for example administration, is taking up a large part of your time, then ask yourself why? How could I cut this down and repurpose some of that time towards sales activities?

I've seen countless examples of sales icons cutting down processes to repurpose time for more valuable tasks. For instance, with one consultancy firm I worked with I found that one of their processes was that they had a regular Monday morning sales meeting whereby all the sales team must attend. Quite standard for a sales team to do this so no problem there. The qualm I had with the process is that they had ten salespeople in the room and the sales director insisted that they went around the room and review every single salespersons past week of meetings. He wanted to know exactly what happened in every meeting, the outcome and follow up, and then he wanted to know the whereabouts of them all in the up and coming week, and the plan.

He did this for every single salesperson. Now, not only was this type of micromanagement disastrous for the sales team's morale, it was even worse for their productivity. On average, a sales meeting would last three hours, on one occasion I was told that it lasted five. It had got so bad that staff were booking Monday mornings off just so that they could avoid the meetings.

The solution was pretty simple. I explained to the sales director this sales icon discipline around time. I made it clear how he was wasting around thirty hours of sales time on a weekly basis (ten salespeople multiplied by three hours). This amounted to 1,440 hours a year for a forty-eight-week year, enough time to add some substantial figures to their bottom line. The solution I came up with was a clear agenda for the meetings, it would have a maximum time limit of one hour. Each salesperson would give a highlight overview of their success in the last week and give an overview of upcoming meetings that were planned if they were notable. A maximum time limit of six minutes per salesperson was put in place so that the sales director could get his visibility but also to cut down on the time spent in the meetings. The result? Well they saved 960 hours a year which was repurposed into selling time.

So where can you save time? Review your time association and see where time can be saved, then repurpose this time for high pay off activities.

1.3 – Note Taking

The award for the most boring part of any salesperson's role goes to…note taking! Hey, let's be honest, it's a boring subject, and we all hate doing admin. It's bad enough taking notes down in a meeting, then when we carry out our follow-up actions we must type the notes up in our CRM system. Who can be bothered with that?

Well let me tell you who, sales icons. It might be dull and laborious but note taking is an important part of any salesperson's role. You're a professional and you should act in that manner. What if other professions were blasé with note taking, take the medical profession for instance. Imagine a doctor prescribing you medicine that you have an allergy to because they didn't take down any notes in your previous consultations. Or imagine an architect planning a bungalow for you when you clearly outlined that you wanted a detached three-bedroom house, all because they didn't take any notes. We as salespeople are qualified professionals and note taking is a big part of our role which we must conduct to maintain our professionalism.

So whether it is in a meeting or over the phone, we need to listen to what a prospect or customer tells us and record that information in as much depth as possible. This vital information may be for imminent use or for use later down the line; nevertheless; it will all be useful at some point.

The trouble with note taking for most people is that it's often cumbersome, and commonly we as salespeople see it as extra effort which isn't needed. I often hear salespeople say, "I'm not good at admin, I just want to sell. What's the point in note taking?" If I've heard it once from a salesperson, I've heard it a thousand times. The truth is though that they're often the average to poor performers that say this, never the sales icons.

So why is note taking important?

I always explain this to salespeople in an example of treasure divers. Picture yourself now as a treasure diver, you're on a boat way out at sea, you're wearing copious amounts of kit from a wetsuit and a mask to an air tank. Your friend has just dived down to the wreck below where it's rumoured that in the sunken vessel lie riches beyond your imagination. Your friend has just finished his dive, he's spent 45 minutes down at the wreck, using almost the last breath of air left in his tank before he surfaced. Now it's your turn, all that lies between you and the treasure is 150 metres of Cold Ocean; then the search begins. Excitement flows abundantly through your body as you leap off the boat, ready to find the treasure that you've been longing to discover.

You hit the water, you descend further and further until you hit the ocean bottom at one hundred and fifty meters. The water is dark and murky, you frantically look around the ocean bed where visibility is poor, you can't see the wreck in sight. You use your intuition and head in the direction you deem to be correct, into the current. Minute after minute passes, you look at your tank gauge and you see that half of your air has gone already, you struggle on and finally find the wreck. In a state of frustration and despair, you realise that you only have sufficient air left in your tank for ten minutes exploration. The dive ends with disappointment, your exploration time was so minimal that you hardly got a chance to look for the treasure – a failed trip.

Now this would never happen to an experienced treasure diver. The reason is that when a treasure diver takes a dive down to a wreck their first step is to always set a downline. This downline is a rope that goes from the vessel to the wreck, usually put at the point of the previous exploration. The purpose of this downline is to save the diver's time when they leave the wreck and go back down for later dives. With this they'll know exactly where they were when they last dived and where to start from on this dive saving them copious amounts of time.

Now the thing with wreck diving is that often you'll be diving at excessive depths, therefore stress levels are high. In addition, there are stringent deadlines you must keep to, as depending on the depth there is only a certain length of time which you can search a wreck before you must make your ascent back to the ship for safety reasons. Vaguely speaking, all of this sounds not too distant from sales when you look at it like this: stressful work with deadlines to meet, a pot of gold at the end if you get it right. That definitely sounds familiar, right?

But honestly this is the perfect analogy for note taking. The downline we mentioned is imperative to an effective dive, often divers will be diving in dark murky waters where it's all too easy to lose your bearings or forget where you left off from your last dive. This is where the downline saves you time, it's your marker to start searching once again.

Now you need to get your mind-set to work in the same way with sales, in that note taking is your downline, it's your marker, the point where you left off. If you fail to take notes you'll be the wandering diver that constantly keeps covering their own footsteps and never exploring new territory to find the gold.

Layout

The layout of your note taking is key; this section of the book is entirely based on time, so it seems rather peculiar to be looking at the topic of note taking. Now I can understand that some of you may think that note taking kind of conflicts with this concept of time, but it's a necessity. Without note taking we have no background, no history and no knowledge, and thus very little chance of becoming a sales icon.

When we partake in note taking we must be conscious of time as ideally we want to keep tasks of this nature down to a minimum so that we can be out selling more. The important thing to remember with note taking is that the layout is king.

Now when you speak to a customer or prospect it's imperative to take notes on what they're saying. How you do this is down to you, some people paraphrase, some dictate everything, for this use whatever works best for you. What is really important, however, is how you write up these notes later into your CRM system, in particular around the layout which you use.

To illustrate the importance of layout, let me take the time to prove this to you in a real-life example. This works with any industry, but especially those industries that are quite complex with many different conversational areas. For this instance I will use the example of an IT provider as this field can be rather complicated at times with many different discussion points in one meeting.

So below are the notes that the salesperson has had with an IT manager (don't worry you don't need to understand the IT parts the point will become clear later). I have written this in two layouts, option 1 and option 2, the information in them both is exactly the same. But I'll let you be the judge of what is a more efficient layout.

Option 1

"Meeting – 27/07/16

I met today with Anthony Johnson, he's the IT manager for BKJ. We chatted for about an hour, he's a nice guy. Their business seems to be doing really well as he mentioned that they will be expanding their team by adding twenty new members of staff in the next year. When it came to the subject of business goals and strategy he said to me that the drive is to enable employees to work inside and outside of the office which I think is a good plan. They're thinking about changing their server infrastructure in the future, potentially looking at virtualisation; he's not sure what platform yet, though. He thinks that they want to make the change before Christmas this year. They have a moderate-sized server estate at the moment, they've got 10 physical dell servers, which are 7 years old, running an old operating system namely server 2008."

Option 2

"Meeting – 27/07/16

Attendees Anthony Johnson – IT manager

Info on BKJ Team expansion
Employing 20 more staff this year

Business goals Mobility
Want to incorporate mobile working for staff

Plans for development
Infrastructure refresh
Potentially virtualisation – unsure which platform
Timescale = before December 2016

Infrastructure
Physical servers
No = 10
Vendor = Dell
Age = 7 years
Operating system = server 2008

Now this is just a small snapshot of information; the average meeting would have a lot more information but this short extract is simply to prove a point. I bet you have navigated around many a CRM system and seen notes written up in the option 1 layout. Now the big issue with this layout is time. A compact paragraph(s) of information takes a good bit of time to read and take in, in this instance that paragraph probably took you around thirty seconds to read. To put this in perspective if you're calling one hundred prospects a day and their notes all take thirty seconds to read then you've spent fifty minutes of your day simply reading notes; again, this is wasted time.

Whereas comparing this to the layout of option 2 this is very simple to read and scan. If you need to quickly find out some key information about the customer such as their business goals or something like that you could simply scan and find the information you need in seconds. This is even more beneficial when you're on the phone with a prospect or customer and want to reference something quickly about your last interactions.

This book isn't about speed reading by any means but our speed of comprehension for both our own and our peers notes is key. Just reflect on some speed reading techniques, standard reading, learning and memorising techniques can see the reader take in between 130 and 300 words per minute. Whereas compare that to the technique of scanning which on average a reader takes in around 600 words per minute. That's at least twice as fast, why wouldn't you do it! Vitally though, we must have a layout that permits scanning, so try using the key tips below the next time you write up your notes."

Key points to a succinct layout

- Use bullet points
- Use bold subheading, for topic areas such as business goals or plans for development
- Lose the jargon – it's not a literature review, be succinct, lose worthless notes such as "I agree with his view on" or "he's a really nice guy" these parts just clog things up and add no value.
- Scannable – the goal is to be able to scan you notes quickly and get the key information

Activity

Try this approach for your next meeting. Make a conscious effort when you're typing up your notes on your CRM system to think about the layout and speed of reading the notes when you next refer to them. Try this once, notice how easy it is to do and adopt this as a discipline in the future.

1.4 – Boost Your Meeting Count

Now I'm a big advocate of using the telephone to book meetings; in my opinion there is nothing better than calling somebody and speaking to them over the phone. It seems to be quite topical that social campaigns are the new buzzwords. I see so many adverts saying things like "never cold call again," or "social networking the most effective sales tool." Now in my opinion they are fantastic tools but by no means are they ever going to beat calling a prospect. I do, however, feel that they can aid your cause as if you have a social campaign with a prospect and also call them then there's a higher probability that they'll at least give you the time of day.

Now the old-school generation of sales works in a very different way than that of the Millennials and later generations. Old-school salespeople grew up in a time of the yellow pages, when mobile phones weren't used, when often they'd queue at telephone boxes at allotted times in the day (along with other salespeople) for their daily call with their boss. The old-school sales technique was much a 'drop in' mentality, mainly because they didn't have many other channels (phone or email etc.). What I mean by this is that they'd create a prospect list, drive and see them, and ask for the person they needed at reception and hope to sit down for a chat/meeting with them. Now I have worked with a number of older salespeople who still use this strategy, not to say that the strategy doesn't work, because it does, but it is not the most effective. Not once have I seen a salesman who uses these old school techniques be at the top of their sales leader board. Why? Because it's humanly impossible to do enough.

Think about it in number terms, with this old-school technique you spend most of the day driving around and speaking to very few decision makers. Even if you're proficient at this you'd be lucky to speak to ten decision makers a day. For a five-day week of a forty-eight-week year you'd speak to a maximum of 2,400 decision makers a year. Add to this the fact that the majority of these chats would be a waste of time as the decision maker can't give you enough of his time as you've interrupted his day and you soon see how you can become a 'busy fool' using this technique.

Juxtapose this with calling. In a real hard graft of calling you can make up to one hundred and fifty plus calls a day with around a 20% conversion rate of speaking to the right person. This would enable you to speak to thirty decision makers a day, again for a five-day week totalling of a forty-eight-week year you'd speak to a total of 7,200 decision makers. That's a total of 4,800 more decision makers a year than the old-school drop-in method, clear to see how this is a more efficient and effective method, not to mention the travel expenses are much less and the fact that you'll book quality, qualified meetings where the decision maker has set aside time to speak to you.

Now if I asked you which technique to adopt right now then you'd most probably say calling, and you'd be making the wrong decision. The old-school drop-in technique may be old but it's not obsolete, nor might I add is it the complete approach. What I would recommend is a hybrid model. What I mean by this is that calling should be your primary technique as the effectiveness and efficiencies are clear to see. But when you book a meeting and attend that meeting that's when you should also adopt the old-school drop-in method. Just think about how long you spend driving to a meeting with a potential customer, sometimes it can be hours, you get there, attend your meeting then drive all the way back – what a waste. The approach I champion is attending your meeting yes, but after or even before look around, see what other businesses are local, to the left, to the right, across the street. Give it a try, pop into that business across the street and ask them the information you need to find out. The worst that can happen is that they say, "Sorry I can't tell you that," the best is that you get to have a quick chat with the person you need. I have adopted this technique myself and have encouraged many other sales icons to do the same and not once have they been refused even a bit of information. The reason is that it's much harder for somebody to be rude or say no when you're standing there in front of them. Chances are that you'll go across the street, ask who looks after X purchasing and the gatekeeper will give you the name. Great what a result, you've just gained one more contact in thirty seconds.

Don't go crazy with this technique but use it to your advantage, make a point of for every meeting you book trying to pop into three to five other local businesses and you'll soon see the fruits of your labour.

Tip – switch board

Now a key tip to consider when you're calling on the phone is the amount of time you waste. Some of your time is wasted which is out of your control, but that which is in your control should be prevented. A tip I recommend when calling prospects is to always write down on your CRM systems the switchboard set up. Why? Well it's not uncommon to wait on a switchboard listening to options for over thirty seconds. I remember one instance where an automated switchboard had so many options that it took three minutes to get through it all. Just think about it, if every switchboard wasted thirty seconds and you made one-hundred calls then fifty minutes of your day would be wasted just listening to an automated switchboard. Imagine how many calls you could make and opportunities you could find with fifty extra minutes a day. That could be twelve thousand hours a year more selling time that I've just given you. The tip is this, next time you call a switchboard, write down the switchboard set up to get to your decision maker or department of choice.

Let's use a quick example to depict this:

If I call an automated switchboard and want to get through to Human Resources, and I'm told press three for Human Resource. Then the second set of automated message says press five for Mrs Smith I would depict the following in my CRM:

Phone number, option 3 then 5

The next time I call I wouldn't have to listen through it all again, as soon as I hear the first automated message start, I would press three. Then as soon as I hear the second set of automated message start, I would press five.

Note if an automated switchboard doesn't have your desired option then just note down the option for reception or the operator and use that every time.

1.5 – Plan Your Drop-In Calls

Now most salespeople who practise drop-in calls conduct them in a relatively one-dimensional manner. They'll most probably have a meeting with a customer and then pop in to other local businesses on the street or estate after or before that meeting. Now don't get me wrong, this is a great practice and I champion it always. However, for most of us it would definitely be more beneficial if we planned our drop-in calls appropriately beforehand.

I take this view as there's a great deal of hope involved when you conduct a drop-in call that's next to a prospect or customer that you're meeting. If you're popping next door you don't know if the prospective drop in business is in your sweet spot of customer, you don't even know a contact name. Now if you sell a product or service that any business can benefit from using then drop in calls next door can work. But if, like many, you have more of a niche offering that only certain customers would use then drop in calls next door won't work. Consider for example selling cleaning services, this would represent a unanimous need service, for this you could pop in at any local business as you know that they're a potential customer.

However, if you sell something more niche or specialist then you can't do this. For instance, if you sell industrial kitchen appliances then it's unlikely that the solicitors firm in the office next door is going to need your products or services. However, the caterer around the corner may do. In such circumstances you'll need to be more particular about your planning, but how do we do this?

Well to add an extra dimension to the drop-in approach sales icons take it upon themselves to plan their drop-in calls. Now I know you may be slightly reticent to planning your drop-in calls, as you're probably thinking that this will be a meticulously time-consuming task. But I'm going to enlighten you with one little technique that will make this planning a breeze.

The technique that I speak of is a drop-in calls sheet. Let me explain.

Remember our goal is to maximise our selling day wherever possible. Average salespeople will drive to an area for one meeting, then drive to either their next meeting or back to their office. Hardly maximising their day. For sales icons we need to set higher expectations, our goal will be to drive to the area and have that meeting. But then to maximise our time by dropping it at potential customers in the area. If we can ensure that these drop-in calls are to prospects who sit in our sweet spot, then we're truly maximising our day.

But what is a drop-in call sheet? Well it's quite self-explanatory; it's a list of potential drop in calls broken down by area. But it's not simply a list of companies, it's a list of vetted companies. Meaning that we have already checked that these businesses fall into our target area or sweet spot. So you know already that they have a need for your product or service, they're the right size etc. It probably doesn't make sense yet but let's start by looking at an example and then I'll talk you through how to build such a list.

Company	Postcode/ Zipcode	Activity
X Solicitors	EC....	01/01/2019 - X
ABC Accountants	EC....	01/01/2019 - X
Y Solicitors	EC....	02/01/2019 - X
Z Steel	EC....	01/01/2019 - X
Z Steel	EC....	03/01/2019 - X
DEF Accountants	EC....	01/01/2019 - X

How this works?

The technique works by first creating a document for your drop-in calls. I personally use my Microsoft OneNote and create an individual workbook for this. I then list a number of core geographical areas. I use postcode areas but these could be more specific if your area is smaller. Then I add to each postcode area any vetted prospects as a potential drop in call with their postcode. I list prospects one after another, categorising them by postcode area.

How do I add to my list?

So currently you'll have a sheet for your drop-in calls with a number of geographical areas as subheadings. You then need to add to your list. This is accomplished by detailing below the subheadings any prospects who are good potential drop in calls in that area. The tricky part is establishing who to add to your drop-in calls' list. Personally, I like to set a threshold. What I mean by threshold is a minimum number of potential drop in calls, my threshold is usually ten organisations for each subheading area. When I use up any of the organisations in this list (use up meaning completed a drop-in call) I add to this list once again. For instance, if I was in tower hamlets London and used two of my drop-in calls from my list, then I would spend some time adding two more prospective drop ins to my list to use at a later time.

Process once the drop in is complete?

So the process once you've conducted a drop-in call is to record it. Go to your drop-in calls list and highlight the line for the prospect who you've dropped in at, I usually mark it in green and state the date for when the drop-in call was completed as well as listing if I left any sales material with them. The reason that you record this is so that you don't make the mistake of conducting a drop-in call too soon after the last drop in. Moreover recording this information will give you a return on investment (ROI) as at a later date you'll be able to look back at your drop-in calls list and see which have been successful.

How do I use this technique?

So great, I've got a list of potential drop in calls but how do I actually use this? Well the best way to use this is in conjunction with your current meetings. Sales icons follow this process, they book a meeting in a certain area, let's say for this example the sales icon books a meeting in Luton. Their next step is to review how they can maximise their day in this area, so they go to their drop-in list and see what other prospects are in Luton. They then add however many drop in calls they deem appropriate or however many they have time for into their schedule for that day.

When should I use my drop-in sheet?

I'm a firm believer that we need to be planning our calendar a week in advance (more on this later). I encourage any sales icon to spend part of their Friday downtime period just planning the upcoming week. Your drop-in call sheet should help you immensely in this planning. So let's say it's Friday afternoon, I'm planning my diary for next week. I review my outlook calendar to see where my appointments are next week. I know my goal is to maximise my selling day. So I review my drop-in calls list in conjunction with my calendar for next week and I evaluate what potential prospects are local to my meeting. From looking at my drop-in list I can see the local prospects to my location on each day, I can then add these to my calendar to maximise my day. Now I've gone from say one meeting a day to one meeting and four drop in calls a day.

Route planning:

Your route planning is imperative here to maximise your day of selling. If a sales icon had two scheduled meetings in a day they'd look at the route between the two and which drop-in calls would be in close proximity to this route. Such as if a sales icon had scheduled one meeting in Bedford in the morning and one meeting in Milton Keynes in the afternoon then they'd review the route. They'd look at their drop-in calls list and see if any were situated between Bedford and Milton Keynes. Then they'd look at how much time they have free, how long the travel time would be and determine an appropriate number of drop in calls to those parameters.

Why is the technique more beneficial?

For sales icons this technique is more beneficial than simply conducting drop in calls aimlessly such as the next-door technique. It's all about the value of your time, as you transition to becoming a sales icon you'll find that the more effectively you can use your time the more successful you will be. Undoubtedly, you'll get to a point where time is so precious that you'll have to turn down other commitments or even opportunities.

Therefore to save you time it is better to focus your drop in calls on credible prospects whose rewards are worth the investment of your time.

All in all that's not to say you shouldn't conduct drop in calls next door. It may be the case that the business next door sits within your sweet spot so they're perfect for a drop-in call. The point is that planning your drop-in calls rather than succumbing to convenience will show greater reward.

Setting expectations:

So what should I expect from a drop-in call? Well I hate to sound cheesy, but the possibilities are endless. Let me explain with an example. I once worked for a man who is up there as one of the most awe-inspiring men I have ever met. He started his career in sales and I will never forget the stories he told me about knocking on doors. He explained to me how when he was a young salesman he went to see a customer to drop off a product, he finished his meeting, dropped off the product and started heading for his car.

He then talked about how the average salesperson would have got in his car and drove off to their next meeting or back to their office. But his thought process was different, he said to himself that he'd driven this far, he might as well see if he can get any more value out of his journey. So instead of leaving he decided to conduct some drop-in calls, and where better to start than the office block he was just in. The customer he visited was situated on the ground floor of the office, and the office had eight floors in total.

He jested with himself that if he worked his way up the office floors that the likelihood would be that he'll get half the way up, become demoralised and then come back down and leave. So he decided to start at the top floor, that way he'll be working his way down with no easy escape.

So he starts his drop-in calls, knocking on the doors of all the offices on the eighth floor. He gets mixed responses as expected, some people say no, others take business cards and brochures from him, some even have a short chat with him. He works his way down the floors, office after office, floor after floor.

Then comes his lucky break, he gets to the fifth floor. He speaks to the receptionist and asks if he can chat to the person who looks after the purchasing of typewriters for the business. Would you believe it the receptionist says, "Well of course, that would be Mr James, and actually we're looking for some typewriters at the moment. I'll just go and get him."

To his good fortunate he sits down with Mr James there and then and has a long discussion with him. It turned out that Mr James was looking for some typewriters for his office. But to make things even better Mr James looked after the purchasing of typewriters for the whole company which was a national corporation.

The result was that this drop-in call lead to a long-standing relationship whereby Mr James regularly ordered typewriters from this man for many years. In today's money, this business relationship would have equated to millions of pounds worth of business every year. This all came simply from maximising his day and dropping in at a few other local businesses.

Now this was sheer good fortune, but the same with any lottery ticket you buy, you've got to be in it to win it; if you never try you can never win. Now from an expectation perspective, it won't do you any good to expect to walk in for a drop-in call and expect to generate a gem of a customer straight away. So what should our expectations be? Well, for sales icons we want to:

1) Find out the decisionmaker
2) Try to see them
3) Information gather
4) Leave something (not just a card)
5) Follow up

Find out the decisionmaker – this is our minimum criteria, for every door we knock on we at least want to find out who the decisionmaker is. So set this as goal number one.

Try to see them – goal number two is to ask to see that decision maker once we have found out who they are. Chances are that they'll be too busy or out of the office but you lose nothing from asking. Who knows, they could be like Mr James, they may be waiting for a supplier to help them with something right now. So ask the question, you have nothing to lose.

Information gather – if you fail to get to see the decision maker then try to gather information. Ask a few questions of the gatekeeper that will help you in your sales process or qualifying such as, 'Who is your supplier for X at the moment?' or 'How many staff do you have?' or 'What other offices locations do you have?' See what you can find out but be cautious not to pester the gatekeeper too much.

Leave something – prepare for the circumstance that you don't get to meet with the decision maker. Put together a brochure pack, something tangible that the gatekeeper can pass onto the decision maker. Remember, the average salesperson will leave just a business card, maybe a brochure at most. Why not go the extra mile, write a letter and include it in your pack, print off some case studies that will be insightful for them or some insight that might be useful for them. Leave something tangible and memorable.

Follow up – the most important step of all, you must always follow up. I very much doubt that the customer will come to you, you need to be the driving force. So make sure that for every drop-in call you conduct that you follow up with a phone call. Ask them if they received the brochure pack and what their thoughts were.

I've encouraged sales icons to use an approach like the following

Day 1 – drop-in call, find out decision maker and drop off brochure pack if they won't see me

Day 3 – phone call to follow up

Day 5 – phone call to follow up (if haven't got through to my desired decision maker)

Day 7 – phone call to follow up (if I haven't got through to my desired decision maker)

If after a couple phone calls I haven't been able to get through then I would send an email and in the subject I will state

(Company name) – Did You Receive The Pack?

For this, I would use a generic yet slightly bespoke email that I've previously written. In one of the latter sections on nurturing I'll show you what this would look like.

Now your follow up approach maybe slightly different from this. Maybe due to your workload you can't follow up with a prospect so soon after a drop-in call. Irrespective of timings the most important thing is that you follow up, otherwise you've wasted the time that you spent conducting a drop-in call anyway.

Tip – No Names Policies

No names polices, the term that makes salespeople shiver. Well not for a sales icon. I used to hate no names policies, every time I encountered a no names policy I arduously tried to get around it but often to no avail. The eventuality would be that I'd cross the prospect off of my list as I'd just waste my time getting nowhere. I can categorically say that for the majority of salespeople when they hear no names policy they deem it as a dead end and move onto the next prospect. This is not the sales icon way.

Now with experience I've come to love no names policies. Think about it, if a business has a no-names policy then competition is already dramatically reduced as most salespeople won't try to get in there because they can't. This presents a fantastic opportunity for you, a golden egg if you will, because if you can get in with the customer they'll guard the gates themselves to prevent competitors from intruding. The question is, how do you get in? The answer is a drop-in call. I am yet to fail to at least get the decisionmakers name from a drop-in call, thus it's a great way around a no names policy.

Don't believe me? Well, in my early career one of the largest opportunities I landed came from this route. The story goes that I had been prospecting an IT director and developed a great opportunity. To my misfortune he left, and to add to my bad luck they implemented a no names policy so I thought it was the end of the road. So I thought to myself what the hell, let's try a drop-in call, I've got nothing to lose. So I went to reception and said I was working with Mr X three months ago before he left, can I ask who looks after his role now? To my amazement the receptionist told me who had taken over the role straight away, no quibble at all, with some more buttering up she also gave me his direct dial and agreed to take a brochure pack to him personally to say I'd popped by. The result? This was the initiator to landing a large deal that made me a large chunk of commission every month, definitely worth the effort of popping in and asking for the name.

So next time you get told sorry we have a no-names policy, don't simply cross them off your prospecting list. Add them to your drop-in calls list, pop in and say, "Hi I was just in with X around the corner and saw the business so thought I should pop in. I just wanted to enquire who looks after Y for the business. I intended to drop something off for them."

1.6 – Route Planning

One oversight many a salesperson has made in their time is route planning. I know I've been a culprit of this in the past. We'll book a meeting in the morning in one area and another in the afternoon fifty miles away and spend the time in between travelling, what a waste. Our ideal scenario is to have our meetings planned out by area so that we can utilise our time in that area as effectively as possible. For example, if you had a meeting in Canary Wharf London in the morning your ideal scenario would be to book other meetings around the Canary Wharf area for later in the day. Obviously take this with a pinch of salt, it's an idealist theory which doesn't play out as easy in reality. The goal is to get in front of customers and sometimes that will mean your route planning is shot, but if you keep this in the back of your mind it will aid you and give you the gift of time.

Tip – Google Maps

Undoubtedly, in your role you'll have a list of accounts and hot prospects, if you don't right now I assure you that you will at some point in the future. Now the tip I offer is to use Google maps, right here I can hear you sigh, "Yes, I use Google maps already!"

Well you may be unaware of a feature that can greatly benefit your route planning. When you get to the later stages of your sales icon training you'll be on the verge of great success and will understand how valuable your time is. At this point you'll have a number of accounts and hot prospects, which you'll continually be contacting and attacking regularly. Anyone in sales knows that the more you can get in front of a customer/prospect the better. So what I propose is using Google maps in line with route planning in order to get in front of your hot prospects/customers more often.

How?

Well in Google maps there is a feature called create your own maps. In this you can create your own personalised maps for anything that you wish. Have a look at an example of such a map from one of the sales icons that I worked with:

The thing that I love about this is that you can colour-code pins in various ways. To see who the pin represents you simply click on the pin and it will show the necessary contact and information. To drop pins all you need to do is search for a company in the search bar, when it's found click add to maps and then colour-code in line with your preferences. Me, I like to use a simple traffic lights colour coding system like this

Red = prospect
Amber = hot prospect
Green = customer

What's this useful for?

You can use this for so many different things, most notable are

- Route planning
- Prospect attack planning
- Area growth plan
- Route planning

This technique is great for route planning, because if you book a meeting with a prospect in an area you can then review your personalised map to see what customers and other prospects are also close to that area. Once you have visualised who is nearby you can contact them and say you're in seeing X company around the corner on Tuesday morning, can you pop into to see them also in the afternoon. You'd be pleasantly surprised how many people say "Well if you're in the area then you might as well pop in."

Prospect attack plan

This is something we are going to address in depth in a later chapter but your personalised Google maps can be great for this. To give you a brief overview when you create a plan of what prospects you're going to attack this can be a useful tool to utilise. For instance you may map out all of your accounts in a personalised map and see how all of your accounts are densely populated to one area, say Manchester. You may review your prospect attack plan and conclude how 80% of the prospects you're attacking are based in Nottingham, which may set alarms bells off that you're not attacking your sweet spot. This will make more sense later.

Area growth planning:

Sales icons have also used this technique for area growth planning. For instance they have looked at an area at the start of the year such as Bristol and said that they'd like to increase their foothold in the area in a certain vertical such as legal. How they go about this, is by creating a new map named legal firms in Bristol, colour coding their legal accounts in the area if they have any and colour coding all the others as prospects. Taking a snapshot (picture in time) of what it currently looks like and making a continuous action to review this map once a quarter to see how it develops. For instance, from one month to another they may see that four of their prospects change from red (prospect) to amber (warm lead) and one prospect change to green (customer) due to their effective prospect attack plan. You may ask how this will help but it is great for motivation and a sense of accomplishment when you can review things visually in this way and see the fruits of your labour.

1.7 – Flagging System

Are you the type of salesperson who enjoys selling but often struggles with your self-organisation? Well you wouldn't be the first person to say this. I've seen so many salespeople fail in this area, they'll have meeting after meeting and forget to put notes on their CRM, forget to follow up with prospects or customers, forget to carry out actions etc. Often it leads to great stress for them and results in having to spend a day or two working late trying to get organised once again. It's common for them to deal with this backlog of work by undertaking all of their follow up activities all in one go for their last ten or so meetings. This, while not ideal for your general enjoyment of the job can also be catastrophic for your relationship with the customer or prospect and can lead to loss of business. Not what any sales icon wants!

The solution is a little technique sales icons like to call a flagging system. This system will help to eradicate such circumstances that I highlighted previously when you have to carry out a binge follow up.

The flagging system fuses together a standard checklist with something coined as logograms. I'm sure you're aware of what a checklist is, but what about logograms. Well simply put, a logogram is a symbol or character used to represent a word or a phrase for shorthand. Think of ancient hieroglyphics, this is an example of a logogram, a symbol which represents another word or phrase. In ancient Egypt, series of logograms would be used in conjunction with each other. But such a technique wasn't only used thousands of years ago. It's still something we use now. Think of your modern-day language, we have numerous logograms which we use every single day, most probably without even knowing that they are. Such examples include:

- 1 is a logogram of the word one
- = is a logogram of the word equals
- # is a logogram of the word hashtag
- $ is a logogram of the word dollar

So logograms aren't actually a new concept for you; they're something you undoubtedly already use but are unaware of what they are categorised as. So when I use the term 'Flagging system', what I mean is fusion between Logograms and a checklist.

Now that we understand the concept, let's look at our work and see where we can use our flagging system. If we start by thinking about a typical working day, as with any day you'll have a number of tasks that you need to complete from things like replying to emails or writing up your notes on a meeting into CRM or even preparing a proposal.

Now some of us are better at self-organisation than others, but the important thing to remember is to focus on the tasks in priority order. I emphasise the word priority as this is key, what we don't want to do is focus on the less important, easy-to-complete tasks. In addition, we want to be weary of becoming reactive.

Becoming reactive is such an easy trap to fall into. If you're like me you'll probably have done this or seen others who have fallen foul. Just reflect for a second, how many times have you been undertaking a task and an email pings up where you immediately stop the task and look at the email? Or maybe the phone rings and you straightaway pick it up unbeknown who the caller is. Sound familiar? Don't worry we've all done this.

Such behaviour as this is known as the urgency treadmill, whereby you act on impulse to stimuli around you such as email, a text, a phone call, a knock at your door. The intentions of a person jumping on the urgency treadmill are harmless and justified, but there's a big downside. Giving into these impulses, in whatever format whether that is a quick email reply or picking up the phone as it rings will dramatically reduce your performance and efficiency. That's because when you come away from a task you lose your chain of thought, which will in turn end up taking more time to revert back to your previous chain of thought when you come back to the task.

So a word of caution before we go into more depth on the flagging system, try and steer clear of being reactive to stimuli and jumping on the urgency treadmill.

Now we're all busy people and I'm not saying that for every task you do that you shouldn't give in to stimuli as otherwise you'd never interact with anyone else. What I am saying, however, is that for the important tasks you need to be completely focused on them and not be distracted by impulses.

So here comes the interesting bit, how do we become more regimented in our self-organisation? Well that's through the flagging system.

Now the word regimented is a rather pertinent term to use. When you think of the term regimented what do you think of? Me, well I think of our military forces like the army. I say regimented and then I think about the words regime and organisation, both archetypal traits of military personnel.

But why are they traits of military personnel? Is someone born with self-organisation skills which make them the perfect candidate to join the military? Well maybe for some, but for most the answer would have to be no. Think about it, any of the armed forces have such a wide plethora of staff. From individuals of upper class, educated and wealthy backgrounds to school dropouts with little to no qualifications or education. Yet somehow the armed forces manage to mould all of their personnel into self-organised individuals and it's completely and utterly down to the training and procedures that they encourage them to follow.

This is great news for you if you're not very self-organised at the moment as it proves that you can learn how to do so. If the military can take on board a troop of candidates, and despite their background be able to teach them conformity and unison then you can achieve disciplines of this nature too. They take on board young sixteen-year-old kids, often they'll be young men and women who have never fended for themselves. Their mum or dad would have made their dinner, washed and ironed their clothes, cleaned their rooms. Then after joining the military they have to learn this all for themselves as well as a host of other new skills such as marching, survival, first aid, tactics etc.

The military entrench practices and regime into their recruits through intense training, proven procedures and repetition. Now I'm not going to grill you like an army instructor; that would be especially hard through a book as you'll just put it down. What I am going to do, however, is train you on a procedure, the flagging system. It's going to sound alien, and chances are that you're not going to pick it up first time. But think of yourself as an army candidate in basic training, you're learning the procedure, but you need repetition to make it a habit. Repeat, repeat, repeat until it becomes ingrained as part of your normal process.

What is a flagging system?

If you were to look at your regular activities I am certain you would see similarities in the processes you use for them. I like to call these my core action processes. Let me explain in a clear example.

If I want to wash some dirty laundry then there are a few keys steps, those being:

1. Collect dirty laundry and place in washing machine
2. Add detergents and other cleaning products
3. Select spin cycle and length

All of which I would call my core actions processes for washing dirty laundry. If I miss one of those steps then I won't have clean laundry.

So now let's apply this to sales, let's hypothesise that I have just had a phone call with a decision maker or even a meeting with a decision maker. Now for such an activity my core action processes would be categorised as the following

- Email
- OneNote/CRM
- Calendar
- LinkedIn

The action required for these would be as follows

Email – for every qualified interaction, through any medium whether that be face to face or over the phone, I would always send an email to the decision maker I spoke with. In this email I would include any salient topics we discussed and actions I'm working on in a succinct way. Take note of the term qualified interaction. What I mean by qualified is that you've had a conversation with some substance. So if I speak to a decisionmaker on the phone about a number of items then I would quantify this as being of some substance and therefore would warrant a follow up email. Conversely, a thirty-second conversation with little to no substance wouldn't usually constitute such an activity.

OneNote – for every qualified interaction I would type up all my notes in my OneNote, for you this may be your CRM system or other medium. This should be a standard process. Think back to earlier in the book, think of yourself as a deep-sea gold diver, your notes are your downline, they help you pick up where you left off and save you time in the future.

Calendar – for every qualified interaction I would add an interaction reminder in my calendar for the future, something like call Jim at X company and set this in my outlook calendar for the date in the future where I deemed best to contact them again, such as July the 10th.

LinkedIn – for every qualified interaction I would always connect with the person on LinkedIn, or if I'm already connected with them then I would go on their profile as they'll be able to see that I had been on there. This way I build up multiple familiarities through a range of mediums, and then the decisionmaker has a better chance of remembering me.

How does it work?

When you make a phone call or have a meeting with a decisionmaker you'll most probably have a notepad in front of you where you jot down all of your notes. The trouble is that we may have multiple meetings in the day as well as make multiple phone calls.

This adds extra complexity, as when you are carrying out your core actions processes it can become confusing as to what you've already done and haven't done. Often we can spend time looking up if we did put our notes in CRM for that meeting last week, or we may find that we became mixed up and forgot to email our customer following on from our meeting the other day.

What we want is a simple system. A system that encourages us to complete all of our core actions processes for any qualified interaction with a decisionmaker. Moreover we want to be able to look back in our notes and identify what's been completed and what core action processes are still outstanding. This is where the flagging system comes in.

So how does it work?

Well let's put this into practice for one of your meetings or phone calls. You need two items here:

1) Notepad – with notes from a qualified interaction
2) To-do list – paper form or electronic

If you haven't got these to hand then you'll just have to imagine having them in front of you.

Step one – review what our core action processes are

We already identified that these are your OneNote/CRM, email, calendar and LinkedIn

Step two – list on our to do list our core action processes in an abbreviated form denoted as a flag, this should take the format

(Customer name) – (O) (E) (C) (Li)

The abbreviations stand for the following:

O = OneNote
C = Calendar
E = Email
L = LinkedIn

For instance, if I had a qualified interaction with Jims Bakery then my flags in my to do list would look like the following

Jims Bakery (O) (E) (C) (Li)

Step three – start with our first core action process, in this case OneNote/CRM. Here I would type up all of my notes from my qualified interaction and put them into my OneNote and/or CRM system.

Once I have completed this action this is where the flag comes it. I would then detail a circled O like so (O) on the page where I wrote up my notes. This circled (O) is my flag, it tells me that I have completed this core action process. I then also review my to-do list and put a line through the (O) that I have detailed on there.

Step four – I repeat the procedure identified in step three but this time for my next core action process, the next one being email. Then the same for calendar and the same for LinkedIn.

So for email this flag means that I have sent a follow up email to the decision maker that I had a qualified interaction with. If this has taken place then I depicted a circled E on my notepad where the notes are like so (E). In addition, I also draw a line through the letter (E) on my to-do list.

Then for calendar, have I rescheduled in my calendar a date or time for my follow up. This could be for a call, a follow up email or a meeting or even all of them. If I have done this, then again I write a circle C on my notepad next to the notes like so (C). Same again too, I draw a line through the letter (C) on my to-do list.

Finally for LinkedIn, this tells me either to add the decision maker on LinkedIn or if I have already added them then I should go on their profile so they know I've been on there. You get the gist with the next bit, I circle (Li) on the notepad and put a line through it on my to-do list.

All in all the finished article should look something like this on my to-do list.

~~(o)~~ ~~(c)~~ ~~(e)~~ ~~(li)~~

The flagging system comes into its own even more so when you're busy. It's human nature for big tasks to become daunting. But if instead of becoming overwhelmed we break the tasks into manageable chunks then it simplifies the whole process and increases our productivity.

Let's take for example a busy day of activity, say that yesterday you had three meetings with new business prospects. You get into the office this morning and you know that you need to conduct your follow up activities. You look down at your notes and see over six A4 pages of written notes. You can feel an angst build up as you wonder where you should even start. This is where the average performers procrastinate, miss parts of the follow up and take a long period of time to carry out the follow up activities.

Whereas a sales icon uses the flagging system. The whole point for this is to break our follow up activities into management chucks so that we

1) Don't miss any of our follow-up activities
2) Can look back and check that all follow activities have been conducted

So let's venture back to that scenario, yesterday you had three new business meetings and today you've just entered the office ready to start your follow up activities. Well, If you were a sales icon then straight away you would start by adding the three meetings to your to do list with the flags ready to tick off.

1) Meeting 1 (O) (C) (E) (Li)
2) Meeting 2 (O) (C) (E) (Li)
3) Meeting 3 (O) (C) (E) (Li)

Note meeting 1, 2 or 3 would be the company name.

Then you'd start with the core action processes for meeting one. Once you'd completed them you'd move to meeting two and so on and so on.

Remember that it's important to use the flagging system on your notepad too after you have conducted that core action process. For example, if you have a page of notes from a call with Mr James at 'Just Plastering' and you have carried out the email part of your core action processes then you would denote a circled E next to the notes. If this is the only core action process you have completed then you would only use the (E) flag until you have completed another core action process.

This has a perfect use case for cold calling. The great thing about this flagging system is you won't waste time questioning if you set it in your calendar or emailed the contact after. You can just quickly check your notes and if you see a flag by the notes then you know which core action processes you've conducted and if any have been left out.

Note you could have other core action processes than that which I've described, these are my four core action processes but yours may be different depending on your business, industry or role. For instance, in one role I had I can remember using a flag called (PSR) which stood for pre-sales request. The reason being is that it was common for me in this role to have a core action process of a pre-sales request therefore I made it a flag.

A word of caution here, however, try and be succinct with your core action processes. It should only be the processes that are regular in the majority of cases, some interactions will require bespoke action, though that does not mean that this one off bespoke action should become a core action process.

The purpose for this is almost like a checklist to tick off the core actions that I need to undertake, which ensures that I always conduct them.

Colour Coding for Completion

If you're anything like me, you live and die by your Outlook Calendar, which can be a good and a bad thing. One of my challenges in sales was that I'd look back in my calendar and I'd question whether I had completed my actions such as my core actions processes or not. It would be a continual frustration and time sapper as I would look back and paranoia would set in. I'd start to question whether I'd sent my follow up email or something of that nature. Then I'd waste time tracing my steps to find out that actually I had sent my follow up email, and the cycle would continue. This was until I found my solution, and a simple one at that. The crux of the solution to this problem was colour coding my diary. Nothing too complicated, just simply that if I had an entry in my calendar where I had completed its relevant actions then I'd colour-code this in purple. Anything left in its standard blue shade would denote actions not completed. This gave me a great way of being able to look at my calendar for the last week or more and see if anything was still outstanding or not. So simple, just

Purple = actions completed
Blue = actions yet to be completed
Below is a depiction of what this would look like:

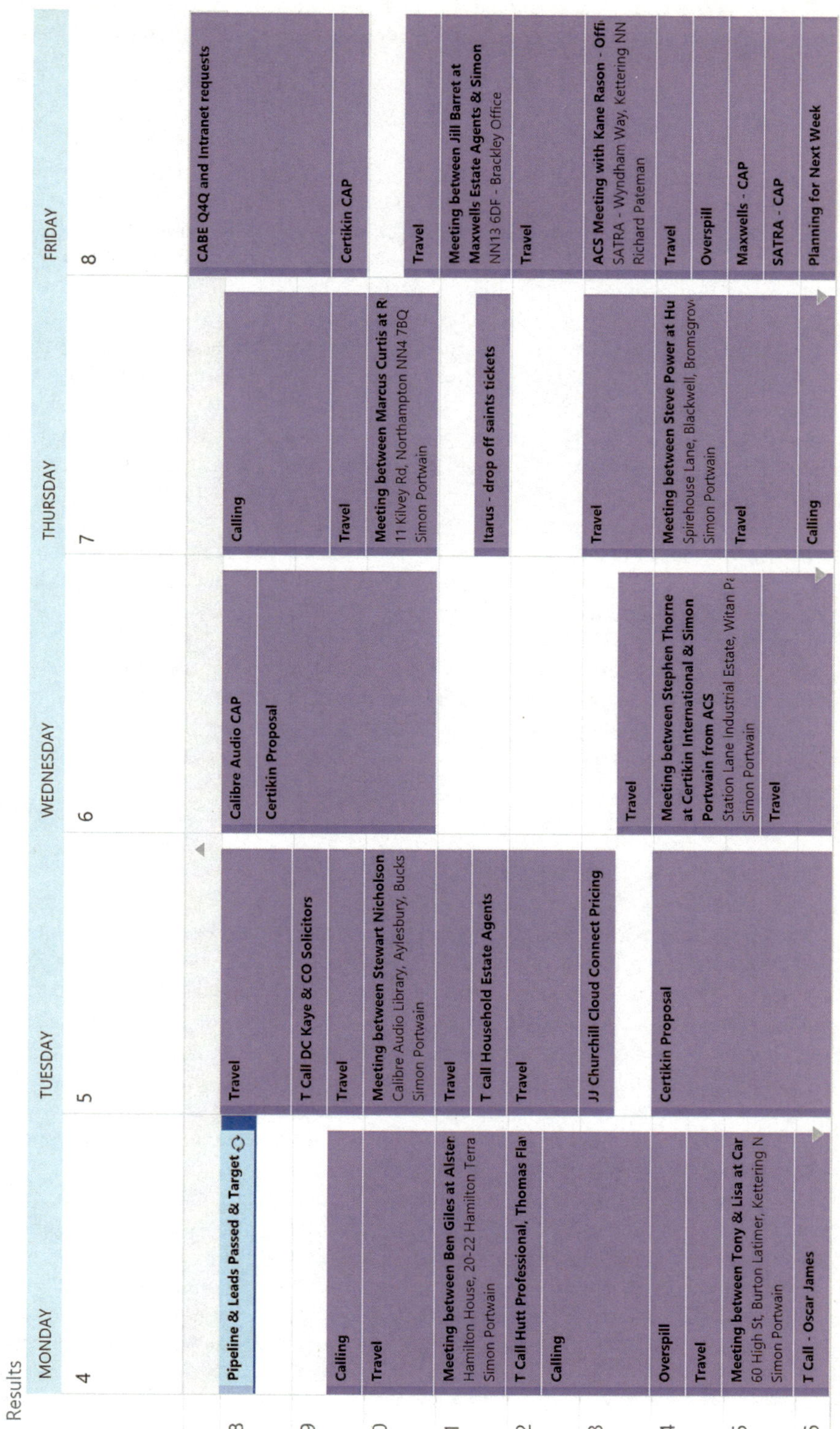
Results
MONDAY 4
TUESDAY 5
WEDNESDAY 6
THURSDAY 7
FRIDAY 8
08
09
10
11
12
13
14
15
16
Pipeline & Leads Passed & Target
Calling
Travel
Meeting between Ben Giles at Alster
Hamilton House, 20-22 Hamilton Terra
Simon Portwain
T Call Hutt Professional, Thomas Fla
Calling
Overspill
Travel
Meeting between Tony & Lisa at Car
60 High St, Burton Latimer, Kettering N
Simon Portwain
T Call - Oscar James
Travel
T Call DC Kaye & CO Solicitors
Travel
Meeting between Stewart Nicholson
Calibre Audio Library, Aylesbury, Bucks
Simon Portwain
Travel
T call Household Estate Agents
Travel
JJ Churchill Cloud Connect Pricing
Certikin Proposal
Calibre Audio CAP
Certikin Proposal
Travel
Meeting between Stephen Thorne at Certikin International & Simon Portwain from ACS
Station Lane Industrial Estate, Witan Pa
Simon Portwain
Travel
Calling
Travel
Meeting between Marcus Curtis at R
11 Kilvey Rd, Northampton NN4 7BQ
Simon Portwain
Itarus - drop off saints tickets
Travel
Meeting between Steve Power at Hu
Spirehouse Lane, Blackwell, Bromsgrov
Simon Portwain
Travel
Calling
CABE Q4Q and Intranet requests
Certikin CAP
Travel
Meeting between Jill Barret at Maxwells Estate Agents & Simon
NN13 6DF - Brackley Office
Travel
ACS Meeting with Kane Rason - Offi
SATRA - Wyndham Way, Kettering NN
Richard Pateman
Travel
Overspill
Maxwells - CAP
SATRA - CAP
Planning for Next Week

So you could look at this and say that for this week all of my actions have been completed barring one on the Monday morning on the subject of pipeline, leads and target.

1.8 – Golden Hours

If I had some solar panels and put them out every night when it's dark to develop renewable energy then it would be a pretty foolish thing to do. Or if I was to go hunting at a time where the animals I hunted had emigrated south for the winter then the chances are that I'd go hungry. It may sound like I've gone off topic but the point I'm trying to emphasise is that timing is everything, and the same is true for your timing of tasks throughout the day. Nothing frustrates me more than working with a salesperson who starts the day checking their emails, carries out a few tasks mid-morning and then when they've finished their tasks they eventually pick up the phone around midday. What a waste of valuable time!

Now don't get me wrong everything here is important to do, but you have to think about planning your tasks as effectively as possible and taking into consideration your golden hours.

What are your golden hours?

Basically, your golden hours are your most productive time for getting in touch with your customers. The time between 0800–1100 hrs and 1400–1600 hrs is the golden time for most industries, but this may differ for you.

How to plan?

The crux of this section is to plan to use your golden hours as effectively as possible. Your mind, creativity, self-esteem, determination and a whole host of other attributes are at their peak as soon as you get to your desk. Below is a good representation of how you diminish throughout the day:

0900 Capabilities = 100%
1000 Capabilities = 80%
1100 Capabilities = 60%

This is not scientific or accurate by any means, as it would be very hard to quantify. But it's undoubtedly true that your capabilities at the start of the day are at their peak. At this point your mind is completely focused, you're not thinking about that email that just came in, the guy who was rude to you an hour ago on the phone or your colleague who has annoyed you all day. Your mind at the beginning of the day is at its peak, and that's why I don't understand why some people use the peak capabilities of their mind for mundane tasks. Imagine if you managed a sports team, say a football or baseball team, it would be like using all your star players in the run up to the cup final and then in the final dropping them to put the rookies in.

What you need to do is take advantage of the time when your mind has its greatest capability available and match it to the time where your prospects are available and willing to speak. This is why the general lunch time period isn't considered part of your golden hours, this is because most of your prospects will be out on lunch. Does that mean you should sit around twiddling your thumbs…no, this is your downtime period, the perfect time for carrying out the mundane but necessary tasks such as replying to emails, writing a proposal, planning the rest of your week, conducting your core action processes.

So take this on board and plan the hours of your day as effectively as possible. If it was me planning I would schedule for creative tasks in the morning when you need as much brainpower as possible so things like cold calling. Admin tasks at midday, then back to creative tasks in the afternoon, potentially meetings.

1.9 – Block Booking Your Calendar

You've probably heard the cumulative saying before that:

"If I have ten good hours work that means I've had a good day, if I have five good days that means I've had a good week. If I have four good weeks that means I've had a good month and if I have twelve good months then I've had a good year."

The science of selling is all about those small increments that we do to make us as effective as we can be. Think of any sporting team; the misconception is that winning a single game, league or cup is made in the time that they play the sport, those ninety minutes or so on the field. The truth is that the winning is made in the shadows, in the countless hours of blood, sweat and tears they put into training. Without the work in shadows no success would be achieved.

The science of selling is no different to this, we need to focus our attention on the small details that enable us to be as successful as we can be. How we do this is by making every single hour we work constitute as worthwhile, then over time them hours of good work will add up to good days, good weeks, good months and good years. This is the art to becoming a sales icon, master your minutes and you will become a sales icon.

Why's this important?

Did you ever once get to the end of the day or a week and think what have I achieved? Or even at the end of the day have a moment of panic where you realise that you've forgotten to carry out an important task and now you have to deal with the stress and have to potentially work overtime? Mastering our minutes will make this a thing of the past. It will give you a clear structure for your day(s) and ensure that any important tasks get carried out when and where required.

How to master our minutes?

One of the most effective disciplines for mastering our minutes is block booking your calendar. What this means is to schedule tasks in your calendar in allocated time blocks, I personally like to use fifteen-minute increments or more.

What's important?

The important things to remember when block booking your calendar are:

- Prioritise
- Headroom
- Unplanned space

Prioritisation – This is always integral when tackling any tasks, the same should carry through for block booking your calendar. If you have a task which is of the upmost priority such as a task that could close a massive piece of business then this needs to be prioritised over the less important tasks. Prioritise in whatever way works best for you. I personally like to number my tasks in priority order, then I block book my calendar respectively for the task and assign an amount of time to that task.

For instance if I had three tasks such as:

- Undertake my core action processes from my prospect meeting yesterday
- Arrange golf day with X client
- Put £500k proposal together for a presentation next week

I would prioritise them as follows

1) Put £500k proposal together for presentation next week
2) Undertake my actions from my prospect meeting yesterday
3) Arrange golf day with X client

Then I would assign time to them that I deem as adequate.

Task one – four hours required, two hours today between 0800 and 1000 hrs and two hours tomorrow between 0800 and 1000 hrs

Task two – thirty minutes today between 1300 and 1330 hrs

Task three – fifteen minutes today between 1330 and 1345 hrs

In this example I have only three tasks so it's quite simplistic, in reality you'll probably have many more.

Headroom – Approximating how long it will take to complete any task is a challenge. No one can plan everything to an absolute tee, and I don't expect you to. After years of using this practice I and many other sales icons still fall foul in that we fail to plan the exact amount of time for a task.

We've all had the circumstance where we think something will be trivial to complete and quick to do so, yet in reality it becomes much more time consuming than originally expected. It may be because something unexpected changed the time it took to fulfil the task or even a change of circumstance.

Don't worry, it's not just you that struggles with approximating this time, it's all of us.

This is just Hofstadter's Law at play, and it's as simple as this:

"It always takes longer than you expect."

Hofstadter studied and coined this concept relating to the human challenge of accurately estimating the time it will take to complete tasks of complexity.[4]

The best thing you can do is to plan for this, build in headroom where you can so that certain tasks can over run and not negatively affect the rest of your scheduling. The time allotted shouldn't be your goal mind, if the task can be completely proficiently in half the time then do so and reutilise the time elsewhere.

Unplanned time – it's also important to schedule in your diary some time for overspill, I usually block a section of time in my diary every day and title it overspill. The purpose for such time is to enable flexibility, so if you get that email from a customer with an urgent requirement you have some space in your diary to fit them in. Whatever the circumstance may be, you have the time available to use. If nothing pressing comes up then you can use the time for whatever you deem fit, potentially one of our regular tasks such as cold calling.

What about gaps in my diary?

Fill the gaps in your diary wherever you can and schedule important tasks, I highlight the point a number of times in the book because it's true…what gets scheduled gets done! Remember to schedule your regular tasks that are important to your success, things like cold calling, training, drop in calls etc.

Activity

Trust me on this one, just try this discipline, even if it's just for a few days. I assure you that block booking your calendar will enable you to get more done, achieve more self-satisfaction as you can see your productivity in a tangible way, improve your efficiency and effectiveness as well as reduce your work stress levels. Simply give it a go and I'm certain you won't look back.

1.10 – Planning Your Upcoming Week

So we've discussed the concept of mastering your minutes through block booking your diary. But to become a sales icon we must always be prepared. So to master your minutes as effectively as you can, it's integral that you pre-plan your diary for the upcoming week.

When should I do this?

The best time to plan your diary differs between sales icons. Most of us prefer to plan this a week in advance, say on a Friday afternoon you could pull up your calendar for the following week and plan all of the tasks then. Do bear in mind that you cannot completely plan your diary a week in advance, sometimes you can only plan things completely the day before or on the day. The exact day or time that you plan your diary for the upcoming week isn't essential, what is essential is doing it!

Example of unplanned diary

Let's take a look at an unplanned diary

Results

	MONDAY 4	TUESDAY 5	WEDNESDAY 6	THURSDAY 7	FRIDAY 8
08	**Pipeline & Leads Passed & Target**				
09					
10		**Meeting between Stewart Nicholson** Calibre Audio Library, Aylesbury, Bucks Simon Portwain		**Meeting between Marcus Curtis at R** 11 Kilvey Rd, Northampton NN4 7BQ Simon Portwain	
11	**Meeting between Ben Giles at Alster** Hamilton House, 20-22 Hamilton Terra Simon Portwain				**Meeting between Jill Barret at Maxwells Estate Agents & Simon** NN13 6DF - Brackley Office
12					
13					**ACS Meeting with Kane Rason - Offi** SATRA - Wyndham Way, Kettering NN Richard Pateman
14			**Meeting between Stephen Thorne at Certikin International & Simon Portwain from ACS** Station Lane Industrial Estate, Witan P Simon Portwain	**Meeting between Steve Power at Hu** Spirehouse Lane, Blackwell, Bromsgrov Simon Portwain	
15	**Meeting between Tony & Lisa at Car** 60 High St, Burton Latimer, Kettering N Simon Portwain				
16					

This is most probably what you work with at the moment. You have a number of pre-booked meetings in your diary and that's more or less the extent to your pre-planned diary.

Well let's take a look at a planned diary to see if we can notice the difference.

Example of planned diary:

Here is a snapshot of a pre-planned diary:

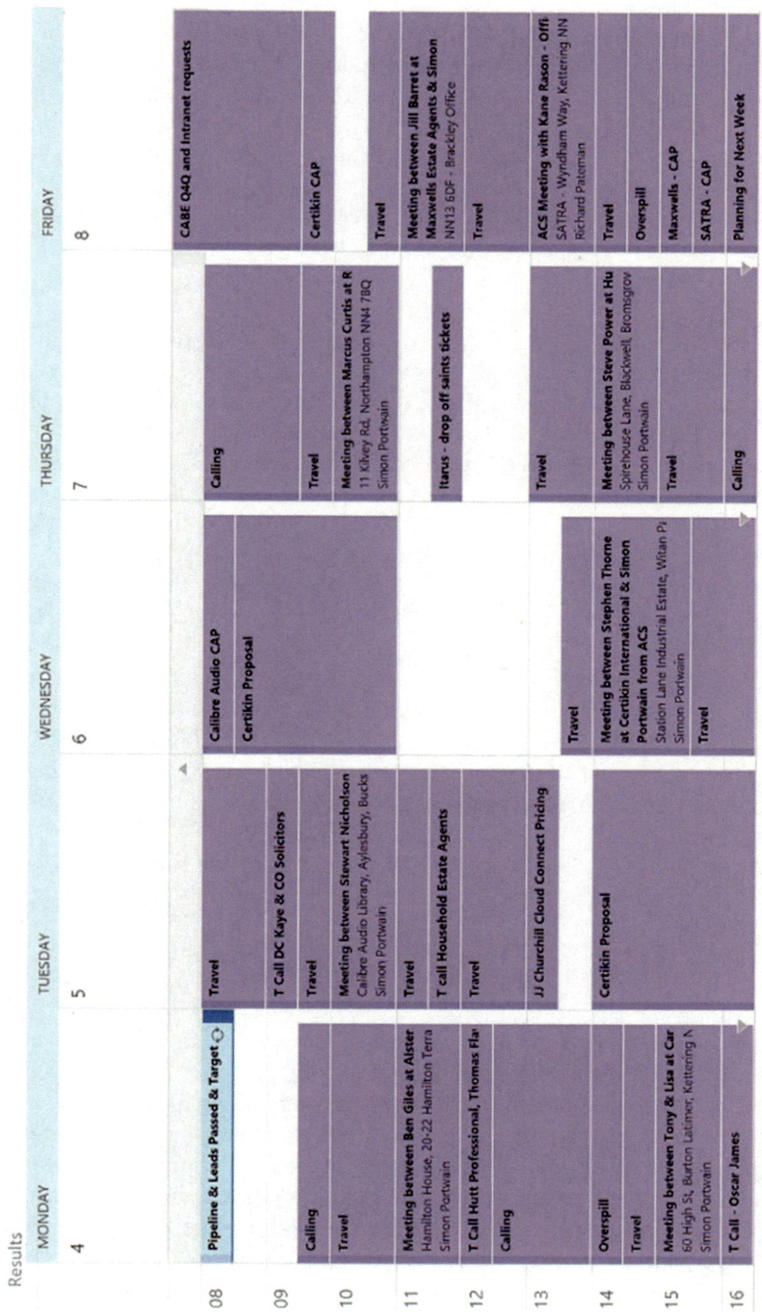

The skeleton makeup of the week is no different than the unplanned diary. The difference being is that the following have been factored for:

1) Calling – you'll notice that calling regularly occurs in the sales icons diary. Come to think of it there isn't a day where calling doesn't feature and that's key. Often when salespeople are busy with meetings and other activities it'll mean that calling takes a backseat and often gets overlooked. Days may pass, sometimes even a week since the salesperson last picked up the phone to make some prospect calls. Now this is terrible for your pipeline as in a few weeks or months you'll be lacking meetings and sales. But it's even worse for your sales skills. Take exercise for example, if you fail to exercise you get unfit and put on weight. Avoiding making phone calls is no different, if you fail to use a skill then eventually you become rusty and potentially lose that skill. If you fail to regularly make prospecting phone calls then your skills in this area will reduce and you won't become a sales icon.
2) Travel – quite self-explanatory, you'll need to factor in travel time to go to your meetings.
3) Drop in calls – notice that these are scheduled too. In this example the sales icon has denoted this as a T call, known as Try call. Bear in mind, here that you can factor in the odd drop in calls next door or over the road, the important fact here is that time has been scheduled specifically for drop in calls.
4) Overspill – as I mentioned in the block booking section, it's best practice to factor in some overspill. This is so that you have some time free to deal with urgent issues that occur that you haven't factored for, or some additional time to deal with some outstanding emails etc.
5) CAP – which stands for core action processes. Note that we have slotted time to carry out these activities to ensure that items do not get missed.

This is but an example. Your diary may look completely different to this. For instance you may receive hundreds of emails a day, therefore it may be best for you to factor regular intervals in the day when you tackle your email inbox. Separately in your role, you may spend much of your time putting together proposals or designing solutions, if this is the case then again you will need to associate a portion of your time to this in your diary.

What you plan for in your diary is down to you, again the important thing that I will reiterate is to pre-plan your diary. If you can do this effectively then you have mastered your minutes.

1.11 – Conclusion to Time Chapter

This chapter revolves around the concept of how can I do more with my time. It may be the case that you're being wasteful with your time, or not utilising your day to its maximum, which I'm sure this chapter will have highlighted for you. We started by looking at time association, something I love to speak to aspiring sales icons about as I'll often start with the question of "What's your time worth?" Remember that we want to focus every ounce of our being on as many high-pay-off activities as we can, if we can delegate the low-pay-off activities then great, do it. Remember that you're an expert, so use your time wisely and effectively, master your minutes and you'll be well on your way to becoming a sales icon.

Then we verge into the subject of note taking, which sounds like a mind numbingly boring topic, but it's an area which can save you masses amounts of time should you do it right! Note taking is your divers downline that you use to seamlessly pick up where you left off, and believe me, when you're speaking with thousands of decisionmakers you need something to reference and jog your memory as you'll never remember it all. The important parts are to always take notes and make them really easy to read and scan for quick reference at a later date.

Following on from this we talk about boosting your meeting count and route planning. Try a hybrid model of hitting the phones as well as conducting drop in calls. That way we maximise the time in our day and make every journey more worthwhile than just for one meeting. Make life easy by planning these drop-in calls in advance, put together a list of drop in calls and sort them by postcode or area. Then when you're planning your meetings you can refer to this and fill the gaps in your diary with drop in calls when you're in an area. Use with this the route planning which is a topic discussed in the chapter and you'll be a time efficiency guru. Try mapping your prospects and customers with Google Maps and then you'll be sure to maximise each and every day with drop in calls or meetings.

Subsequently, we talk about the flagging system which has to be one of the most efficient tips I can give for mastery over your time. Don't get this misunderstood, this isn't simply for sales, the flagging system can be used for any process which requires that same set of activities. On the subject of the flagging system I've given you my core action processes - OneNote, calendar, email and LinkedIn. Yours maybe different, but the important thing to do is identify your core action processes and come up with a flag for them. That way you can mark any notes or to do lists with that flag once it's completed, this way you'll never again miss a follow up activity. The term I use is 'CAP' my call or meeting, if I have 'CAPed' a meeting then I've conducted all of my core action processes.

Finally we get to our golden hours, dubbed as golden as they're the hours that are most fruitful and will produce gold like returns. Remember that you should organise your day with activities that match the time of day, our focus is to be results driven. Therefore, don't use the golden hours of the day for admin, make sure you focus on prospecting here and then do your admin in the downtime period.

Key Takeaways – Discipline 1 – Time

- Time Association
  - You're a skilled specialist and your time is more valuable than other people with less valuable and expert knowledge
  - Our goal is to increase our level of high pay off activities to their maximum and reduce our level of low pay off activities to their minimum by delegating tasks
- Note Taking
  - Remember that this is your divers downline, it's a discipline to save you time
  - Layout of your typed-up notes is very important, notes need to be succinct and be scannable to read quickly
- Boost Your Meeting Count
  - Try a hybrid approach of booking meetings and dropping in to prospects when you're in the area

    - Note down the switch board configuration to save you time the next time you call
- Route Planning
    - The goal is to book meetings in close location to one another
    - Google maps can be a good tool to plan routes efficiently
- Flagging System
    - Identify your core action processes
    - Use flags to identify when tasks have been completed both on to do lists and on your notepad
- Golden Hours
    - Utilise the right time in the day for the right tasks
    - Creative tasks should be conducted when your capabilities are at their peak
    - Admin tasks should be undertaken in downtime such as lunch periods for customers

Discipline 2 – Planning

Planning, also called strategy, is a concept we as salespeople often overlook. The trouble is that we're so eager to succeed that we perceive that the best approach is to go all out gung-ho. Now while this ambition and work rate is admirable, it's never going to turn you into a sales icon. The advantageous route is to take a step back, put together a plan or strategy and then commit to executing that strategy. If our strategy doesn't become fruitful then we adapt it as we go, but each time taking a step back to analyse our pitfalls and ways to improve, and then executing the altered plan.

In this section we're going to discuss some of the disciplines you can adopt in your planning process in your pursuit to become a sales icon. We'll begin at the start, looking at what we define as your reverse-funnel planning. In this part, we convert a sales target into its activity steps because let's face it, a target of one million or ten million gross profit means nothing. What any salesperson needs is the guidelines to achieving that goal, such as X number of opportunities that close, or to make Y number of calls a month.

When we've developed our activity requirements to surpass our target we're on track and focused, then comes the application. That's where the next part of the planning process comes in, your prospect attack plan. We highlight that all too many salespeople make the mistake of being overly cavalier in their approach, costing them a great deal. Sometimes it only costs them time but other times it will cost them their job! In the book we'll focus on astutely planning which prospects to attack and the key criteria that we should be assessing.

Prospects aren't the sole focus of this planning process; we'll also look into our account attack plan. We all know that accounts will be our easiest and sometimes quickest wins, so we'll deep dive into some techniques for account maximisation, meaning to get the most business out of an account.

So if planning isn't your forte or you're looking to improve the way you plan currently then venture into this chapter and plan your way to becoming a sales icon.

2.1 – Reverse Funnel Planning

If you want to be successful in the world of business then a book you must read along the way has to be Steven Covey's The Seven Habits of Highly Effective People. The habits identified in this book are revolutionary and imperative for success. It's a book that inspired me more than any other book, and there's not a day that passes when I don't use the habits he speaks of. One of the habits highlighted in Steven's book is the following

Habit 2 – Start with the end in mind [5]

In layman's terms what this means is that for any activity we conduct we should also be looking at what we want the resulting outcome to be. Take a diet for example, usually our motivation for changing our diet is to be healthier or to lose weight. It is this principle of 'start with the end in mind' which is the foundation to our reverse funnel planning.

In sales, you will undoubtedly have been given a target of some sort, whether it be number of sales or gross profit or turnover. If you haven't been set a target or you'd like to be more ambitious, then set a target for yourself and write this number down. Once again I'm going to use an example to explain this principle, so for this example we're going to set a target of £1m gross profit.

Task – write down your target

Now picture in your mind what a funnel looks like, you all know the sales funnel and how it works therefore I'm not going to bore you with that.

We have the leads at the top of the funnel, moving down to opportunities and then to sales decreasing part by part. Now comes the bit of analysis. You may have reviewed this before but if you haven't then this will be really exciting. What we want to find is our conversion rates through the stages of the funnel. Here are the things you need to analyse (don't worry if you don't have these, you can use the sales averages and adapt yours to be more accurate in the future):

1) How many opportunities on average do I convert to a sale?
2) How many warm leads on average do I convert into an opportunity?
3) How much activity on average do I need to develop a warm lead?

Task – answer these 3 questions and note them down (if you don't have the answers then use my rough averages and develop your own over time).

Industry averages.

As a good starting point a valid approximation would be to use the following:

Conversion rates:

- Opportunities to sale – 33%
- Warm leads to opportunities – 50%
- Activity to warm lead – 10% (varies on channel)

So here is where Steven Covey's Habit 2 – start with the end in mind comes into play. We know our end goal, for this example I'm using £1m gross profit. However, there is one thing that we're missing and that's the average size of opportunities, this will vary per industry and if you don't know yours I'd ask a collective group of your colleagues to get the answer or just take a best guess if you are unable to do that.

Sales Icon Example

For this let's say the following:

- average opportunity size is £20k Gross Profit
- Opportunities to sale – 33%
- Warm leads to opportunities – 50%
- Activity to warm lead – 10%
- End goal – £1m GP

Identifying how many sales we need to make?

We know that our average opportunity is worth £20k Gross Profit, our target is £1m Gross Profit and with this we can deduce how many sales we need to make on this basis by undertaking the following:

Step 1 – divide my end goal target by my average opportunity size

£1m/£20k = 50

This tells me that I need to convert 50 opportunities to sales which amount to an average size of £20k, this will mean I can hit my target of £1m Gross Profit.

Identifying how many opportunities we require?

Now that I know the number of sales that I need to make I can now work out how many opportunities that I need to develop to meet my target.

Step 2 – divide my number of sales required (in this case 50) by my opportunities to sale conversion rate (in this case 33% or a third)

50 / (1/3) = 150

This tells me that I need 150 opportunities in order to reach my end goal of £1m Gross Profit.

Identifying how many warm leads we require?

So I know how many opportunities I need to meet my target, but to gain these opportunities I need to know how many warm leads I must have/build, which I can find in the next step.

Step 3 – divide my number of opportunities required (in this case 150) by my warm leads to opportunity conversion rate (in this case 50%)

150/ (1/2) = 300

This tells me that I require 300 warm leads in order to reach my end goal of £1m Gross Profit.

Identifying how much activity we require?

I will discuss more on this activity piece in greater depth later in the book. This is an important step to formulate and then use your reverse funnel analysis. Without giving away too much, later in this book we will discuss channels that you can utilise to develop warm leads, all of which have different conversion rates. For simplicity in this section though we'll say that your conversion rate for activity to a warm lead is 10%. I can then use:

Step 4 – divide my number of warm leads required (in this case 300) by my activity to warm lead conversion rate (in this case 10%)

300/0.1 = 3,000

This tells me that I need to be prospecting 3,000 external stakeholders with a conversion rate of 10% in order to meet my target of £1m Gross Profit.

This sounds like a tall order initially, wow 3,000 prospects, that's loads! But remember this is based annually, plus if you consider that if you made 100 calls a day for a five-day week over forty-eight weeks this would equate to 24,000 calls a year. That 3,000 doesn't seem so vast now when you take this into account.

So to conclude, in order to reach our end goal of £1m Gross Profit we would need:

- To have 50 sales of average size (£20k) per annum
- To generate 150 opportunities per annum of this size
- To develop 300 warm leads per annum of this size
- To prospect 3,000 organisations per annum of this size

Why does this help?

If someone sat me down and said your target is £1m GP, go out and get it then I'd probably take a big gulp of coffee, then I'd start to sweat and panic. Then as the worry slowly diminishes I'd start to think how I'm going to achieve this goal! The point is that it's daunting, and that's the case no matter what your target is.

What reverse funnel planning will do is to break down your target into manageable chunks. Once you've done this you can understand how you're going to achieve the goal and in fact find that the goal is actually very achievable, especially when you break it down into manageable chunks.

Let's take our example once again of a target of £1m Gross Profit. If instead of thinking about this in its complete entity I instead used my reverse funnel analysis to break it down into manageable chunks it would look like the following.

Per month I need:

- 25 leads
- 13 opportunities (£20k Gross Profit each)
- 4 to 5 sales a month (£20k Gross Profit each)

Then straightaway my stress levels and worry about my target have dissipated. I can see how this is more achievable. I just need to focus on my activity goals and the results will come. By activity goals I mean developing leads and opportunities. There's much more on this topic later so again don't fret.

Skewing your target:

Think back to our flagging system earlier. The whole point in the flagging system was to break up your workload into manageable chunks, those being your core action processes. You can do the exact same thing for your target, what I mean by this is breaking it up into manageable chunks and skewing that target.

I can skew my target in whatever way I deem appropriate. For example if I was new to the role I would obviously start off slow and build from there. Therefore I may want to skew my target to be weighted more in the backend of my year. For this my reverse funnel planning may look like the following:

- £1m GP target for the year
- 10% in Q1
- 20% in Q2
- 30% in Q3
- 40% in Q4

Which would work out as the following:

Quarter	Target
Q1	10% = £100k GP
Q2	20% = £200k GP
Q3	30% = £300k GP
Q4	40% = £400k GP

I can then take the quarter as a single entity to work out the activity requirements, such as for Q1 below.

Quarter 1

- £100k Gross Profit required
- Average opportunity size is £20k GP therefore I need to close 5 deals
- Opportunities to sale = 33% therefore I need to open up 15 opportunities minimum

- Warm leads to opportunities = 50% therefore I need to generate 30 warm leads
- Activity to warm lead = 10% therefore I need to be prospecting 300 prospects

This now gives you the plan to achieving your £100k target in Q1, now you can carry this out for the remaining quarters and you have your rough version of reverse funnel planning in a staggered, achievable approach.

Be mindful when you conduct your reverse-funnel planning that you're identifying your minimum threshold, not your maximum target. Take the previous example, we discovered that thirty warm leads are required to hit £100k Gross Profit in the first quarter. But this is a minimum thirty leads, ideally we want more. If we can get more, then chances are we close more and surpass our £100k Gross Profit target in the first quarter.

2.2 – Prospect Attack Plan

For those of you who have been lucky enough to go on an African wildlife safari you may have a head start on the rest of us. Those lucky folk have witnessed how predators set their plan of attack for their prey. Take a pride of hunting lionesses for example, their success rate for hunting prey and making a kill is on average thirty percent. Now they have learnt from experience that it makes no sense to attack just any prey, they are selective and calculated in their plan of attack. They know that conservation of energy is key, and the more hunts that go unsuccessful the higher the chance of peril for them and their pride.

The approach they take is on a risk/reward basis. They will judge whether the reward of taking down a mighty water buffalo is worth the risk it presents, they gauge whether their pride has the resources to take down such a large animal, they asses the health of the animal and any weaknesses it may have. If they deem the risk too high then they will call it before the attack and move onto the next target. The key point is that lionesses will evaluate their prey thoroughly before they begin a hunt, they want to find the easiest kill that has the highest chance of success therefore they look for the old, young, weak or injured as their prime targets.

This is a lesson we should take on board from these animals. We need to be calculated and selective in planning who to attack as prospects as this is one of the most important facets of the planning process, and potentially the whole sales process. Get it wrong and you could waste vast amounts of time prospecting the wrong people, and in essence becoming a busy fool. I've seen many a salesperson fall by the wayside, not because they lack the ambition, work rate or proficiency, but because they didn't appropriately plan who to attack as prospects. So if you're new to sales or a sales veteran just take the time to assess your current attack plan and see if your approach is as efficient as it can be.

"Vision without action is a daydream. Action without vision is a nightmare." – Japanese proverb [6]

I really like this quote as it sums up most salespeople in their prospect attack plan. Commonly, the actions of salespeople are often unquestionable, it's the vision, or should I add intelligent vision that they lack.

Businesses spend inordinate amounts of time and capital on their strategy so why should we as salespeople be any different. Take the car manufacturer Chrysler who saw first-hand the flourishing benefits of an effective strategy. In the early 1990s, they experienced somewhat of a decline in sales. In a bid to turn things around they appointed a new CEO, Dieter Zetsche. They needed to act fast as their financial woes increased as they saw performance problems, rising costs and economic downturn affecting their bottom line. Zetsche focused on changing their strategy, and so he appointed Bill Russo as the vice president of business strategy. They saw great success from focusing on their strategy and gaining buy in from their staff which led to $1.2 billion in earnings, to which they also rolled out a new team, the Chryslers office of strategy management of 13 full-time employees dedicated to strategy. If a business such as this turned things around by focusing on its strategy then doesn't it show you how vital strategy can be. If Chrysler employ a dedicated team solely for strategy then doesn't this demonstrate that its of imperative value to any business and to any individual? Your strategy should be no different, you should run things like your own businesses and evaluate and plan accordingly.

In this section we're going to divulge how a sales icon incorporates intelligent vision into their prospect attack plan.

What's the end goal of this section?

The end goal of this section is to have a sweet spot for your prospects. We want to identify a set of criteria which tells us whether a prospect is worth pursuing or not. If they are worth pursuing then great we qualify them in. If they are not worth pursuing then that's still great as we've saved a lot of time and heartache later down the road. Therefore, we'd qualify them out. So at the end of this section we want to have those set of criteria so we can put our prospect attack plan in motion.

Think of our prospect attack plan as a spirit level, we'll call it our sales spirit level. We want to able to hold our spirit level up next to a prospect and if the spirit level says that the prospect falls within certain criteria then great, they're in our attack plan. If, however, it leans too much to one side then they're not right, they may be too big or too small or just not right for one reason or another.

How to plan?

There is an abundance of different things to consider when planning your attack, but I've detailed the main topics I consider essential to review, the core five criteria:

- Geographical location
- Business turnover
- Number of employees
- Vertical
- Need

Geographical Location – it may depend on your type of business whether this is very important to consider or not. Obviously, I assume that you're smart enough to not attack prospects overseas if you can only facilitate the needs of businesses in your country. What I mean by assess your geographical location is that you may have a better chance of prospecting businesses in a certain area than opposed to other areas. Take a simplistic business model such as a window cleaners, it would be naïve for such a business to attack prospects who are 50+ miles away as it may not make commercial sense. Moreover, often customers like to use local businesses just in case they require them urgently in an ad hoc manner. Therefore, take the time to look at either your own or your peers' accounts, this way you will see if there is any geographical trends to which you can stick to. Believe you me it's much easier that way. For example if you found that all of your accounts were in a 50-mile radius of your head office then you'd know to attack prospects also in this vicinity or potentially slightly further afield such as 60 miles.

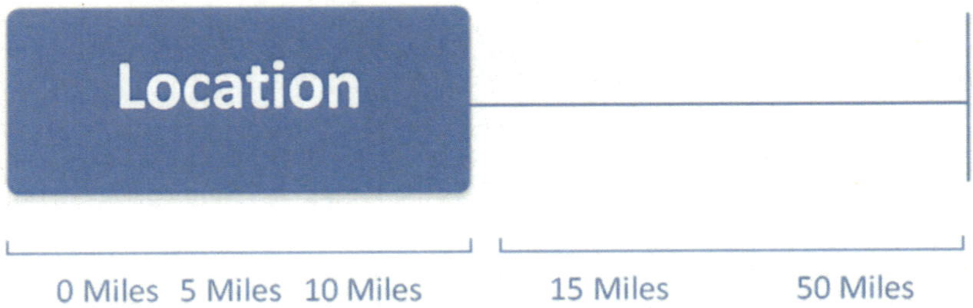

Business Turnover – business turnover is often key to consider as this could make or break your prospecting attack. I once worked with a consultancy business that has a product offering that was so costly that only companies with a turnover of £30M+ had sufficient budget allocated to be able to afford their offerings. Therefore one of their prospect attack criteria was businesses whose turnover was more than £30m. For those of you thinking that this only is necessary for a lower limited threshold, you'd be wrong. Another example I would give is that I worked with an IT outsourcing company, their business was based on being an IT support partner for the SMB market. Research with them found that their sweet spot for company turnover was between £500k<£7M on average. Anything below £500k and the prospective business wouldn't have enough IT requirements to constitute outsourcing to them. Anything above £7M turnover and the business would usually employ an internal IT person therefore relinquishing the need for an outsourced IT solution.

Number of Employees – for many organisations this is very important as it often dictates what the size of opportunities will be within a prospect. Take for example an external HR consultancy, it would be ludicrous for them to attack very small businesses such as single man organisations or up to 5-man organisations. In most circumstance an organisation of this size just wouldn't require enough HR support for it to be commercially viable for the Human Resources consultancy. Conversely though if you consider a Human Resources software company this may be their bread and butter market, SMBs that have between 2 and 5 employees as they're too small to either outsource to a Human Resources consultancy or hire a Human Resources manager. Human Resources illustrates perfectly how different businesses may target different companies as prospects based solely on their number of employees. Again for your business it may not be as clear-cut as this. What I'd advise is to look at your current accounts or your peers' accounts. See if there are any trends in relation to employee size.

If you find a trend such as 80% of your accounts have between 20 and 100 employees then hey presto you have some criteria to follow as you create your prospect attack plan.

Vertical – you might say that this is rather self-explanatory as a factor to review, but you'd be surprised how often this is overlooked by salespeople. In the majority of industries, a new prospect will ask for some form of reference customer, and often will ask for a reference of a customer in their industry. Take for example with education, if you were pitching a software solution to a school they most probably would ask what other schools use the software already. Therefore to make your life easier and your prospecting as efficient as can be take the time to look at your own and your peers accounts and see whether there are any vertical trends. This doesn't mean that you should exclude those potential prospects who you don't have a reference customer in that vertical. It just means that you may have better luck focusing on the verticals where you have a large number of references. For instance if you found your product offering was popular within the professional services vertical at 60% of your customer base, then it would make sense to cater for this and have the majority of your prospects within this vertical also.

Need – is there a clear and obvious need for your products or services? Simply put you may find an organisation that's in the right geographical location, has the right business turnover, number of employees and in a strong vertical for you. But the fact remains that they don't need what you provide; if that's the case then you can disqualify them straight away. Sometimes you can identify that there's no clear and obvious need from first glance. For instance a chain of bakery stores won't have an avid requirement for bouncers on the doors as security services. On other occasions it may not be so clear however, for instance a business may have a head office internationally that look after strategic decisions. Nevertheless, be careful not to assume too much. You never know who could be your best customer so when in doubt keep them as an option and disqualify them out later if you find out more insight.

What do I assess?

In order to determine what the most helpful prospect-attack plan is, we need to assess our businesses' customers. So take a look at your CRM, or conversely sit down with a few peers one on one or maybe your boss and go through their customer list one by one.

Here's the process:

Step 1 – identify customer
Step 2 – assess their five core criteria and write them down

Step 3 – repeat step one for a different customer and then repeat step two, do this for as many customers as you can, try for a minimum twenty customers
Step 4 – review all information that you have on your analysis of your customers

Step four is key, the review stage. From this what you should see is common denominators between customers. For instance these common denominators could be that all customers sit within certain verticals or have a turnover of a certain amount etc. If you're lacking any common denominators then increase your sample size, if you've only assessed twenty customers then try assessing fifty or one hundred.

Ask your peers for help!

This can be a hard task just on your own so don't be afraid to ask your peers for help. Select a few of your peers, preferably those who are experienced in their role and are successful in sales. Take them aside and ask them to highlight two of their smaller customers, two of their average customers and two of their largest customers. Once they have done this then ask them about the core five criteria such as the customers' vertical or number of employees.

From this you can formulate your outliers as depicted in the diagrams for location, business turnover and number of employees. On the lower end you'll be able to see the minimum threshold of a customer and on the other end you'll be able to see the maximum threshold of a customer. A word of caution here though is not to take one peers feedback as gospel. Just because their largest or smallest customer is of a certain criteria doesn't necessarily mean yours should be that way too. So instead converse with multiple peers and compare this with your own analysis of customers from your CRM system.

Identifying our sweet spot?

So now that we've assessed our customer base we want to formulate our sweet spot criteria. Again, I highlight that this will be our sales spirit level, we will use this to assess all future prospects against these criteria to either qualify them in or out as to whether they're worth pursuing.

Our sweet spot for prospects are

- Geographical location = within X miles of Y
- Business turnover = X<sweet spot<Y
- Number of employees = X<sweet spot<Y
- Verticals = in verticals X, Y, Z
- Need = bespoke to your organisation

Note – It may be the case that for your business there are mixtures of criteria. What I mean by this is that it may incorporate a number of criteria such as turnover and employee size. For example your analysis may show that your strengths are within the manufacturing vertical and for businesses who have between 30 and 200 employees. Therefore analyse all of these areas and see if there are trends in multiple areas, if there are then you have a very solid prospect attack plan.

How do I use my prospect attack plan?

Your prospect attack plan is a tool and only a tool. If you use it then it will be beneficial, if you overlook it then it adds no value. If I talk personally for a second, what I always found hard in sales is disqualifying prospects. If you're anything like me then you're an overzealous optimist, and for good reason. I like to think that I can help everyone in some way or another. But this leaves me in a lurch, as with this mentality I'll have the whole world on my prospect list.

This mentality is shared by most sales icons. They feel that there isn't a prospect they couldn't help despite the makeup of their business. Now whilst this point is valid it's not the easiest road.

Let's use an example, you're in a time trial-running race. Your goal is to set the fastest time possible and you're given the option of running one of two courses. They are both a mile in distance but one is entirely flat and the other is uphill throughout. Which course do you choose? Well it's a no brainier, the flat course, this is the course that I have a better chance of setting a faster time.

Your prospect attack plan is no different than this. It is a set of criteria that highlights the easiest path for success. If you go outside of that criteria it's not saying that you won't be successful, but what it is saying is that it will be a more difficult task. Why take the difficult road to success when the easy road is guaranteed and you'll get there much faster?

This will truly be a godsend for those optimistic salespeople that struggle to disqualify prospects. It enables you to be ruthless with your prospect attack plan; you now have a set of key criteria to follow.

So we've justified our point as to why this is useful, but what do you do with this criteria once you've identified it? What I encourage sales icons to do is assess all their current and future prospects against this criteria. So take your prospect list right now and assess them. Do they fall within this criteria or outside? If they fall within then great, but if they fall outside then a decision needs to be made. Either you disqualify them or if you have valid justification then you can qualify then in. But for any future prospects assess them with this criteria and disqualify early on to save time and resource.

Note – as you take a deeper dive into this analysis you may find that your criterion is product specific. What I mean by this is that there are certain products or offerings of your business that are more suited to certain criteria. For instance with an IT solutions provider I worked with we found that one of their offerings namely for proactive server monitoring was strong in many corporate businesses, but weak within the education sector. The reason for this is that education couldn't stretch its budget to afford the offering and because their operations weren't as business critical as corporate businesses it wasn't as imperative to have a high level of business uptime. You may be wondering how this is important but it truly is imperative when you look at the big picture. If that knowledge wasn't passed throughout their company I'm certain many a salesperson would waste a great deal of time trying to push this offering into education prospects, once again becoming a busy fool.

Activity

If you're new to sales, been doing it a few years or even a seasoned veteran I encourage you to stop your day-to-day activities just for a moment. Take just ten minutes out of your day and assess your prospect attack plan with these five core criteria. Honestly, it could save you days, weeks and months of wasted effort on prospects that won't materialise into customers.

2.3 – Prospect Plan Structure

So far we have ascertained our sweet spot for prospects which is a great step. With this information we can easily identify which prospects are worth pursuing by using our sales spirit level. The trouble is that though you may have disqualified a number of prospects, you still have a wide range of criteria which represents a real challenge. For instance, you may have criterion that leads you to focus your prospecting on organisations with a turnover between £1M and £15M, which is a massive range. The challenge many salespeople will have is who to target from there, often they'll make the mistake of focusing on one type of prospect.

You've probably seen it yourself when a sales peer has focused only on a certain type of business, very often it being the large business that they hope with one sale will reward them with a year's target worth of sales. Whilst I would never want to deter somebody from attacking the big fish I would encourage them to structure their approach just to be safe. What I mean by structure your approach, is to proportion your time between a mixture of prospects based on size, i.e. small, medium, large.

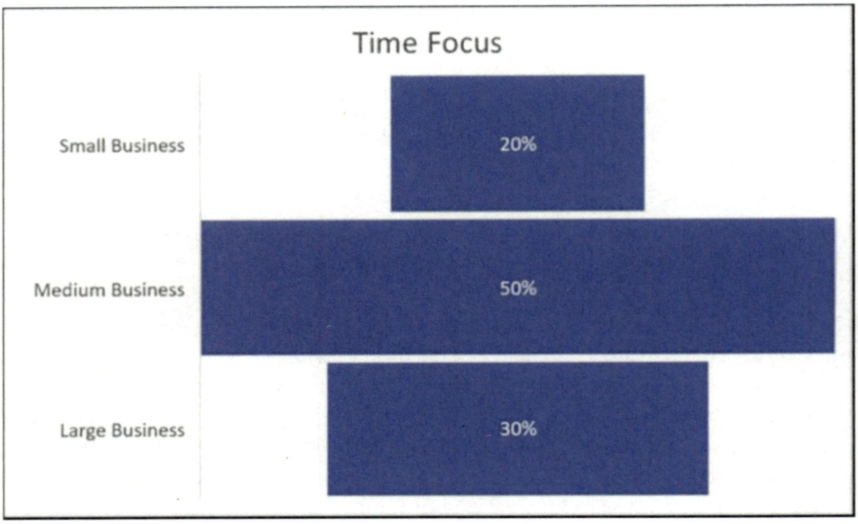

That's the focal point from this section. We want to take our sweet spot and categorise it into subcategories. The subcategories that you use are completely down to you, for most sales icons they use three categories, small, medium and large.

Why is this important?

Well we've all heard of the saying 'don't put all your eggs in one basket' and it holds true for your prospect plan structure. Take the salesperson who only goes for the big fish, in the circumstance that he loses one or two opportunities, then he may be in a very difficult position indeed. I've seen many a salesperson in my career make this mistake, and often had to pay the price with their job. A better approach is to have the big fish as prospects but also be bringing in some smaller business in the meantime to bide you over on your sales results.

How to do this?

The best way to start is by using your prospect attack plan we discussed previously to gauge what your sweet spot of business is. Then you use this to segregate your structure. For instance if I found that our sweet spot of business was the following:

- Vertical = accountants
- Turnover = £500k<£7M

I may determine that my structure would be the following
Small business = accountants with turnover between £500k<£1M
Medium business = accountants with turnover between £1M<£4M

Large business = accountants with turnover between £4M<£7M

What I'm trying to say is that it's all relative to your prospecting attack plan as to how you structure your prospect attack plan. What constitutes as a large opportunity for one company may be small fry for another company. Yet by keeping within your sweet spot here you have a much better chance of winning the business.

Be Flexible:

Always keeping the same approach of proportioning what prospects to attack will not be the most beneficial, try to alter your approach as you gain more accounts and foothold in the industry. For example when you're first starting out the following approach may suit you:

- 30% small business
- 50% medium business
- 20% large business

But as you gain more and more accounts which are supplementing a good part of your sales target you may choose to adapt this to something like:

- 20% small business
- 40% medium business
- 40% large business

I can't tell you how to proportion your approach as it differs per business but I would recommend trying to proportion your approach. If it is not working take note and adapt accordingly, or if it is working but you can alter it to be even more successful, then do so.

Example:

So let's use an example to make this clear to understand. Let's hypothesise that I'm starting out in a new sales role and I deem that the appropriate skew for my focus is as follows:

- 30% small business
- 50% medium business
- 20% large business

I then review my sweet spot criteria which, let's say for this example that my sweet spot criterion is what I depicted before, that being:

- Vertical = accountants
- Turnover = £500k<£7M

I decide that my subcategories would constitute as:

- Small business = accountants with turnover between £500k and £2M
- Medium business = accountants with turnover between £2M and £5M
- Large business = accountants with turnover between £5M and £7M

I then add prospects to my prospecting list in conjunction with this focus. So for simplicity's sake let's say I wanted ten organisations to prospect. Then when I'm building that list I would look for:

- 3 x accountants with turnover between £500k and £2M
- 5 x accountants with turnover between £2M and £5M
- 2 x accountants with turnover between £5M and £7M

I have used ten prospects as an example. In reality you may want a few hundred, but throughout you must keep this structure of size proportion, that's the key thing.

What are the steps?

The key steps you need to remember are

Step one – Review your sweet spot criteria

All of the below steps must comply with your sweet spot criteria so start by reviewing what they are.

Step two – Quantify your subcategories

You need to decide what quantifies a sub category. For instance, for small businesses should I categorise this between £500k and £2M or £500k and £3M? This step isn't easy, but if you take the time to assess your accounts you'll get a good understanding of what you'd deem as small, medium and large. Don't over analyse this too much, you can always change the parameters of a subcategory later.

Step three – Develop a skew

Is spending 20% of your time on large business right for you or not? I can't give you this answer, only you can. Think about your experience, how long you've been in your role and industry and make a judgement call of what you deem is best. If you're really unsure then try an equal split for a period of time. Then review the split in a few months' time and assess whether you can manipulate this skew to your benefit.

Step four – Find prospects to fit into that skew

So there are two scenarios here, either you've been selling for a while and thus have a prospect list, or you're starting out a fresh, i.e. developing a prospect list from scratch.

If you already have a prospect list then you'll need to segregate each prospect into its subcategory, such as small, medium and large following the criteria you set. What you may find is that your current prospects list doesn't fit the skew that you decided. Say for instance that you had a prospect list of one hundred prospects, you segregated your prospects into their perspective sub categories and found that:

Small business = 40% – 40 organisations
Medium business = 10% – 10 organisations
Large business = 50% – 50 organisations

But you have decided on a skew of:

- Small business = 20%
- Medium business = 50%
- Large business = 30%

Then you will have to spend some time rationalising your prospect list. It may be that you have to cut a few of a certain subcategory to comply with the skew that you've decided on. Or the more positive approach is to add to your prospect list in the subcategory you need to even the skew out.

Take that example above again. For this I would increase my prospect list from one hundred to two hundred in the following proportion:

- Small business = 20% – 40 organisations
- Medium business = 50% – 100 organisations
- Large business = 30% – 60 organisations

Thus from my original prospecting list to comply with this skew I need to add:

- 0 organisations to small business
- 90 organisations to medium business
- 10 organisations to large business

If you're starting out fresh it's much easier. Just decide how many prospects you want as a total number, then add prospects in compliance with the skew you've decided on.

Assessing our prospect plan:

It's important to assess the strategy for your prospect plan every so often, regular intervals such as quarterly or bimonthly would be best. The reason for this is that if we're going to become a sales icon we need to evolve as salespeople. Your strategy now compared to three months' time maybe completely different. Maybe the market changes, or your offering, or your proficiency. Whatever it is, we must make sure that we re-evaluate our approach every so often. We should be asking ourselves:

- -Am I pursuing the right size businesses?
- -Would it be more beneficial to change my skew?
- -Are my subcategories of the right criteria? For instance if I changed my maximum turnover to include businesses with higher turnover would I benefit?

2.4 – Sales Cycle

Oh do I wish that I could speak to a prospect and they buy from me straightaway. Unfortunately on most occasions, this isn't feasible as there's a sales cycle to consider.

What's a sales cycle?

For those of you unaware of what a sales cycle is it can basically be defined as the average time in which it takes a prospect to make a decision to buy from you. For instance, below I've depicted some examples of a sales process for two opportunities and the interaction steps that the sales icon followed.

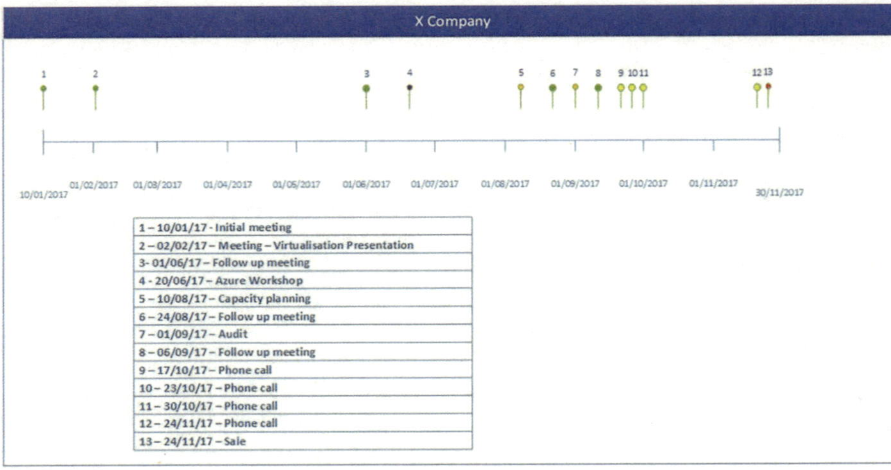

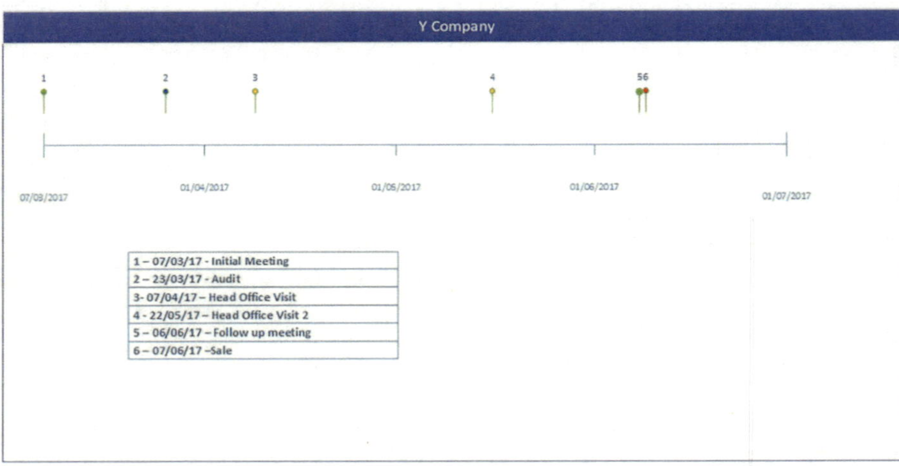

I'm not going to dissect the sales process here but what I am going to draw your attention to is the sales cycle. These two examples are the sales process for exactly the same solution yet selling to two different prospects. Note how the opportunity with X Company took ten months to make the sale with twelve interaction steps. Whereas the opportunity with Y Company took three months to make the sale with a mere five interaction steps.

The point I make here is that sales cycles will vary, of course you'll have outliers, those that close in a very short window or those that take much longer. For some industries the sales cycle can be a matter of days or weeks, for others in can be more like months or even years. Every single business will have an average sales cycle though, so work out what yours is and use this information to your advantage.

Why's this important?

The simple answer is that you can't become a sales icon without taking this into account. Say for instance, that I'm hosting a dinner party and I invite a number of friends over for 1900 on Saturday night. I spend the whole day preparing my meal that I'm going to cook, it's a beautiful 5kg turkey. I spend hours and hours preparing my side dishes, the potatoes, the Brussels sprouts, the parsnips, the swede and the gravy. I, however, forget to factor in the cooking time of my prized bird. It's gets to 1830 and I only just put it in the oven, by the time it gets to serving dinner at 1930 my bird isn't even partially cooked. I'm left with the dilemma of either waiting for the bird to cook for a few hours or not serving it at all. Either way the meal is ruined!

Your sales cycle is just like this, you need to factor in time. You can do all the preparation and work that you want to but if you're not mindful of the sales cycle then you're unlikely to become a sales icon.

How to find out my sales cycle?

If you are unsure of your sales cycle then either ask your peers or work it out yourself. You can do this by looking at some of the opportunities you have closed. Try reviewing when you first met with a customer or spoke to them and how long it took till the sale closed. Don't do this for simply one opportunity, assess multiple to get a good range of data so that your findings will be more accurate.

Sales cycle variations:

To add a fun bit of complexity to this piece, you may notice some variations in your sales cycle. For instance, if you were to compare say education customers with corporate organisations you may find that the sales cycle in the education market is much longer than it is in corporate. Separately you may find that smaller business have a faster sales cycle than larger business.

Often you find that variations in sales cycle relate to:

- Size of business
- Vertical

Conversely you may find that for your business the sales cycle is always the same, such as it's a roughly three months for any opportunity. If that's the case then great, you can plan appropriately for that and forecast more accurately. Therefore, if you were just joining a business and found this out, your plan would detail how in your first quarter of work it's unlikely that any sales could be achieved due to this sales cycle, no excuses for quarter two, however.

Using my sales cycle to my advantage:

Where this point becomes really key is when you find your sales cycle varies depending on certain factors. For example, from your analysis above you may find that for small business your average sales cycle is only one month with an average sale of £2k GP. In addition for corporate businesses with a turnover between £2–7m you may find that the sales cycle is nine months with an average sale of £30k GP.

This is where you can take advantage. Think back to the skew we decided upon earlier. It might be fruitful to adapt this skew now that you know more about your sales cycle. For instance, you may decide that you want initially to have a higher skew of your time focused towards the small businesses, just to get some sales on the board in the short term. In conjunction with this you may want to position some time on the corporate prospects for a longer-term approach as this will have a higher pay off in the future.

For instance, in this example an appropriate plan may be to position your focus as follows:

Quarter 1

- o 75% of your time on small businesses
- o 25% of your time on corporates

Quarter 2

- o 60% of your time on small businesses
- o 40% of your time on corporates

Quarter 3

- o 50% of your time on small businesses
- o 50% of your time on corporates

Quarter 4

- o 40% of your time on small businesses
- o 60% of your time on corporates

In this way, you're working with your sales cycle parameters, and planning appropriately to counteract them, but also to have a long-term and short-term approach. When joining any business you may need to focus more initially on short term and then change the skew bit by bit to longer term as you have more success.

Note – your analysis may be more complex than that which I've outlined above, for simplicity I have only used two criteria, small businesses and corporates. You may find for you have more criteria than this. A word of caution though is to not have too many criteria, try to band together categories where possible, ideally you want less than six criteria as this will be easier to work with and analyse.

Note – don't forget the mix we discussed before. It's a risky approach to only focus on one area such as solely large opportunities where you only have a handful a year, therefore be cautious not to focus your approach on just one area as you become more successful.

2.5 – Account Attack Plan

This chapter is all about planning, but thus far the entirety has been around prospect planning. Now is the time in the chapter where we turn to account planning, as whether or not you have accounts now, you definitely will do soon. Then what's important when you have those accounts, is maximising their spending. This is both through longevity of service and by selling multiple if not all of your offerings.

Account maximisation:

The famous, or in some cases infamous upselling. Mystical to some, a godsend to others and an avenue, which shouldn't be overlooked in your pursuit to become a sales icon.

'The probability of selling to an existing customer is 60–70%, the probability of selling to a new prospect is 5–20%' – marketing metrics.[7]

This is such a profound statement and statistics prove this. Now we're all guilty of overlooking or being ungrateful for the customers we currently have. Often much of your time and your focus is on new business development, and commonly that's the fault of your business as they think that the best approach to growing is through new business. Now whilst this holds some merit, another proven technique is to maximise the spending from your current accounts. Just look at the statistic above again, it's proven that the easier sell is to your current accounts.

As such it's important that I share with you some nifty techniques for account maximisation, by that we mean extracting the greatest amount of spend from your accounts.

Techniques for account maximisation include:

- Account review meetings
- Scheduling time
- Education

Let me explain these techniques in greater depth.

Account Review Meetings

Now account review meetings may be something that you have currently with customers, if they're not then I seriously recommend adding these to your process.

What is an account review meeting?

Quite self-explanatory, an account review meeting is a face-to-face meeting with a customer. It's a chance for them to voice their feedback with you and to discuss ways that you can develop and change your practices for the future. But it's not simply for feedback purposes, it's also to understand further where else you can help your customer in the future.

The purpose at an account review meeting is to obviously keep your customer happy, but it's also an opportunity to upsell. To find out where else their budget is going, if they are still using competitors for some aspects, if there are any offerings of yours which they were unaware that you offered or an offering that they hadn't considered using before that may benefit them.

Regularity:

The regularity of an account review meeting will differ from customer to customer. For your top spending customers, I would say that you need to have regular account review meetings, such as one every quarter. However, not every customer will be accepting of this as they may be too busy. The best approach is to talk about account review meetings with your customers, push their value and your ideal regularity for them and why.

Forward Appointments:

It's important to forward-book meetings with accounts so make sure to agree with your customer when they should be held. The regularity for these I leave to your judgement, say every quarter or maybe more infrequent for some customers. Make sure to send the calendar invites over well ahead of time, for instance if you've agreed a regularity for the year then get them emailed out for the next year. Such as if you've agreed one account meeting every quarter then you should be emailing out four calendar invites for the agreed meetings. Your ideal scenario is to have regular account review meetings scheduled with your top customers. For instance, if you have say twenty top accounts, you may want to have quarterly review meetings with them all equating to eighty account meetings set in your diary already.

Who for?

You need to judge which accounts are worthy of an account review meeting. I would always recommend that you have account review meetings for your top 20% spending accounts. The other accounts are left to your judgement. Many sales icons in the past have used a sliding scale, such as the top 20% spending accounts are worthy of a quarterly review meeting. Those who sit below the top 20% but above the top 50% (top 20%>X>top 50%) we can justify for an annual review meeting. Any accounts that are in the bottom 50% may not be worthy of an account review meeting but it's completely down to your judgement. You need to be the judge of this, some sales icons I've worked with have had hundreds of customers and therefore it would be humanly impossible to visit every single customer. In this case, they were forced to be rather strict and only select a set number of customers who qualified for an account review meeting. On the other hand, I've worked with sales icons who have very few customers, but all of who are big spenders therefore for them all of their customers require regular account review meetings. The point is that this will be different for all of you, the important thing to take on board though is to have account review meetings with your customers from here on in.

Account Potential:

This is another factor to consider when looking at how regular you should have account meetings. As discussed a minute ago you may take on board this approach for account review meetings and use the sliding scale approach. However, the circumstance may arise whereby one of your customers sits in the bottom 10% of your customers by spend, yet their account potential is massive. For instance, this account may spend only £10k GP with you but you're aware that they spend £100k GP with a competitor. In such circumstance you would class this account as high potential, therefore it may be advisable to increase the regularity of contact time with this account such as by having more regular review meetings.

Example

Description	Spend status	Potential
Account A	Top 20% spending account	Minimal
Account B	Top 20<50% spending account	Minimal
Account C	Bottom 50% spending account	Large
Account D	Bottom 50% spending account	Minimal

Now if we solely judged accounts on their spending, then it's obvious to see that account C and D are only going to be worthy of an annual review meeting at best. But when we add to this the account potential then the story changes completely. As such the account review meetings I would recommend are as below:

Description	Regularity of account review
Account A	Every quarter
Account B	Annual
Account C	Every quarter
Account D	Annual or none

So the key take away here is not to overlook an accounts potential; we'll delve into this part in more depth shortly.

Activity

I recommend that you review all of your accounts to understand their potential in greater depth. The only way you're going to be able to do this though is by asking the questions, through either a review meeting (ideally), or over the phone or by email. From this you can then class your accounts by potential. What I mean by potential is the ability to spend more with you. You can then come up with a classification criteria, something like:

- High potential = Potential to spend £50k+ more
- Low potential = Potential to spend below £50k

Then you can class your accounts. What you'll find is that if you've perfected your account maximisation then all of your accounts will be classed as low potential. If, however, you find some top spending accounts with high potential then that's your sign to attack them more, improve their customer experience and keep them as happy as can be. If you find some low-spending accounts with high potential then put some focus on them, increase the regularity of your account review meetings, improve their customer experience, build rapport with the customer, everything you can to extract their potential and turn them into a top account.

Prerequisites?

Of course there are prerequisites to any account review meeting. You want to understand everything about the account that you can in order to maximise their spend.

Important prerequisites

- Spend history
- Offerings map
- Alike customer comparison

Spending history – take the time to review your customers spend for the history that you have been working with them. Is there a regularity to their spending? Have there been peaks or troughs in the past? What are they purchasing?

I worked with a sales icon who had a long-standing relationship with one of his customers, a government institution. They had a six-month sales cycle and a 'use it or lose it' budget mentality. I conducted some analysis of the customers' spending with the sales icon and we found that the vast majority of their spend came every year in March. This coincidentally was the month that their financial year-end fell. So we concluded, we must make it our mission to be meeting with them six months before March and in late February or early March at minimum just to increase our chances of maximising their spend.

Offerings map – is the customer purchasing many of your offerings or only a set few? If it's just a few then map these out and review if any other offerings may also be advantageous for them, they may be purchasing one offering that goes perfectly with something else. Put yourself in their shoes, think about their drivers, their everyday hardships and worries and from that review what offerings could make their lives a little bit easier. Plan what offerings you want to promote to them, it may not be something that they want to take up straight away but it could be food for thought for the future.

Example

Why not try an offerings map such as below?

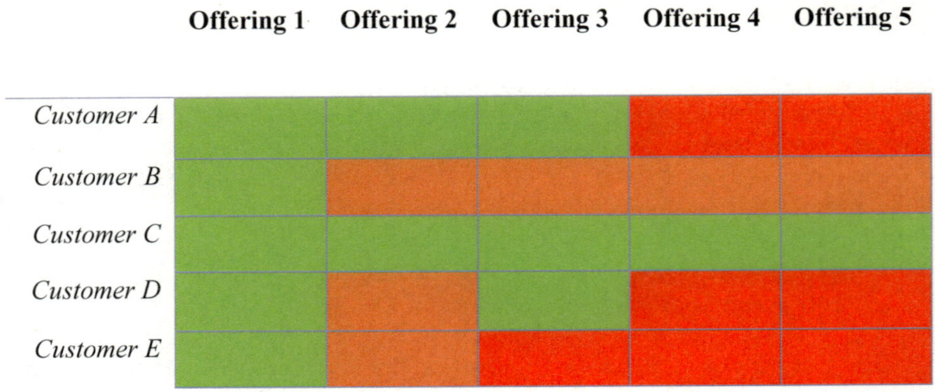

Simply write down your offerings and list them in the column headers, then list your customers in the descending rows. Then colour-code your map so you can read it easily, for simplicity I've used a traffic light system here denoting:

- Green = use offering
- Amber = discussed with customer but not using
- Red = customer not using haven't discussed

So if this was a real offerings map for a customer I'd read a great deal from this such as:

- Offering one is used by all my customers, why is that? Is that where my strengths are or is this a strength of my business?
- Customer C lacks potential as they use all of my offerings
- Customer E I need to spend time with educating them on additional offerings
- Customer B has potential
- Offering four and five haven't had much uptake, why is that? How can I adapt my approach to increase business here?

Alike customer comparison – review the customer with other alike customers you have, that could be by vertical comparison, by size, location, turnover etc. In this comparison, compare their varying spends and the offerings each of them take up with you. Are there any discrepancies? For instance, if I was a manufacturer selling showers, and I had two housing associations I worked with and the offerings we sold to them differed I could analyse why. Is there potential to sell the showers that I sell to housing association one to housing association two and vice versa. By reviewing the alike customer comparison you've also got reference ability, take the example above, you could say to housing association one that housing association two use these showers of yours because of X to get them interested.

How this Helps?

This topic revolves around account maximisation and we've discussed account review meetings and why they're essential to getting the most out of your accounts. If you simply speak to your customers blindly meaning without background then the chances are you're not going to get the most out of them. However, if with every customer you know everything beforehand, their spend history, account potential, offerings map and alike customer comparison then you're in a fantastic position to maximise their account. Flick back to the offerings map earlier, if I was going into see customer A then my goal would be to promote offerings one and two.

Activity – conduct the analysis of these areas now, they will help you to get the most out of all of your customers spend, and well on the road to becoming a sales icon.

Scheduling Customer Time

If you're like any other ambitious salesperson out there then much of your schedule is probably dominated by new business activities, whether that be cold calling, initial meetings, proposal meetings etc. Whilst this new business focus is a fantastic practice to follow it can also lead to your peril.

That's because it's easy to get caught in this pattern of having much of your time focused towards new business. The downside to such an approach is that you take your eye off the ball when it comes to your current customers, which can lead to them leaving you or most probable that you don't maximise their account spend.

So we need to do something, customers are hard enough to bring on board at the best of times, so we must ensure that they stay with us and that we maximise their spending. The good thing is that the solution is simple, all we need to do is to schedule regular customer time, emphasis on the word regular. Whether that be an hour a day, one day a week, ten days a month, whatever you deem is appropriate but be sure to schedule it. Have it as a reoccurring reminder in your outlook calendar that for example every Wednesday afternoon is dedicated to customers.

Regularity and amount:

The regularity and amount will differ from person to person. If you have a large number of accounts then one hour a week may not be adequate enough to partition off for your customers. Maybe you need to set aside a full day a week or even two days a week. Conversely if you have very few customers, you may deem that one hour a fortnight is sufficient. The way to determine the regularity and the amount of time you should give to your customers depends on two factors

1. How many customers you have?
2. How much time it takes to keep those customers satisfied?

Contact time and regular familiarity is the key here. There's no exact science as to how you should do this, but any action is better than no action. One action I've undertaken in the past is to spend some time adding value to my customers, such as by researching into innovative solutions for them and sending this over via email for each of my customers. I remember one customer of mine in the past who was really into his motivational speaking; he absolutely loved attending seminars where they'd be some form of thought leadership or a prolific speaker there. For me this set my sales alarm bells off straightaway, as I knew that I could add value to this customer personally in the future. What did I do? Well, I took it upon myself to set in my calendar at regular intervals to get in touch with this customer. I would send him things like exciting up and coming seminars, examples and extracts of new books he may be interested in, YouTube videos of talks or podcasts I thought he'd like etc. None of this activity got me a direct sale, but what it did do was build our relationship, and ensure that he sees me as more than just someone who he buys things from.

A word of warning though is to be conscious of time again. For any activity such as this you would need to look at how much time the content takes to develop. For example let's say that for each customer you decided to dedicate fifteen minutes to research and put together content which you then would email over to a customer. If you had twenty customers you would multiply this to uncover the overall amount of customer focus you require, in this case five hours of customer focus. Then you'd need to gauge the regularity of this engagement, for example you may deem that monthly interaction with customers is sufficient. In this case you could stagger your approach, such as one hour a week (for a five-week month) or block this in monthly instalments such as five hours on one day of the month.

Personally my preference is that little and often is better, so I'd go for the staggered approach. Plus with dedicating just an hour you could conduct this in your downtime such as the lunch period, so you don't waste vital selling time in your golden hours. The staggered approach may look something like this:

Regularity = 1 hour every Wednesday lunchtime

Time per customer = 15 minutes

Customers per week = 4

With this approach each customer would receive at least one interaction of this form each month.

You may want to mix up your approach for scheduling time for your customers. Sometimes you may want to send them insightful information, other times you may want to arrange a call for a catch up. Vary your approach, find out what works for you and what your customer values.

Note – to save time, try and reuse content as much as you can. For example if you developed a great email on how an offering can help a certain customer and why then try to adapt this in a way that it can be reused for other customers. For instance if you have a number of customers in the same vertical, say estate agents, create an innovative email relating to estate agents which you can use for all of them.

How will I know if I'm succeeding here?

The two items that will help you understand whether your succeeding here are:

- Customer retention rates
- Offerings map

With regards to customer retention rates, if they remain high then you're doing a good job. If I were you, I'd ask my peers what our customer retention rates are, if yours aren't higher then you're failing here. My rule of thumb is that every sales icon should have a customer retention rate of 90% plus, if you don't then you need to address why and how you can raise your retention rates to that level.

Your offerings map will also be a great indicator. If you notice that the vast majority of your customer base has a green segment for most of your offerings then you're maximising your accounts. Conversely, if it transpires that the majority of customers have a red or amber segment for most of your offerings then you're failing and thus need to focus more on account maximisation.

Activity

Have a tester month for me. For the next month schedule in regular customer time in your diary, that could be a few hours a week or a day every week, whatever suits best. Then at the end of the month judge where you are, do you feel that this is working? I'd be surprised if you say no. I very much doubt it will have instant results, but if you remain true to the cause it will have profound results.

Educate Customers

Another principle to account maximisation is educating your customers. The relationship shouldn't simply be all take. The scenario we are striving for is a win-win for both parties. Anyone who has read the challenger sale will know that the concepts outlined in that book consist of teach, tailor and take control. If you haven't read this book then don't worry too much as the approach is simple, though I would recommend you read this book soon.

This educate customers part is the same concept of teach in the challenger sale, yet this is focused towards your account base. You need to educate your customers on aspects that add value to them, their operations, their business and their unique set up. A lot of the time this may have no short-term effect, but the long-term benefits can be immeasurable.

Why do this?

So why should you do this? Why should you spend your valuable time trying to educate customers? Well the first reason is for familiarity. It's something we strive for with our prospects and customers. We want to be the first name they think of when it comes to our field of expertise. So when your customer is thinking about their next big project you want them to think, 'ah yes, James at X can help with that.' That's the familiarity we want.

In this age of unlimited access to data and resources this level of familiarity is hard to achieve, especially if you're in a competitive market. But educating your customers will differentiate you from the rest and ensure that you are the first name that your customers think of.

The second reason for doing this is for longevity. If you get your education approach right then your customers will see you as more than just a supplier or someone they buy from. They'll see you and your business as a value add partnership and when you achieve this you'll have longevity and a loyal customer that keeps coming back to spend with you. We've all been there when we've tried to prospect someone who has a very strong relationship with a competitor which is almost impenetrable to break. That's because they've become more than just a supplier to them. Obviously, the education part isn't the sole aspect to achieving this, rapport with the customer is a big aspect too. But educating your customer can build a very strong relationship and value perception also.

In addition to this, the education approach will bit by bit ring fence your customer from competition. How? Well as I explained previously, your customer will see you as more than simply a supplier, you now go beyond the call of duty. You add value to them and for that in their eyes no other supplier could do the same so why would they look elsewhere. But the important fact to remember is that if you don't do this, someone else will. If you choose not to assist your customer with educating them in various ways then a competitor at some point will come along and they will do so. Then you have the hard task of trying to coax them back to you, which is a harder task then if you had just taken the time to add value to them in the first place.

Problem resolution is another reason to educate your customers. Undoubtedly at some point in the foreseeable future something is going to go wrong, no matter how good your company is or the processes that you follow. Whether that is a wrong delivery, a late delivery, a service mishap, whatever it is problems will occur. Now if you build your status to become perceived as a value-added partner of your customers (through educating them) then problem resolution will become much easier. Your customers won't threaten to run off to competitors every time something goes wrong and the risk of them leaving is minimal. Why? Because they know that the value add service you're providing couldn't be found elsewhere.

What to educate with?

This is a common question that is asked. The easy mistake to make is to always be pitching your offerings, that's not educating, that's you trying to sell, pushing your own self-interests. That's not to mean you can't educate and push your own products, but they have to suit your customer.

Ideally you want to educate customers with information that will be insightful for them. Here some ideas of what may fall in this category:

- Articles on what their competitors are doing
- Market research
- Offerings that would be beneficial for them
- Innovations in the market
- Info on things you don't sell but may be helpful for them
- Exhibitions that they may want to attend
- Webinars that are upcoming
- Newsletters
- Offers

The list could go on and on. The point is that these need to be suited to your customer, something that they see as useful and makes them perceive the relationship between you both to be valuable, emphasis here on value add.

Expectations

Be realistic with your expectations. This education principle won't show results tomorrow if you start today, it's a long-term approach.

Note – despite the best intentions with account maximisation, the chances are that you will never dominate 100% of a customer spend in your industry. There are many reasons for this but most prominently customers want to reduce their risk, and if they rely solely on one supplier in a single field then there is heightened risk associated to this. Sometimes you might receive 100% of the spend, but not on most occasions. Your goal is however to encompass the large majority of their spend, as close to that 100% as you can.

Education Matrix

We've already discussed how educating our customers is an important practice, now how do we execute it. The sales icon technique is to have a plan for how we do this in the form of a simple matrix. For every customer we create an education matrix, all this consists of is a list of topics that have or could potentially be used as subject areas for educating them. These should be bespoke, as some product offerings may fit better for a certain customer therefore educating them on a particular topic is best.

Seasonal Variance

This is a subject which rather frustrates me. I'm sure you've heard it in the past when one of your peers stated how seasonal variance has caused them to have a bad month. Seasonal variance isn't a myth, it's a real thing, but by knowing about it and doing nothing to counteract it is a mistake, and that is why seasonal variance should not be an excuse. I worked with a salesman once who sold into the education market and this was his favourite phrase. Now the education sector did have some seasonal variance to their spending habits, which meant that his sales figures were littered with peaks and troughs and every time it was brought up his defence was seasonal variance in his market.

The problem I have here is that if you are aware that your accounts have seasonal variance then why haven't you done something about it. In this case, the salesman knew that his market vertical was the reason for his peaks and troughs in sales, the solution, look for other opportunities in different verticals than education to counteract this. Take for example if you owned an ice cream store, this is a market of great seasonal variance as its rare for someone to want ice cream when it's cold. The owner could decide to continue with his business plan of only selling ice cream or he could diversify into other markets in order to counteract the seasonal variance. For instance, he could focus on selling hot drinks in the winter months, he could look at exporting to other countries, or even look at something completely different like providing ice cream making courses at home or selling ice cream making machines. There are endless opportunities you can take advantage of to counteract seasonal variance, the crime is to just accept it.

Just imagine if the rest of the world simply accepted seasonal variance as an acceptable excuse. There is no such excuse. Let's use Starbucks as our inspiration. Historically they had seasonal variance, they found that winter periods were their busy time and summer periods were their slow down. The driver was the fact that people rarely wanted a hot drink when the weather was warm. So what did they do? Did they sit back, rest on their laurels and accept this seasonal variance. Did they heck! Instead they created a blue ocean, a submarket in itself that they'd be first to market in and soon to be copied by many major competitors. That submarket was iced coffees. This plugged the gap that they had, they now had an offering that prevented against any excuse of seasonal variance.

Activity

Take some time now to analyse your accounts to review if you have any seasonal variance. Many a salesperson I've worked with in the past have been surprised to find they do have some form of variance that they were unaware of before. Simply review the spending habits of your customers by listing all their orders month by month for how many years they've worked with you. From this you may see some patterns emerge such as 50% of one of your accounts spending is in March which is the end of their financial year. Or that for all of your sales the month of December every year only equates to 2% of your overall sales on average.

From taking a look at this graph on a person's sales shows that they have some season variance. Their boom period seems to be the summer months, yet the winter period sales are subdued. Once you know this you must do something about it, living with seasonal variance isn't acceptable, put a plan in place to change things.

Once you have collated your sales information and looked at seasonal variance, you can then put together a strategy as to how you can counteract it. Not every strategy you put together will meet its desired outcome but it's much more affective to try than not.

Example strategies:

So what are some strategies we can use? Well let's discuss some of these, be mindful that the strategy most suited is dependent on the type of seasonal variance that you have.

Verticals – if from your analysis you see that you have some form of seasonal variance then try to analyse why. It may be that the common denominator is that you have strengths in a certain vertical and in order to counteract the variance, you need to branch out into other verticals.

Business size – your analysis may show that the variance is related the size of business of your customers such as their turnover is below £1m or they're less than a fifty-seat organisation. If this is the case then explore whether looking at a different size of business to prospect would help to alter the variance. It's quite common for businesses sales to fluctuate dependant on when their financial year starts and ends. Take for example government institutions, they're often given a budget for the year which they know if they don't use then the next year their budget may be cut. It's a ludicrous system I know, you would think that the government would incentivise cost savings and champion departments who look to reduce their spending and not use all their budget. Instead it's a 'use it or lose it' approach, which is quite appealing if you're selling to them. So for government institutions you may find that their spending is highest at the end of their financial year as they try to spend their budget in a means to ensure that their budget the following year isn't cut.

Product offerings – this is usually your first step for changing your strategy by looking at your product offerings. As you analyse your accounts look at the offerings you sell to them and see whether you find anything in common. It may be the case that the reason for your seasonal variance is that you're focusing on a product which has seasonal variance therefore all you need to do is mix up your approach and promote some of your other offerings at certain periods of time.

My work with a ventilation manufacturer is a perfect example of this. With the ventilation industry you find that their boom period is in the winter months. The reason is that when the weather gets cold and wet, people start putting their wet washing on radiators to dry them or on clothes horses inside their house instead of hanging them outside to dry. Now this may get the clothes dry but what it also does is add additional moisture to the interior of the house which is the perfect breeding conditions for mould. The after effect is that to counteract the mould build up a homeowner thinks that the fix would be better ventilation and thus goes out to purchase a new or more powerful extractor fan.

Now the solution with this ventilation manufacturer was to counteract this boom period in the winter with some form of product in the summer. The solution, well in the summer the temperature rises and people want to try to cool themselves. Therefore, the goal for this ventilation company was to push their cooling fans in the summer. This way they can reduce their seasonal variance as effectively as possible by promoting their extractor fans for mould prevention in the winter and their air movement fans for cooling in the summer.

Tip – the easiest way you can develop your strategy for counteracting seasonal variance is to see what your peers do. Chances are that when you speak to one of your peers you find that your down period is actually their boom period. If that's the case then great, ask them about their customers and their approach and find out why this is their boom period. Then analyse what you're doing different and build the perfect strategy with no seasonal variance.

Training Plan

'When you're green you grow, when you ripen you rot' – Ray Kroc.[8]

Explain to me what the theory of relativity is, ready go! Ok you might know that one. How about interstellar travel, tell me what the challenges are for interstellar travel. Struggle more with that one? Well I'm not surprised, and I don't expect you to be able to answer either of these questions.

If I asked Albert Einstein about relativity though I'm sure I'd get a detailed explanation. Or indeed if I asked Stephen Hawking about the challenges of interstellar travel I'm sure he'd educate me on this a great deal. The point I'm making is that we only know what we know, and answers to questions only come from specialists who have that knowledge.

So where does this come in? Well in order to satisfy our customers we must be knowledgeable about what we do. Am I saying that we need to live and breathe our business and know every single minute detail? No I'm not. But you need to at least know enough to get by and be striving to increase our level of knowledge to improve the service we personally provide our customers.

Let's reflect, we're talking in this chapter about account maximisation. We've taken a focus here on educating customers and how such a practice can aid us in maximising our account spend. But think about it, isn't this concept of educating customers an oxymoron if:

1. Personal knowledge – You don't have the knowledge yourself or
2. External knowledge – You don't have someone else (internally or externally to your business) who you can call upon with said knowledge

Personal knowledge:

If you lack the knowledge yourself then you're prohibited in selling and you'll be unable to educate customers. You must at minimum understand the concepts that are spoken within a meeting or over the phone, if you don't then you will barely be able to lead the meeting/call, let alone steer the opportunity towards a sale. So whether we have some knowledge or none at all, we must first understand the concepts and then have a stringent training plan to regularly stretch our knowledge base. But how do we do this? Well, we undertake training. I know it doesn't sound revolutionary but let me aid you in this with a little technique, a training plan.

How to build personal knowledge?

Every sales icon will have a training plan. Irrespective of where the salesperson is on their sales icon journey, their career or knowledge base, every single one will have a training plan.

Think back to your last meeting, or several of your last meetings. Was there any aspect, maybe the smallest facet of a discussion where your knowledge on the topic was poor or average? I bet there was! I still now have multiple instances where my knowledge in an area isn't proficient enough. Now the average salesperson does nothing about this, they carry on as before, they'll go to other meetings and when this topic comes up again they are once again not too knowledgeable and thus may potentially lose credibility or fail to spot or close an opportunity as a result.

So how do we counteract this? Now by no means can we know everything, but what we can do is put ourselves in the best position by having as vast a knowledge base as we can, or at least above our competitors or average salespeople. The sales icon technique to enable this is to create a personal training plan.

What's a personal training plan?

A personal training plan is exactly as it sounds. Too many average salespeople use the excuse of 'oh I haven't had training for that therefore how can I know?' Well, for a sales icon this isn't a prohibitor, yes we'd all love formal training, but the onus is on the individual to fill any gaps in their knowledge base.

The sales icon technique is to develop a personal training plan. I personally use my OneNote but feel free to use whatever works for you whether that be written paper consolidated in a folder or a word document etc.

Your personal training plan will consist of a number of documents, the first and foremost being the training plan matrix, this is your master document. The training plan matrix is simply a holistic view of your training plan, that being the topics you have studied and when you last conducted some training.

The other documents will be the individual training topics and their notes.

How do we know what to add to our plan?

I would start with a brainstorm, write down everything in your sales portfolio and highlight any subjects that you're not confident with or have strong knowledge of. Then prioritise which subjects are most important, this could maybe be those that have the best margin or those that can be a good door opener to other business, whatever you deem best.

After you've brainstormed subject areas I recommend adding topics as you go. So the next time you're in a meeting with a customer and they mention something that you're not too sure about, note it down in your notepad and then when you're back in the office add it to your training plan.

Schedule training time

What gets scheduled gets done! Don't just fit it into your schedule when you have a minute free, schedule training time from the outset. Because if you don't then training will always take a back seat to something else, and chances are it'll never get done. Schedule training time in your calendar, whether that is for one hour a month or one hour a week. Any amount of training is better than no training at all, the fruits of this will present themselves over time.

Train, train and train again, you should never stop learning, period!

> 'If you're not growing, you're dying.' – various people [9]

Personal development should be a big part of your life if you wish to become a sales icon. Training is part of your growth and personal development, at no point in your life will you know everything or have all of the answers therefore you need to strive to always be better. Your training plan should never come to an end, even if you have trained on every topic in your sales portfolio you should not end there. Revisit the topics, study finer details that you may have missed the first time, study new techniques for selling skills, study everything you can. To become a sales icon, training and personal development are staple to your success.

Training Plan Breakdown:

So let's break our training plan down into steps so that we understand how to put this together.

Step one – brainstorm offerings:

Start with just listing all of your offerings. I suspect that each offering will comprise of a few components, so list them too underneath each offering. Let's use an example to make this easy, you've probably all heard of the Microsoft solution called office 365 and Microsoft Dynamics (CRM system). For ease of understanding let's say that these are the only two offerings that I sell. If so then my training plan list would be the offering and then all the components within that offering. Therefore if I was brainstorming my list of offerings then my brainstorm would look something like this:

- Office 365
- Email
- Office applications
- Planner
- Yammer
- Etc.
- Dynamics
- How to navigate the platform
- Integration with office 365
- Sales forecasting and pipeline
- Activity tracking
- Etc.

For your brainstorm, I'm sure the list will be much longer as you'll have more than two offerings. But you understand the basic layout we're encouraging for this brainstorm.

Step two – score your knowledge in those offerings:

Think about the goal here, we're trying to educate ourselves so that we can pass this onto our customers. If we do this correctly we'll be able to have informed conversations which will in turn improve our ability to steer and close opportunities. What we don't want to do is just train ourselves on the things we know, or things we enjoy, this gains us nothing. Therefore, we need to score our knowledge on our offerings, and in doing so we must be candid in our scoring. We need to review our list of offerings (only offerings not their components) and honestly say yes I'm good at that or no that needs some work. A great way to conduct this is by scoring them which also helps you to prioritise where to start your personal training plan.

The scoring criteria I encourage is 1 to X, X being the total number of offering that you have. We're going to denote:

1 = most knowledgeable
X = least knowledgeable

Let's explain in an example, say I work for Microsoft but I'm specialising in selling five of their offerings those being:

- Microsoft Office 365
- Microsoft Dynamics
- Microsoft Azure
- Microsoft Surfaces
- Microsoft Surface Hubs

I then score my knowledge in those areas using the scoring criteria I mentioned previously, so after evaluating my knowledge it may look something like this:

Offering	Knowledge score
Microsoft Office 365	1
Microsoft Dynamics	5
Microsoft Azure	3
Microsoft Surface	2
Microsoft Surface Hub	4

To conclude, here I've stated that the offering I'm most knowledgeable in is Microsoft office 365 and the offering I'm least knowledgeable in is Microsoft Dynamics.

Step three – develop training plan matrix:

Now we need to develop our training plan matrix. This should be your dashboard of all your training. We want to be able to look at it and see what offerings we have trained in, when and how much time we've trained in those areas. It should also demonstrate those offerings that we haven't trained in.

The format you use is down to you. I personally encourage sales icons to use some form of spreadsheet (could be a spreadsheet in OneNote). To show you the type of layout I recommend let's continue the example of selling Microsoft solutions. So in this step I take all of my offerings and their subcategories and insert this into a spreadsheet. I then list any training dates where I carried out training and also the time spent, it looks like the following:

Offering	Component	Training date	Time spent (hours)	Total training time (hours)
Microsoft office 365	Email			
	Planner	01/01/2017	1	
		12/07/2017	0.5	
	Yammer			
			Total	1.5
Microsoft Dynamics	Navigation			
	Integration with office 365			
	Sales forecasting and pipeline	03/04/2018	1	1
			Total	1
Microsoft Azure	Site recovery manager	12/12/2017	2	
		02/03/2018	0.5	
	IaaS			
	Cold storage			
			Total	2.5
Microsoft surface	Specifications			
	Compatibility			
	Mobility benefits	04/03/2018	2	
			Total	2
Microsoft surface hub	Specifications			
	Compatibility			
	Use cases			

The layout of your training plan matrix is down to you, if this way works for you then feel free to steal it. What's important is that you have a training matrix which shows your training activity, that way you have no excuses and nowhere to hide.

Step four – record your training content:

Imagine you're painting a beautiful canvas of a serene landscape. It's a deep green valley of grassland surrounding an aggressively flowing river with cascading flurries of water crashing over a collection of river rapids. Well envisage being halfway through this painting. You've spent hour upon hour outlining the finer details, the small fragments of water flying through the air, the contrasting colours of the yellow and brown flashes of dying grass within the fields of a green plain. Despite your dedication to the painting you decide to call it a day and come back to things tomorrow or in a few days. Then when you return you completely start afresh, right back to the start. The hours you'd put in on the last canvas are disregarded and you initiate the painting once more.

Sounds like ridiculous behaviour right? What a waste of time, and you'd be right! So when I explain this in painting a canvas it sounds like madness, but when most people conduct training they follow this exact approach. The thing is when most people participate in training they sit, write, listen and comprehend. Then when they've finished their training on a topic, often their notes get neglected and/or thrown away or lost. The big downside here is that when they need a refresher or want to add to their knowledge in that area, they're unsure how far their training went to previously. As a result they often start again or end up retraining on a number of aspects that they've already invested time into.

To counteract this we must record our training. Take electronic notes of each training session you persevere with and list down pertinent points. Then when it comes to a refresher or picking up where you left off you can do so in a quick manner. This will take your training plan from being average to that of a sales icons.

Step five – schedule regular time for training in your diary:

Schedule training time, put it in your diary right now on a recurrence. If this is simply for fifteen minutes on a Monday morning, one hour on a Friday morning or a regular slot every day. How often you train I leave to you; you must make the judgment call on how regular it should be. My advice though is that if you want to become a sales icon you must train at least once a week. If you can spare an hour then great, but even if you can only spare fifteen minutes then this will have to suffice. Regular training far outweighs bingeing with one full day of training every few months.

So these are the core steps to putting your training plan together. All I can say is try it, you'll notice that as your knowledge base improves so does your confidence. You'll find that prospects and customers listen more astutely to your input and actually come to you for advice. It should, if applied correctly, aid you in your pursuit to maximise your accounts spend, as well as your new business development.

What should I train first?

This is a common question asked in sales icon training. Previously we discussed scoring what your knowledge is of certain offerings. Now it would be easy if we just said to train that which you're least knowledgeable in, but it's not that simplistic. We score our knowledge for good reason, we want to know where our strengths and weaknesses lie. But simply training on an offering just because your knowledge of that area is less than others is foolish.

Think about it, what's our goal? Well we want to sell more so that we make more commission and become a sales icon. Consequentially, when we're addressing which areas we should train on first we need to be thinking about all of the following:

- What offerings can I make the most money from?
- What offerings are there an opportunity for? I.e. market demand?
- What offerings am I failing to sell?

If we address all of these questions in conjunction with our scoring on knowledge then we'll be able to identify where to focus our time.

Let's use an example to make this point clear. Think back to the previous example, say we're selling Microsoft solutions and we have scored our knowledge as follows:

Offering	Knowledge score
Microsoft Office 365	1
Microsoft Dynamics	5
Microsoft Azure	3
Microsoft Surface	2
Microsoft Surface Hub	4

Well then we could add to this our further analysis, let's say that it looks something like this:

Offering	Knowledge score	Potential £	Market opportunity	Selling status
Microsoft Office 365	1	Low	Mild	Good
Microsoft Dynamics	5	Low	Mild	Mild
Microsoft Azure	3	High	High	Low
Microsoft Surface	2	Mild	Mild	Mild
Microsoft Surface Hub	4	Low	Low	Low

Now if this was my actual analysis there would be a great deal to conclude. If we simply looked at our knowledge base on the face of things and invested time in training on those topics then we may be making life hard for ourselves. Take the Microsoft surface hub for example, knowledge may be lacking in this area but I've also found that there's little money to be made. Whereas Microsoft azure I have a fantastic opportunity here from my analysis; therefore, in such circumstance I would prioritise this in my personal training plan. Do bear in mind this is just an example. I'm sure there's money to be made by all of these offerings, it's an example to help you understand the point. Just because knowledge is lacking doesn't mean we should invest time in training in this area. Look at the bigger picture, where will my training be most effective and by most effective we mean have the largest return on investment.

Tips for your training plan

Tip one – Regularly review – the world changes every day. We see new applications released on our phones, new products we can buy in supermarkets, new markets that were never there before. So if our world is constantly revolving then why should our training plan be any different? The tip here is to protect against complacency. It's common that the wise old dog thinks he knows it all, then the new young kids come on the block and blows his performance out of the water. Don't let this be you. Regularly review your training plan. Have your offerings changed? Has the market changed resulting in you needing to change your training plan? If you reapplied your knowledge scoring would it be different now? Just be mindful to rule over your training plan, don't let it rule over you.

Tip two – Personal development – much of the time when we think of training we think of our businesses offerings, the products that we sell or services we can offer. This is but a drop in the ocean of your training. Most of your sales don't come down to knowledge of your offerings, they boil down to your sales acumen. As a result we shouldn't overlook our personal development training, so what's yours going to be? Do you need to learn tips for closing? Or maybe cold calling techniques? Or maybe it's more about managing time appropriately? Whatever it is personal development should feature in your training plan too, selling is so much more than just knowledge about the products or services of your business.

Tip three – Competitor training – if I was a mixed martial arts fighter then I'd most probably spend hours studying my opponents before we entered the ring. I'd know their strengths, their weaknesses and have a clear strategy to defeating them in hand-to-hand combat. For instance if I found that they're a great boxer but their floor work was poor then that would be my strategy, get the fight to the floor as quick and as often as I can. If I can do this then I have the best chance of winning. Your training plan should mimic this with your competitors. By no means should your focus be on the competition, but if you understand the pros and cons to their offerings then straight away you have an advantage. You can steer any conversation away from a competitors strengths to their weaknesses if only you know what they are. So include in your training plan some competitor training, use the most common competitors and offerings that you come against for the best results.

Tip four – Overtraining – I once worked with a young lady who was incredibly intelligent. She was university educated and could pick up knowledge far easier than most. Her trouble was that she hated the hard parts of selling such as picking up the phone and making cold calls. She fell into the trap of overtraining. She would prioritise training over most other activities and her sales began to reflect that. Her knowledge was impeccable, trouble was that she spoke and saw no customers as she never took on the other sales activities. The result was that she lost her job, the most knowledgeable salesperson who didn't practise selling. I don't want you to fall into this trap. Whilst training is important, sales activities are more important. So try to regularly train, but don't make it the focus of your work, otherwise you're a student and not a salesperson.

So now we have covered the first part of your training which centres around your personal knowledge. But let's reflect again, this part of the chapter is about account maximisation and how this can be achieved through educating your customers. The limitation you have is that you're only one person. Despite how smart you are and how hard you try you can't know everything. Thus to conquer the art of education you must also look external to oneself.

Look externally:

So what do we mean when we say look externally. Well what we're trying to say is look for knowledge from outside of your own, this could be from a colleague, or a person in an external business such as a partner company you work with.

Why look externally?

Many average salespeople are reticent to looking externally. They want to keep hold of everything and they're fearful that if other people are involved and they act in the wrong way or let the customer down then it'll reflect poorly on them. Now whilst these reservations are valid, the upside far outweighs the downside. The positives to looking externally are:

Reduce workload – this is massive perk, most of the time when you look external to your knowledge you're doing so because someone else has invested a great deal of time specialising in an area. So for you to be able to replicate this you would have to invest the same amount of time in your study. So if I said to you that you've got two options, introduce John at X to your customer or go and spend twenty hours studying Y I'm pretty sure you'd opt for John. It's a massive time saver, with this you can invest your time on high pay off activities elsewhere.

Passive income – most of us want an easy life and passive income is the route to an easy life. Passive income is income that you haven't had to work for, well at least not hard anyway. If you use external sources correctly then you can have passive income, most of the time they'll do the majority of the selling for you. Yes you may need to arrange the odd meeting or call or even take the notes, but they'll be doing most of it.

Strengthen relationships – using external resources will 100% strengthen the relationship you have with customers and will give a positive perception of you and your business. If a customer knows that you can help most of the time, but if you can't then you'll call upon people to assist them then the result will be the same. They'll come to you for everything! That's our dream scenario, we're the first thought in their mind when they need something.

Why externally?

There are two outlets to looking external, those are:

- Internal to business
- External to business

Internal to business – this includes anyone in your organisation. People like your boss, managing director, colleague in the technical department, colleague in research and development etc. The best person to involve will differ depending on the opportunity.

External to business – this consists of anyone outside your business. For instance do you resell a vendors products, if you do then could you get a sales rep from that business involved who specialises in that product or service? Or maybe you have a partner business who offers something that would aid your customers?

What should we be going external for?

Knowledge is the answer. You should go external for anything where you believe external knowledge will add value. I encourage sales icons to ask themselves, will looking external help me win this deal? If yes then go for it! So when you have an opportunity just think about the following:

- Is there anyone in my business who would add value to this opportunity?
- Who can I use outside my organisation who can help my customer with this?

Let's use a few examples to make this easy.

Example one – external resource – I was working with a company who were reselling a software solution. The salespersons' knowledge of the product wasn't too in depth so I encouraged them to introduce the vendor. They did so, the vendor went to have a meeting with them to provide a demo. Subsequent to the demo they provided a proof of concept trial, it all went well so the customer bought the solution.

Example two – internal resource – I was working with a consultancy firm who implemented a new scheme with a customer. The solution wasn't going 100% to plan, much of the time it was being utilised in the wrong way by employees in the business. I encouraged the salesperson to involve other team members with the customer. They did so and had an account development manager and technical officer meet with the customer, they tweaked the solution to make it more user friendly and hey presto utilisation from employees dramatically improved. The result was a happy customer and more money for the salesperson.

Regularity of external resource:

This is always a good question; how often should we use external resource. Well for me it's all about value add, again ask yourself the question, will using external resource help me win a deal? If yes then use it. If that's for every opportunity or for once in a blue moon, whatever you feel is right. My advice though is to use it regularly, as we highlighted it'll reduce your workload, create passive income and strengthen your relationship with customers.

Activity

Try a bit of analysis now of your customers. Look at what opportunities you have, or maybe topics that are on your customers' strategy list and uncover whether external resource may add value. Try this a few times and see what you think.

Conclusion to Planning Chapter

In this chapter we dived into many concepts which might be completely new to you. In my opinion planning is where most salespeople make their biggest mistakes, they opt for the overzealous approach of attacking whatever they can as soon as they can. This often can cost them a great deal of time, money and ultimately could cost them their job.

The first concept we discussed for counteracting such pitfalls is the reverse funnel planning principle, which is the tool we can use to hit and surpass our target. This tool works by using your target to identify what activity is required to develop such a sales output. It'll look at your conversion rates and spit out some minimum criteria that you need to meet in order to hit your target such as number of meetings etc.

We then addressed the holy grail of new business through looking at the prospect attack plan and prospect plan structure. In these sections we analyse what's the right fit for your business and offering. This will help you to stay prospecting within your sweet spot so instead of wasting time with prospects that you'll never have a chance with you'll instead have a regimented focus on those prospects that are suited to you. The end result, more time, more opportunities and more sales, all simply through spending a bit of extra time planning your new business approach.

Later on in the chapter we took this concept one step further and applied it to our accounts. This planning is to maximise the spend we get out of our accounts, for instance by outlining which accounts have more potential, putting together a spend map and agreeing regular meetings. Undertaking such practices will mean that not only do you write more business, you also ring fence your accounts from competitors and have a higher chance of successfully attaining future referrals.

We close the chapter with some items in relation to training, both for your customers but also for yourself. We talk of the concept of educating your customers to become a value-added partner as opposed to simply a supplier, do this and once again we ensure lengthy retention rates of customers and maximum loyalty. Although this is impossible should you fail to educate yourself, so be sure to schedule regular training time. No matter where you are in your career you can never know it all, so avoid complacency by continually training and retraining, that way you'll be an expert in your field.

Key Takeaways – Discipline 2 – Planning

- Reverse-Funnel Planning
    - Remember the habit "start with the end in mind"
    - Discover what your conversions rates are for each stage in the sales process
    - Use this to plan how you're going to hit your target
    - You can utilise a staggered approach to make your target feel more manageable and achievable
- Prospect Attack Plan
    - Always start with a plan before attacking any prospects
    - Review your businesses current accounts by looking at factors such as their location, turnover, number of employees and vertical
- Prospect Plan Structure
    - To mitigate risk it's best to proportion your prospect attack plan, thus not solely focusing on large opportunities for instance
    - Define what constitutes as a small, medium or large opportunity for your business
    - Set what percentage of your focus that you will spend on small, medium and large opportunities
    - Regularly review your approach as you progress as to become a sales icon you will need to adapt these percentages of what you focus your time on
- Sales Cycle
    - This is the time that it takes for a sale to close
    - The sales cycle may differ for different opportunities
    - For your businesses account base, some factors to assess are their turnover, number of employees and vertical
    - From this you may find the sales cycle differs
    - Review your sales cycle statistics and plan your approach
- Account Attack Plan
    - The probability of selling to an existing account is 60–70% compared to 5–20% for a new prospect
- Account Review Meetings
    - Agree regular, forward booked meetings with your accounts
    - Assess which accounts are worthy of your time and how regular you can afford to meet with them
    - Remember to look at an accounts potential as well as their current spend history

- Map out upselling opportunities

- Scheduling Customer Time
    - Plan time for your account base in your calendar
- Educate Customers
    - Take the time to help your customers and educate them in some way
    - Goal is to become a value-added partner
- Seasonal Variance
    - Review if your accounts have any seasonal variance
    - If so plan how you can counteract this
- Training Plan
    - Put together a personal training plan
    - Schedule in your personal training

Discipline 3 – Sniff Out What Sells

The concept of 'sniff out what sells' basically means to find something that works then continue doing it. Sales icons are always striving to sniff out what sells. We want to identify the fastest and easiest route to success; if something we do doesn't work then we need to be ruthless and drop it. But when we uncover a practice that works then we need to replicate it and if we can do so in a mass scale then we'll be successful and become sales icons.

In this chapter we're going to talk about a multitude of areas that we can refine our approach to receive the best results. We'll kick off by looking at lead generation as let's face it, most of the time this is the hardest and most gruelling task. In my view the rest of the sales process is the easy bit, whereas getting in front of motivated buyers is the hard part. So we'll start the chapter with lead generation and looking at the vast plethora of channels which are at your disposal to use.

Moving on from lead generation, we'll look at our activity, mainly in relation to lead generation and the channels we've mentioned. Here is where we will digress into how we can put together an effective plan for our activity, using multiple channels.

But wait, stop right there, how do we know what channels to use? Well we'll spend some time looking at the conversion rates of channels to help you answer this question. Frankly, if a channel doesn't work then why use it? That's what we want to determine. As well as which channels do work so that we can exercise those channels to a greater extent. In doing this we will also incorporate our reverse funnel planning from the last chapter, this way we'll know both the activity required to hit target as well as the medium through which we're going to focus our activity.

After all the groundwork on lead generation is completed we can then put our plan together. In this chapter we'll talk through our campaign planner, how it can be used and put together. To add a proactive stance to our approach we'll also talk about forecasting our results so that we can act when results aren't in our favour instead of having a deficit in our lead generation which dominos on to our sales.

The discipline of sniff out what sells can apply to any part of your sales process, but for best results, we're going to start by looking at lead generation and applying this discipline.

3.1 – Lead Generation

Lead generation is often a sore subject with most salespeople. If you're the type of salesperson who expects to be fed with leads continually then you won't become a sales icon. If, however, you're the type that would like to increase your lead generation but also put in the grind of other arduous tasks such as cold calling then this section will help.

We will discuss in this chapter how to utilise your channels effectively and by that I mean maximise their lead development to retain the best return on investment for your time. Just to clarify if you're confused, the term channel stands for outlets of lead generation, for instance emails, events and cold calling are all examples of individual channels.

Once we've identified what channels you have at your disposal we'll talk about measuring their effectiveness. I'm often dumbfounded that this doesn't occur in many organisations, they invest time, money and resource into a channel but never actually record if it's working.

The best part of the section comes next. When we've highlighted the channels and their effectiveness we can then talk through its application in terms of your reverse funnel planning. We will be able to predict with a high level of accuracy what our minimum lead activity will need to be in order to meet and surpass our target.

So let us begin, let's dive into how we can sniff out what sells through our lead generation.

Your lead generation:

So to start have a think about your lead generation. What channels do you use? If your answer to this is simply cold calls and emails then this section is going to truly open your eyes and blow your mind when you see the results.

So what channels are there that you can take advantage of? Well there are many, I've highlighted some of the notable channels below:

- Cold calling
- Cold generic emails
- Personal emails
- Email surveys
- Events/exhibitions
- Web tracking
- Inbound
- Direct mail
- Whitepapers
- Live chat

These are just a few examples of channels that you can use.

Lead Generation Trap:

Before we go any further let's talk about the lead generation trap. It's a common throwaway comment that half of your marketing is wasted, the trouble is that you don't know which half. I hate the thought of this, so what we want to do is find out the half that's working and that which is not.

Now what many businesses do is to utilise many channels for lead generation and good on them as their intentions are correct. The pitfall, however, is that they aimlessly conduct campaigns yet never record their results. They'll put together an email to customers and not focus on whether the content invoked interest. They'll arrange events and not review what resulted from such an activity. They won't plan their campaigns in conjunction with their business targets, everything is just hit and hope and action for actions sake.

It's like playing a game of darts, you're desperately trying to get to the 501 score but you're not taking down the score every time you throw a dart. How will you ever know if you win, or if you're close or if that was a bad shot? The answer is you won't!

So this is the pitfall that we're trying to avoid and what this sniff out what sells concept revolves around. We want to know what works so that we can cease exercising those activities that don't work and replicate those that do.

Recording Your Activity:

From here on in I want you to look at all of your channels independently and to start to record both the use of a channel and results of each channel. You may be thinking that this sounds like hard work and too much effort but it's not. I can promise you that adopting this concept will hand you the gift of time. I remember conducting this analysis with one organisation I was working with a few years ago and we found that their lead generation was only 66% effective. That meant for a third of their campaigns there were no results at all, meaning that really they could have taken a third of the year off on holiday. Think about the big picture, it's not simply about the campaign development itself, it's all the work after too. A great deal of time can be wasted on a single campaign and if it has no benefit then we are just working for working's sake.

So to become a sales icon you must regimentally record and assess your activity through any channels. A simple way to do this is to build a campaign planner, if you don't have one of these there is a piece on the campaign planner later in this book. The purpose of the campaign planner is to record activity of channels, when you used the channels and the results it gave. For example if you sent one hundred emails you would note down the following:

- Email overview i.e. selling points of XYZ
- No. of emails sent
- Date sent
- Results – i.e. replies, or meetings booked subsequently after calling the customers regarding this campaign

Whenever one of my newer students starts this process they struggle with this as they fail to see the benefit initially until I explain it to them. They say, "Simon, this is such a laborious task, I'm sending all these emails which is time consuming as it is, why should I record it all down also, surely this is just adding more to my workload?"

My answer to this is to ask another question, "How do you know what works if you never have any results?" Imagine being a salesperson who never received any sales results, you'd never know if you're doing well or not and whether to change the way you're working or stay the same. The principle holds true also for campaigns, you need to record your activity and results in order to determine what works, what to spend more time doing and what is deadwood.

Remember discipline two – planning, it is impossible to plan appropriately and become a successful sales icon without assessing your campaigns thoroughly. The beautiful thing about assessing your campaigns is that in the long term it will save you vast amounts of time. You'll be able to understand your conversion rates by channel and therefore be able to forecast appropriately and increase your activity levels to meet your overall sales goal.

So the things we need to start recording are:

- Use of a channel – i.e. email, cold calling, survey
- Date
- Description – if email it will be the main topic, if cold call it will just be cold call
- Meetings booked related to that activity

Note – only associate prospects to one campaign at a time, not multiple. If, however, time passes, and a new campaign follows with the same prospect, the previous campaign activity will be closed down and activity will be associated to the new campaign.

Example – this is much easier to understand in an example

If I carry out an email campaign on the 2nd of February to Johns Milles at Adamant Electrical PLC, I later call to follow up on the email but have no luck getting through to John. Several calls proceed over the next 2 weeks and I still struggle to get through to John. As a result I try a new campaign, this time sending through a survey to John. In this instance due to the more recent activity being the survey I would close down the previous campaign response of the email, and associate this to the new activity of the survey. Thus there only being an association to one campaign at a time.

Improvement

If we're not growing we're dying, and I don't think there is a sole on this earth that doesn't want to improve. At the end of this chapter you'll know how to optimise your entire lead generation approach, all in all improving your results and saving you time.

Improvement is the key point, when we have campaigns that don't work we will do something about it. For instance we may choose to run it again just to see if it was a one-off failure. This second or even third test should be conclusive though, if the campaign continues to have poor results then it must be struck off and not used again. Sniffing out what sells and continually improving.

The converse is true also, a campaign that works well can be utilised again or replicated and slightly changed to achieve the same results. The beauty of this is once you 'sniff out what sells' your conversion rates will start to improve over time as you focus on what works and discard what doesn't. Finally, you have found a formula for success.

A word of warning – don't let this stop you from experimenting and trying new things. We never know what works and what doesn't work until we have tried it. I'm a real advocate of experimentation. I'm often caught saying 'throw a load of shit at the wall and see what sticks.' Crude, I know, but the point is clear. I always bring up the example of Thomas Edison, it took Edison one thousand failed attempts until he found out a way to make the light bulb work. If he didn't experiment and persevere then we'd still be using oil lamps every day. But with every failed attempt Edison made he was one step closer to the right answer. He was sniffing out what sells, finding what doesn't work and crossing it off his list until after nine hundred and ninety-nine attempts he found the answer. So don't be afraid to experiment, see what works and then replicate it.

3.2 – Planning Our Activity

Let's be frank, planning our activity isn't the easiest of tasks. In the previous chapter we talked about our reverse funnel planning and identifying the minimum activity we need to achieve our target. Here we're going to take that reverse funnel planning one step further. Not only are we going to find out our activity required we're also going to forecast our results so that we can work proactively to ensure our input to the funnel is sufficient enough to produce enough output, i.e. sales.

So to begin with let's recap the reverse funnel planning we discussed earlier using a short example.

We already know that in order to calculate our reverse funnel planning we must first find out our:

- Average order size
- Target
- Conversion rate from meeting to opportunity
- Conversion rate from opportunity to close

So for this example let's say the following:

1) Average order size – I have an average order size of £10k
2) Target for the year is £100k
3) Conversion rate from meeting to opportunity = 33%
4) Conversion rate from opportunity to close = 50%

So I have a target of £100k and an average order size of £10k for the year. This means that I need to close 10 opportunities this year.

100/10=10

I close 50% of my opportunities therefore the number of opportunities I need to close to make 10 sales must be 20 opportunities

10/(1/2)=20

To have 20 opportunities I need to find out how many meetings I need at a conversion rate of 33%. This tells me that I require 60 meetings.

20/(1/3)=60

So now I know I need 60 meeting for the year.

But this is pretty much where we left things earlier in the reverse-funnel planning section. So instead of a target we've broken things down into activity, in this case meetings. But does this honestly help yet? Well I suppose slightly, but the next question is how do I achieve this number of meetings?

In reverse-funnel planning, we talked about activity to convert a prospect from being cold to warm and booking a meeting. But the question is what activity is required to convert this prospect to a meeting.

What is activity?

Well really any use of a channel counts as activity, so if you run a survey and sent it to one hundred recipients then that constitutes as activity, or if you've attended three events/exhibitions in a year then that's activity too.

This is the point where we're going to add to our reverse funnel planning, as we're going to put something tangible to our activity. At the end of this section we want to be able to say categorically how much activity we need and through what channel. But not only that, we'll also forecast our activity and be ready for the circumstance where certain forecasts don't come to fruition. For instance we will get to the stage where we'll be forecasting that a survey we run will develop say ten meetings for us. But because of our discipline in recording our results if we can see that that we're not going to achieve that result then we can be proactive. This can be achieved by adding an additional campaign in at a later date to supplement the deficit of the poor performing campaign.

3.3 – Channel Conversion Rates

'However beautiful the strategy, you should occasionally look at the results' – Winston Churchill.[10]

It might be surprising for you to learn that the conversion rates of channels differ. So if you ran a campaign with the same level of activity through two different channels the resulting output wouldn't be the same. So if we took for instance an email campaign and an email survey as two separate channels. If we were to conduct a campaign to five hundred people through both channels the results wouldn't be the same as each other. What would happen in most cases is that a survey would reward you with more meetings than an alike email campaign. This difference in what we call channel conversion rates carries through to other channels, there are some that will reap greater rewards than others.

This is why it's important to measure the conversion rates of a channel. If we do this, we have a much better chance of being successful and becoming a sales icon as we can focus on channels that give us the results we need.

But without recording our activity and results we will never know the conversion rates. So as you move forward, I plead with you to start recording this activity and the outcomes. If you do so then you will be able to assess conversion rates by individual campaign and by channel.

As I mentioned briefly just before, the conversion rate that we're looking to discover is the percentage conversion rate to a meeting. This is for each individual campaign and channel.

It would probably help at this stage if I just explained what a campaign is. Well a campaign would be described as a group of activity within a channel, let me use a quick example. Let's pretend I work for a clothing retailer, I compose three emails that I'm going to send out which are:

Email Number	Content	Date
Email 1	Summer wear	January
Email 2	Hat collection	February
Email 3	Men's footwear	March

Then to simply put it these are each individual campaigns, so it would follow that:

- Campaign one = summer wear
- Campaign two = hat collection
- Campaign three = men's footwear

So now hopefully it makes sense what a campaign is.

Each campaign will have its own conversion rate and the total average of all campaigns within a channel will give you the conversion rate of that channel. Let's continue this example to explain what I mean. Just for example purposes, we'll say that we sent these email campaigns out to five hundred prospects and the conversion rates of each campaign were as follows:

Email Number	Content	Date	Conversion rate to meeting
Email 1	Summer wear	January	5%
Email 2	Hat collection	February	0%
Email 3	Men's footwear	March	1%

So what does this tell me? Well, if each campaign was sent to five hundred recipients each then I booked the following meetings relating to each campaign:

- Campaign 1 = 25 meetings (5% of 500)
- Campaign 2 = 0 meetings (0% of 500)
- Campaign 3 = 5 meetings (1% of 500)

Plus I can also find out my conversion rate for email as a channel by equating:
Sum of conversion rates (per campaign) / number of campaigns
So in this instance the conversion rate for email is
-Email conversion rate = 2% (6%/3)
Bear in mind this is still only an example, I very much doubt that emails will be as fruitful as this for you but you might surprise me.

Activity

If you have the data to hand then work out your conversion rates of each channel and campaign you have run. If you don't have this data then start recording activity and results now.

So now that we understand what channels, campaigns and channel conversion rates are, we can move forward. Now we'll start to interlink this into our reverse funnel planning.

Now for your business and industry you will have your own personal channel conversion rates. For some salespeople events might be the most prolific channel for results, though for others it could be web tracking. The point I'm making is don't take my conversion rates as gospel or someone else's, work out your own.

Now I'm going to give you some channel conversion rates below. These are for a consultancy business I worked with previously:

- Events = 29%
- Inbound = 22.5%
- Surveys = 17.5%
- Web tracking = 3%
- Email = 1%

As I said your results may differ to this, it all depends upon your industry, your brand, the quality of your campaigns etc.

Before we go any further I want to dissect what constitutes as activity within a channel so let's spend a bit of time breaking this down. Let's have a more focused look into the channels that I've listed above and what the consultancy businesses deems as activity within the respective channel.

Event leads – this stood for activity where the business had exhibited at an event. Every event that the company exhibited at would count as a campaign. Plus at each event the company would use a survey sheet to uncover information about prospective customers. So if they attended three events then they would have three campaigns through the event channel.

On average that company would convert 29% of event leads (prospects who filled out a survey) to a meeting, so if they had one hundred survey sheets filled in they would expect to book twenty-nine meetings. They also found that for every day that an event lasted for they would expect one hundred and twenty survey responses. So if they had a two-day event they would expect to book seventy meetings just from the event survey responses alone. The key criteria for event leads are:

- Conversion rate of event leads to meetings
- Average number of survey responses per day at events

Inbound leads – this stood for inbound traffic to their website where a prospective customer had filled in a form on their website. On average the consultancy business converted 22.5% of inbound leads to a meeting, so if they had one hundred inbound leads they'd expect around twenty-two meetings from this channel. On average they recorded four inbound leads a week which amounted to one meeting booked every week.

It would be difficult for the business to assign specific campaigns to the inbound channel. So what I encouraged them to do was to look at activity to increase traffic, things such as Google ad words etc. The key criteria for inbound leads are:

- Conversion rate of inbound leads to meetings
- Average number of inbound leads per week or month

Survey leads – this stood for survey campaigns whereby prospective customers had been emailed a survey to fill out for the chance to win a prize. On average this consultancy business would convert 17.5% of survey leads. So if they had one hundred surveys filled in they should expect seventeen meetings from this activity. On average they would record around forty survey response per survey sent out, equating to seven meetings. This was to a survey sent out to five hundred recipients. The key criteria for survey leads are:

- Conversion rate of survey leads to meetings
- Average number of survey leads per survey sent to X number of recipients

Web tracking leads – this stood for contacting prospective customers who had visited their website and maybe focused on particular content. On average the business would convert 3% of Web tracking leads. So if they had one hundred prospects who visited the website they would expect to book three meetings from this. On average they would record around five prospects on their website daily equating to around four meetings a month. Again alike inbound leads it would be difficult to assign specific campaigns to Web tracking. Hence again, I encouraged the business to look at activities to increase traffic to the website but also to increase the time spent on their website by prospects. This is through having ease of navigation and interesting content on their website. The key criteria for Web tracking leads are:

- Conversion rate of Web tracking leads to meetings
- Average number of Web tracking leads per month

Email leads – this stood for contacting prospective customers following on from an email campaign that was sent out to them. A prospect would become an email lead if they opened the email that was sent out. On average the business would convert 1% of email leads. So if they had one hundred email leads then they would expect to record one meeting from this activity. On average they would receive eighty email opens from an email sent to five hundred recipients, hence they would book around one meeting from each email campaign to five hundred recipients. The key criteria for email leads are:

- Conversion rate of email leads to meetings
- Average email leads per campaign to X number of recipients

Hopefully, this clears up the point about activity. This is an example of how a consultancy business addressed activity within their main channels and how they determined what classified as a lead for each channel. You may work different than this in the future, what I'm attempting to do is help you see how your lead generation can work through each channel.

3.4 – Integration with Reverse Funnel Planning

We now know all of the prerequisites for channel conversion rates, now it's time to integrate this with reverse funnel planning. In order to demonstrate this I'm going link back to two examples. I'm going to use my channel conversion rates from this consultancy business which are:

- Events = 29%
- Inbound = 22.5%
- Surveys = 17.5%
- Web tracking = 3%
- Email = 1%

I'm going to also link back to a previous example in the start of this chapter that we are yet to finish off, and that was:

1) Average order size – I have an average order size of £10k
2) Target for the year is £100k
3) Conversion rate from meeting to opportunity = 33%

4) Conversion rate from opportunity to close = 50%

We had already conducted our reverse-funnel planning which told us that in order to hit our target we must book at least sixty meetings. Now we're going to fill in the gap for our lead generation activity by using our channel conversion rates.

We need to find out what combination of activity within a channel will lead to us booking sixty meetings. I'm going to start by reviewing one channel to show how we do this. Subsequent to this, I'll draw up a table to map out what each channel could achieve by itself, then we can look at combinations of campaigns within channels.

So we're starting with a channel in isolation. For familiarity let's use email as a channel in this example as we're all clued up as to how this would work.

I need to source sixty meetings to meet my target, if I use email as my only source of lead generation then how many campaigns do I need to run?

Let us start by looking at the conversion rate.

For this consultancy business we have found that email leads have a conversion rate of 1%. This is for a campaign sent to five hundred recipients recording eighty email opens. So for every single campaign (to five hundred recipients) I should expect roughly one meeting.

1x Email Campaign = 0.8 meetings

So to find out how many email campaigns I would need to hit my target all I need to do is divide the number of meetings I require (sixty) by the number of meetings I expect from a campaign (0.8)

Campaigns needed = 60 / 0.8 = 75

So to conclude, to book sixty meetings I must conduct seventy-five email campaigns throughout the year. That's seventy-five email campaigns to five hundred recipients, meaning that I'll have to email thirty-seven thousand five hundred prospects to achieve my goal! Now it sounds a bit more difficult.

This is why I've used the email channel in this example as it demonstrates how you'll need to use multiple channels in your approach or even just focus on those channels with the highest chance of success.

So now let's look at each channel in isolation and compare them within a table, we'll call this a table of channel output:

Channel	Conversion rate	No. Meetings expected	No. required (for 60 meetings)
Events	29%	34.8 per day at event	2 days of an event
Inbound	22.5%	0.9 per week	67 weeks
Surveys	17.5%	7 per survey to 500 prospects	9 campaigns
Web tracking	3%	0.75 per week	80 weeks
Email	1%	0.8 per campaign to 500 prospects	75 campaigns

Just take a glance at this again, how much easier has your lead generation now become. For me this makes things so simple. Just focus on using the right channels, aiming our campaigns in the right way and we'll have enough lead generation to smash our target to pieces.

Combination approaches:

Previously we used an easy target in our example. We needed to make £100k and to do that we must book sixty meetings. In retrospect, this was too easy for us, especially when you consider how high our channel conversion rates were. What it meant was that our target could be surpassed easily, all we need was say a two-day event and we'd surpass it.

It won't always be this easy though, for you it could be the case that you have a higher target. Or maybe you have channel conversion rates that are much lower than that which I used in my example. If that's the case then you're going to have to use a combination of channels and campaigns to meet your target. Let's demonstrate how this would work in another example. So let's use the same example as before but let's say that we're a sales manager and we're planning for all of our salespeople that report into us. To make it easy let's multiply our output by ten, so instead of £100k we need £1M. Correspondingly that means that instead of sixty meetings we need to source six hundred meetings. Sounds like a massive headache doesn't it, six hundred meetings that's crazy.

Well let's strip it back again, we'll put together another table of channel output which would look like the following:

Channel	Conversion rate	No. Meetings expected	No. required (for 600 meetings)
Events	29%	34.8 per day at event	18 days of an event
Inbound	22.5%	0.9 per week	667 weeks
Surveys	17.5%	7 per survey to 500 prospects	86 campaigns
Web tracking	3%	0.75 per week	800 weeks
Email	1%	0.8 per campaign to 500 prospects	750 campaigns

So now that I have formulated this I need to think about what combination of campaigns will enable me to meet my target.

If this was me, I'd start by looking at my passive lead generation. That's Web tracking and inbounds, if I do nothing else through the year then these two channels alone will develop some meetings for me. So if I based this over the year (fifty-two weeks) these two channels will record:

- Inbound = 46 meetings
- Web tracking = 39 meetings

So if I do nothing more, I will record eighty-five meetings through these two channels alone. But a sales icon would never think this way, how do we get the rest?

Well the leftover deficit is five hundred and fifteen meetings. All I need to do now is to use a combination of the three other channels to plug the gap.

Try looking at the channels in isolation again.

Channel	Conversion rate	No. Meetings expected	No. required (for 515 meetings)
Events	29%	34.8 per day at event	15 days of an event
Surveys	17.5%	7 per survey to 500 prospects	74 campaigns
Email	1%	0.8 per campaign to 500 prospects	644 campaigns

Then brainstorm some combinations like so:

Channel	Combination 1	Combination 2	Combination 3
Events	10 days	10 days	12 days
Surveys	10 campaigns	20 campaigns	10 campaigns
Email	122 campaigns	34 campaigns	35 campaigns

The combination you use is down to you, I can't tell you what the best approach is. It's dependant on a number of factors such as your budget, resources and workload. For some maybe they can't afford to attend lots of events, if so then they'll have to look at other channels. For others they may not have the resources to put together and send emails campaigns. Use the combination that works best for you and your business.

Now we have finally put the last piece of the puzzle together. The final part of reverse funnel planning is complete as you can map out the level of activity required to achieve your goal.

What If There's a Deficit?

In an ideal world we don't have a deficit in lead generation. This ideal world would denote that our lead generation matches the requirement for meetings set by our end sales target. Honestly, this is rarely the case, and I'm a believer that there should be a deficit. I hate to see salespeople fed all of their leads, it makes them complacent and lazy. Ideally though a salesperson should be fed the majority, but the rest should be from their own devices.

So if you find there is a deficit and you need to find ten, twenty or more meetings throughout the year then do you know what the answer is? Find them! Pick up that phone and make cold calls, ask for referrals, go to networking events, conduct drop in calls, send letters to people. You must do whatever it takes to overcome that deficit as the numbers and conversion rates speak for themselves. If you know that you don't have a sufficient number of meetings in the diary then they'll be no hiding, the truth will come, you won't hit your target and won't become a sales icon.

But do you know what, even if there isn't a deficit, make one for yourself. Human beings respond best to being challenged, it excites us and gives us a feeling of self-worth and achievement. So if the circumstance arises whereby your lead generation is enough to meet or surpass your target then don't settle for that target. Challenge yourself, up it by ten or twenty per cent and tell yourself that's what a sales icon would do so I'll do the same!

Improving Your Campaigns

Remember that this discipline in the book is sniff out what sells. We have focused thus far on finding the channels that work best for lead generation and utilising them effectively. There's something ill fitting; however, we stated that we find our conversion rates for a channel and use them moving forward, well a sales icon wouldn't simply be happy with that.

For any sales icon we're always striving to be better than the rest and better than we were before. So why should we take our historical results a gospel? The answer is we shouldn't. What we should be doing is using our channel conversion rates as a benchmark and then embark on trying to improve them. That's the point I'm trying to make, if we can improve on our channel conversion rates then we book more meetings and make more sales, it's as simple as that.

We've highlighted how a channels conversion rate is made up of the average of the campaigns within that channel. Let's take emails again for example, you may find that you carried out three email campaigns last month which resulted in the following conversion rates:

1) Topic = newsletter – 0%
2) Topic = advantages of X – 5%
3) Topic = why choose Y – 7%

Now it's clear as day to see that the newsletter campaign is negatively skewing your results here. If you looked at the average result of all of these campaigns then the conversion rate of the email channel would be 4%. However if you took the newsletter out of the equation then the email channel would have a conversion rate of 6%.

We must be ruthless, if you find something doesn't work then scrap it. But if you find something that does work then replicate it. For every campaign try to ask yourself the reason why? Why did it or didn't it work? What could I change to make this better, maybe content, maybe commitment, maybe approach? We're looking for the formula for success, find it and we become sales icons.

3.5 – Campaign Planner

What gets scheduled gets done!

A simple but effective concept which is so true. The fact is that if you just have something in your mind such as I need to call John at some point, then often it gets pushed back further and further. But the moment you take a few seconds and say no, I'm going to put this in my calendar for next Tuesday at 1000 hrs to call John then it's pretty much a certainty that you will do so. Now the same is true with your campaign planner.

What is a campaign planner?

A campaign planner is basically a yearlong plan on the structure of all of the campaigns that you are going to run. Now you may be in the position where you have a marketing department or not, but irrespective of this fact you should put together a campaign planner of what campaigns you will personally conduct throughout the year. What get scheduled gets done, so plan this to the day.

What should it look like?

Your campaign plan should list all of the weeks and days in that week like the following:

	Monday	Tuesday	Wednesday	Thursday	Friday
Week 1					
Week 2					
...					
Week 52					

Then you should schedule the days within the week/month that you plan to run a campaign. The important thing here is to remember what we have already learnt in the previous chapter for both our reverse funnel analysis and our channel conversion rates.

Let's use an example to make this clear. If my reverse funnel analysis found that in order to hit my target I needed to develop fifteen meetings this month and my budget allows for us to utilise one survey, no events and the rest emails then what would my campaign planner need to look like. Well if my analysis showed that for a database of 10,000 recipients my marketing channels received on average the following results:

- Survey = 30 unique/new responses
- Email = 100 opens

And the conversion rates to meetings for the channels were the following:

- Survey = 30%
- Email = 1%

One survey this month would therefore equate to 9 meetings as 30 x 0.3 = 9

My deficit of meetings required is 6 as 15 – 9 = 6. I can then work out the number of email campaigns required by doing the calculation which is:

6 / 0.01 = 600 – leads required
1 email campaign equates to 100 leads:
600 / 100 = 6

Therefore this tells us that 6 email campaigns are required to develop 6 meetings.

With this information I can then plan out my month accordingly. As I know now that in order to hit my meetings target (as well as sales target) I will have to conduct one survey and 6 email campaigns. All that I need to do now is schedule in my calendar when these are going to be.

Quarterly or yearly plan:

I would highly recommend being proactive here and putting together your campaign planner at least a quarter in advance, ideally you'd have at least a rough plan for the whole year. The benefit of this is that you can counteract pitfalls along the way. Let's use an example to make this clear. If you were selling education software, a quiet period at least on the meetings front may fall in August, the reason for this is that this is the school holiday period. Now with your campaign planner, you can use this insight to plan ahead accordingly. For simplicity, if you needed one hundred and twenty meetings a year i.e. ten a month but knew any campaigns in August would be unsuccessful then you could increase the goal and therefore activity for the other months to counteract this. Such as if you set your goal of zero meetings for August but 11 meetings for the other months then you'd achieve one hundred and twenty-one meetings for the year. This way you've acted proactively and will have actually surpassed your target.

Events play a big factor here. For simplicity, let's take some easy numbers, let's say for every exhibition you attended you gained fifty leads. For this example, let us also say that the conversion rate of an event lead to a meeting is 30%. This would mean that if you attended one event you would expect fifteen meetings to be the result. Now events play such a big factor here because the months where you attend any will skew your results. So continuing this example, if this business attended three events in the year in say January, February and March this would equate to forty-five meetings. Now if the company only required ninety meetings for the year then they would only need a target of five meetings a month for the other nine months which they can then plan for in their campaign planner appropriately.

Note – my advice here would be to over achieve on your meetings target as much as possible. Take this previous example, let's say the business in the other nine months only ran email campaigns to develop the five meetings required a month. If we assume that this was achieved by undertaking four email campaigns in each month. Now the conservative approach would be the following

- January, February, March = three exhibitions
- April – December = four email campaigns a month whereas the more aggressive and successful approach to become a sales icon would be to continue the email activity through the months of January to March. That way you're ensuring that you'll surpass your meeting target. This way you would achieve fifteen or more meetings.

So put together a campaign planner and detail where you'll conduct campaigns and what channel they will be from. Use the combinations we discussed in the channel output tables earlier. This should give the blueprint as to how many campaigns we need, how regular they need to be and from what channel they must be. When you know this put it into your campaign planner, schedule it and get it done!

3.6 – Forecasting Results

Through this book we have highlighted that the sales icon way is to use your targets to put a strategic plan together, whether that be a meeting target or a sales target. Your campaign planner should be no different. It should be the resource that you put together months in advance and actively use your conversion rates to predict results.

Take a second to look at a forecast for a standard sale. If you had forecasted to make a £10k sale that didn't come in then you wouldn't fail to act after. What you would do next is try your hardest to find that £10k that you're now short of. Chances are that you couldn't make it straight away but you'd factor it in to a subsequent month, or even spread it into multiple subsequent months.

Forecasting meetings from a campaign should be no different than this. It's all interconnected, if my input at the start of the chain isn't sufficient then my output won't be sufficient at the end of the chain. Imagine baking one hundred muffins. I prepare my recipe, heat the industrial oven, clear my surfaces, I'm all ready to go. Then I start the process and find that I only have 80% of the ingredients that I need. Well if I continue as normal I can hope as much as I want that my output will be one hundred muffins but in all honesty only eighty are going to be the result. I won't reach my goal unless I make up the deficit in the ingredients.

So let's link this to our campaign planner, just imagine that we planned for a month with the following campaigns

- 4 x email campaigns
- 1 x survey

By using our conversion rates of these channels we can predict the results that we expect. For this example four email campaigns would equate to four hundred opens with a conversion rate of 1% to a meetings. Therefore the four email campaigns would result in four meetings. The survey would equate to thirty responses with a 30% conversion rate to a meeting. Therefore one survey would result in nine meetings.

So with this we can predict our results and empower ourselves. That's because we can adapt and change our approach in the circumstance that our results don't meet our expectations. Continuing with this example, if the first email campaign went out and we predicted that one hundred opens would be the result, but in actual fact we only received fifty opens then this deficit would diminish our success. Think back to the muffins reference again, we've only got half the ingredients.

So we can go two ways, an average salesperson would settle, a sales icon would fill the gap. It's the forecasting results that are key here, if we know what we expect the results to be, if the circumstance arises that we don't hit that requirement we can do something to counteract these shortcomings. In this circumstance, if one or a number of campaigns had not achieved their expected results then instead of just taking the hit on our sales figures we would instead adapt our campaign plan and find the deficit. This could be by adding an additional campaign in such as an event or survey at a later time.

Note that it's imperative to review why certain campaigns have successful results and why others do not. If you can discover the reasoning behind failed campaigns then you can adapt your approach to eradicate these.

It's also imperative to remember that campaigns don't always have a direct affect and the majority of the time you will be working in arrears. What I mean by this is that if you conduct a campaign in May you might not see the results of that campaign until say June or July that being a result such as a meeting and the sale may not be until months down the line depending on your sales cycle. This magnifies the importance of effective campaign planning as you need to plan ahead of time. The month that you relinquish your control and discipline in the field may not have a direct result on that current month, but it will do in the succeeding months.

Tip – for email and survey campaigns a resend can be a great resource. A resend would be classed as the same content of the first campaign the difference being is that you have taken out the recipients who previously responded. You probably won't get as high results as the initial campaign, but you may get some. The benefit of this is that the content is already created so it's a massive time saver. Note that if you utilise resends keep them as a separate entity to original campaigns. The reason for this is that they may bring down your conversion rates. Thus for your conversion rate you may have:

- email campaigns = X% conversion rate
- Email campaigns resend = Y% conversion rate

And the same for surveys.

Campaign Topics

You would be surprised how the topic of a campaign can be so significant to its success. Topical, imaginative and unique campaigns are often those which triumph and stand out from the crowd and achieve brilliant results. My work with an IT company highlights this beautifully. They were in somewhat of a rut with their campaigns, they sent emails out almost for the sake of it in a hope that they would be in their customers' minds. Granted that the effort was there but the execution was poor, most of their campaigns were just fact drops that more or less every other company in their position was doing also. At the time the national news was rife with stories on cybercrime, and how day-by-day more multinational companies' security systems were being hacked and leaking valuable information on the companies themselves or their customers. At this time I said to the IT company, "Let's take a topical approach. Cybercrime is something everyone is talking about and concerned with so let's focus on this for a campaign." From this we put our heads together and came up with a thought leadership campaign on cybercrime. I won't bore you with the details but this small change of direction of focusing on a topical subject made a profound difference. That single campaign hit the same results as four of their other email campaigns.

I have depicted below some examples of campaigns I have seen sales icons utilise in the past:

- Chinese New Year – as it sounds I worked with a company that utilised the time of the year that being Chinese New Year for a topically themed campaign which stood out from the rest.
- 'Back to the future' – I worked with a technology company who used the film back to the future as a topic of their campaign as the time period was the date in which they travel to in the film. In this campaign, they dwelled on what their views on future technological advancements would be and whether we could truly be on hover boards soon and how this related to their brand and offerings.
- Rugby World Cup – this campaign was not only based around the rugby World Cup but also gave away free tickets in a bid to entice stakeholders.

For creativity, there are no parameters or set criteria, you need to experiment and see what works. In my experience the best campaigns are those which stand out from the crowd in some way. Your best approach is to try different things and keep assessing your results, using the 'sniff out what sells' concept to find the formula that works for you and your business.

3.7 – Exhibition Maximisation Principle

If you've ever attended an exhibition before or even exhibited at one yourself then you'll know how exhausting they can be. You can be on your feet for up to twelve hours for potentially five days in a row and throughout that time you must continually strive to attract prospects, wearing a constant painstaking smile and working your hardest to gain the information you need.

Reflecting on this now you're probably thinking 'is it really worth all of this hard work? I have to take time out of my daily routine, often stay away from home, not to mention the expense to the business is immense.' Well the answer to this question is yes, it is massively worth it, but only if it's done in the right way.

In my experience, I've seen it done wrong so many times, even by massive corporations. One company I worked with spent thousands on exhibitions every year across the country and across the globe. They'd rock up with their sales guys on the day, set up a stand and that'd be it. They'd have a few conversations with passing by prospects, maybe get some business cards but that was the extent to their effort. What a waste! Where's the return on investment on that?

Key Criteria for Exhibition Maximisation

1. Preparation

Probably the most imperative part of the process, if your preparation isn't right then you have no chance. Live by the mantra

'Failing to prepare is preparing to fail'

This preparation starts way back in the planning stage, as first off you need to ensure that you are attending the right exhibitions.

An exhibition will be defined by its stakeholders, you need to know with confidence that the right number of decision makers will be there who have the level of spending power that matches your customer's sweet spot. For example, if you are working for a large blue chip who looks for £100k deals then a local exhibition with SMEs won't be sufficient for you.

The vice versa is true also, if you're a small firm don't spend money and time on exhibitions where the stakeholders are too large for you to facilitate their needs. With any exhibition if you're unsure about the number of decision makers attending and their spending power then it's a big risk. You could be throwing away your money and time and thus losing your chance to become a sales icon.

Many people when researching exhibitions get too hung up on the title such as 'the home show' or 'cloud expo Europe.' Obviously you need to take this into consideration, but more important is how many of your targeted decision makers will be attending. For example in the past I worked with a large manufacturer in the construction industry. They were 'umming' and 'arghing' over whether to attend an event called the 'The Eco Show.' Their reservations were that their products weren't strictly Eco, some were but not all. My response was to disregard this, instead I asked them to look into who would be attending (information any reputable exhibition company will provide) and tell me their thoughts after that.

They did so and found that 80% of the participants were going to be their desired stakeholder such as project manager, building officer, head of housing etc. and 10,000 people would be attending on the day. More so, the majority of people who had confirmed their attendance were from businesses whose size was in their sweet spot of prospects. From this they concluded that it was a no brainier that they should attend.

So once you've conducted this analysis I would shortlist a number of exhibitions and cross analyse them. Use our reverse funnel planning to predict the output and expectation of these exhibitions. You can then decide upon which exhibitions have a higher priority due to their better output.

Let's explain this in some examples. If I have £10,000 budget for exhibitions, I have shortlisted two exhibitions which have the following:

Exhibition 1 – 1 day, 4,000 attendees predicted, 80% are the right stakeholders, cost equates to £10,000 for everything.

Exhibition 2 – 2 days, 3,000 attendees predicted, 50% are the right stakeholders, cost equates to £6,000 including everything.

On first glance when we look at how many of the stakeholders attending would be the 'right stakeholders' we find the following:

Exhibition 1 = 3,200 total
Exhibition 2 = 3,000 total

Therefore exhibition 1 looks more appealing, although it's £4,000 more expensive.

Next step is to analyse this using our conversion rates, best to use your own conversion rates but for this example I'll use the following:

- 30% exhibition lead to meeting
- 50% meeting to proposal
- 50% proposal to sale
- Av. Sale of £10,000
- Av. Lead gained at past exhibitions = 10% of expected right stakeholder attendance

This will work out as the following:

	Exhibition 1	Exhibition 2
Leads gained = 10% right stakeholders	320	300
Meetings booked =30%	96	90
Proposals = 50%	48	45
Sales = 50%	24	22.5
Av. Sale = £10k	£240,000	£225,000

What we have just developed is our ROI of exhibitions. The analysis may be so profound that when you present it to your manager/board/FD/MD, they say, "Wow! Let's increase our exhibition budget and do both!"

Primarily though this is a beneficial exercise to determine what priority exhibitions should take over one another, especially when you only have a finite budget and want to gain the best return on investment.

2. Survey Sheet

Another mistake I've seen many businesses make, large and small is their lead-generation practices at an exhibition. Some organisations will simply turn up to have conversations with prospects and claim that the point of attending was for brand awareness. Others may stretch to trying to gain business cards from prospects which is a useful exercise but not everyone will give theirs away for nothing. Plus after an event if you have 100+ business cards how is this really going to help your sales? Yes you may have their contact details now but probably so do many other exhibitors/competitors who attended also. When you call or email the prospect who you have a business card for and say, "We met at 'x exhibition,' you passed me your business card." The truth is that they won't know you from Adam, and they would still be considered as a cold lead.

What you need to do at an exhibition is extract as much essential and useful information out of the prospect as possible. Here are a few reasons why:

A. Qualify – you can save invaluable amounts of time by getting an understanding of the prospect and whether they would qualify as a sales opportunity and be worth pursuing. Let's use an example, if you worked for a shower manufacturer and a prospect said to you I fit a total of 2 showers a year you know not to waste your time with them. Conversely, if he said his business fits 30,000 showers a year your ears may prick up.
B. Credibility – as a salesperson we know that perception is everything. We need to build as much credibility with prospects as we can in as short amount of time as possible. By extracting a good level of information from a prospect at an exhibition we'll gain credibility when it comes to our follow up. Let's use an example, take two firms that are in competition.

Firm 1 – asks prospect Mr Hill for his business card

Firm 2 – asks prospect Mr Hill about what his business goals are, his challenges currently, his plans for development etc.

When it comes to the follow up, it goes as follows.

Firm 1 – calls Mr Hill and says, "Hi Mr Hill, it's Simon here from Firm 1 we met at X exhibition, you passed me your business card, I wanted to speak to you about…"

Firm 2 – calls Mr Hill and says, "Hi Mr Hill, it's Simon here from Firm 2 we met at the X exhibition where you mentioned you were really having difficulty with x,y,z, you wanted to carry out a,b,c, projects this year but were sceptical about how they would comply with your business goals of d,e,f, how have things progressed with you from our last conversation?"

Already it's clear to see who has built more credibility out of these two firms and who has a greater chance of success with the prospect.

How to gain this information?

In my experience, sales icons have used a range of methods, but the most effective by far has been a survey sheet. This is usually just an A4 piece of paper with a number of questions on for the prospect to answer. The survey sheet should be as self-explanatory as possible. Because let's face it when your exhibition stand is brimming with activity you may have to resort to handing out surveys to prospects to fill out whilst you speak to somebody else. Obviously, the ideal situation is that you'd be talking to the prospect directly, educating them on your unique offerings, extracting more information from them than simply the questions ask for on the survey sheet and noting this down as supporting information.

You may be unsure how to put a survey sheet together so for some guidance let's use some examples that other sales icons have used.

Sales icon 1

Company – IT managed service provider

Survey questions

1. Contact information
   a. Name
   b. Job title
   c. Phone number
   d. Email
2. What are your plans for development over the next 12 months?
   a. Virtualisation
   b. Backup
   c. Disaster recovery
   d. Cloud
   e. Other, please specify
3. What does your infrastructure look like at the moment?
   a. No. of servers:
   b. Amount of storage (TB):
   c. No of users:
   d. Size of IT team:
4. What's important to you in a solutions provider?
   a. Price
   b. Quality of service
   c. High expertise
   d. Referenceability
5. Your organisations strategy is best described by the following:
   a. Be more profitable
   b. More agile
   c. More efficient
   d. Higher customer satisfaction
   e. Other, please specify

Sales icon 2

Company – ventilation manufacturer

Survey questions

1. Contact information
   a. Name
   b. Job title
   c. Phone number
   d. Email
2. How many extractor fans do you fit/specify per annum?
   a. None
   b. <200
   c. 200<1,000
   d. 1,000+
3. What types of fan do you fit/recommend?
   a. Axial
   b. Centrifugal

c. Heat recovery
d. All of the above
e. None of the above

4. What's important to you when selecting an extractor fan?
a. Price
b. Ease of installation
c. Efficiency
d. Volume

5. What merchants or wholesalers do you predominantly use?
a. Edmundson's electrical
b. Screwfix
c. Travis Perkins
d. City Electrical Factors
e. WF Senate
f. Newey & Eyre
g. Other

6. Please rate these brands in line with what brand you perceive to have better quality, 1= lowest quality, 5=highest quality
a. Greenwood
b. Ventaxia
c. Xpelair
d. Nuaire
e. Airflow

So next time you're exhibiting, try using a survey sheet alike the above. Such a medium will elevate your lead generation and consequently your sales output too.

3. Client Attraction

An imperative factor in the success of an exhibition is your ability to attract clients. There are hundreds of stands at any exhibition and thousands of people too, therefore the key is how you're going to attract clients to come and chat to you as well as differentiate yourself from the rest.

Giveaways – a giveaway is something I would always recommend as it gives you some bargaining power as to why people should fill out a survey or give you a few moments of their day. Pitch it to prospects that if they enter your survey they'll have the chance of winning your free give away. What the giveaway comprises of will be completely down to you and the budget you have. I've seen sales icons have giveaways ranging from excursions, to iPads, to vouchers to sporting tickets. Be creative as that is what will help you to stand out.

Tip – something I won't encourage (for legal reasons) but have heard is a good technique is to not award the prize in a lottery fashion. Instead pick out the winner who you have the best opportunity for.

Bear in mind that irrespective of who you award the prize to and the process you follow for selecting the winner, I would advise that you make the award after the exhibition. The reason for this is that it will become an almost guaranteed meeting. Once you have deduced who has won the prize you can call them and tell them they're the winner and ask to come and see them for a short chat and to present the prize to them.

Conclusion to Sniff Out What Sells Chapter

To become a sales icon we must effectively use our time. Really we need to be in front of people in meetings as much as possible, therefore our lead generation is essential to becoming a sales icon. In this chapter we uncovered how there are multiple channels we can explore for our lead generation. If we're going to be successful we must exercise all or the vast majority of channels and plan the way that we do this.

Following this we must record such activity to identify what channels are most effective and find our channels conversion rates. From here we can integrate with our reverse funnel planning to determine the exact combination of activity that is required through each channel in order to meet our goal. Then we need to incorporate this into a campaign planner and follow the schedule that we set.

Though a plan shouldn't just be followed, we need to constantly check our results and see where we are in line with what we have forecasted. If we do this then we can adapt when we have a poor campaign by adding in additional activity to cover any deficit. This way we're sure to meet the target that we have set.

Key Takeaways – Discipline 3 – Sniff out What Sells

- Lead Generation
    - There are multiple channels that you can use for lead generation
    - The key is to record your activity to uncover what works and what can be improved
- Planning our Activity
    - We need to plan our activity and determine what channels to use and how often in order to meet our target
- Channel Conversion Rates
    - Some channels are better sources of lead generation than others
    - Find out what the most successful channels are for you
- Integration with Reverse-Funnel Planning
    - We've already calculated how many meetings we need to meet our target
    - Use this to find out what combination of channel activity is required to generate the number of meetings we need
- Campaign Planner
    - What gets scheduled gets done
    - Put together a plan for when you'll run campaigns and through which channel
    - Follow that plan
- Forecasting Results
    - We forecast our sales, so why wouldn't we forecast our lead generation
    - Predicting our results enables us to act in the circumstance that a campaign underperforms on our expectations
- Exhibition Maximisation Principle
    - A survey is a great medium to capture vital information

Discipline 4 – Preparation

There is always a sense of amazement when an average salesperson sees how a sales icon works. Amazement at their ability to speak so confidently and proficiently over the phone and in front of customers. Amazement at their wide spanning knowledge of their companies' offerings, history and customer base. But overall amazement at the results they achieve.

Honestly, it's so simple to become a sales icon through the preparation discipline, but first we must bear in mind that primitively we are only human beings and that is often where our downfall lies, let me explain more.

Human beings have brains which can be rather inefficient, you've probably heard before that at any one time we're using less than 10% of our brains potential. That's an awful fact, as I write this book I'm thinking to myself imagine if I could just use 20% or maybe 30%, think how much better my book would be and faster I'd get it written. But seriously 10% efficient, if an electrical device had that poor an efficiency we'd probably throw it out and get a new one.

So with this in mind the secret that sales icons use is to not solely rely on their brains, sounds strange I know. What you need to do is free up as much capacity in your brain as possible so that you have a higher ability of creative thought. Why might you do this, well let me demonstrate in a simple example. Take two identical computers, they are both identical in every way, the only discrepancy is that computer A has 80% of its memory free and computer B has only 10% free. If I gave both of the computers the same task to compute which one would be more efficient? Of course the answer is computer A as it has more resources free to process the task you have asked of it.

You need to treat your brain in the same way as this, you must free up as much resource as you can by stopping the following:

- Trying to remember things – write everything down in some form or another preferably in an electronic format
- Have reference literature (see later)
- Put sales journey plans together

You need to empower yourself through preparation, and here is how:

4.1 – Reference Literature

I want to start by introducing you to a little known medical condition called hyperthymesia. Now there are reportedly only six true known cases of hyperthymesia in the world so it's incredibly rare. What is it? Well it's a medical condition whereby the person has an autobiographical memory. The individual has the ability to recall specific events from their personal experiences from major incidents to trivial details such as dates when things occurred, the weather on a specific date, what a person wore when you met them once eleven years ago etc.

So where am I going with this and what does this have to do with sales? Well just reflect for a second about your past experience with say cold calling. Have you ever stuttered on the phone? Or maybe forgot an important part of your pitch? Or even failed time after time to interest the prospect on the end of the phone enough to have more than a thirty-second conversation with you? Honestly, we all have, whether we are veterans of our trade or newcomers.

The reason I began by talking about hyperthymesia is that it's so rare, yet day to day in our sales roles we act as if we have the condition, especially when it comes to cold calling. How many of us undertake a cold call and simply rely on our memory? The answer is most of us! Yes we might have a notepad in front of us or maybe even our CRM system up on the screen to show us our previous interactions with the prospect, but how much is this really helping us?

The truth is that in these circumstances we're relying heavily on our memory, and unless we suffer from hyperthymesia we may struggle to recall all the information we need on demand. Cold calling in particular is difficult enough, why make it harder by relying on our memory for recall? On a cold call when we get through to a decision maker it maybe our one and only chance to have airtime with them and invoke some form of interest, I'll reiterate, one and only chance. It's quite pressurised!

Now what I'm going to propose is a technique that's simple to use and incredibly effective, but most of all it will ensure that you are in the best position to speak to prospects or customers.

Let's start by going back to basics, if I'm on a call with a prospect or customer I need to be prepared for anything they may ask. They could be an Oxford PhD educated professional who knows more about my field than I ever will, so sitting on a call with a blank piece of paper in front of me simply won't cut it.

There lies the mistake that most salespeople make with cold calling, it all resides in their preparation. They sit on the phone, potentially with the email they sent to the prospect open on the screen in front of them. They get through and bang they're pressured, they're nervous, they lose track, they forget parts of their pitch etc., in essence they make a mistake. The result, they lose that prospect, which could have been their gem, their next £100k or £1m account gone.

Sales icons take a different approach entirely. They don't rely on their brain to remember everything, they need their brain firing with every free and available resource in case the prospect asks a difficult question. Juxtapose to the normal sales approach, sales icons remember to do one thing, and that's prepare, here's how you can too by using reference literature.

If you took my advice previously and started a OneNote document then great, because you can have a whole notebook on reference literature which you can refer to seamlessly through a single click or search. If you didn't, however, then not to worry, but you will need to come up with a system to refer to for your reference literature, such as having a central document where all of this is stored.

Why do you need reference literature?

There are various purposes of reference literature. Firstly, it gives you confidence. How, well compare these two, I call someone with a blank piece of paper in front of me for notes, compared with calling someone with a list of reference customers you have in their vertical, local customers to them, offerings that have interested competitors of theirs etc. Just having this supporting information easily accessible to you will give you a profoundly more confident approach and a higher chance of being successful. Secondly, it enables you to build credibility in a short space of time. Thirdly, it allows you to deal with reservations easily, as more or less any question someone on the phone asks you'll have an answer to in your reference literature. If you don't then add it to your reference literature, then you can never be flummoxed by that question again. I could go on and on with the list of pros about reference literature but hopefully these points paint a positive picture for you.

What should it look like?

When developing your reference literature you may find that there are some unique points to your business or how you work which you want to include. The basic template of information that is important to have though is the same for most businesses. Those are:

- Customer base
  - Vertical
  - Location
  - Offering
  - Renowned
- Offerings
- Elevator pitches

Customer Base

- Vertical – a simple name drop is an effective approach to build instant credibility with a prospect over the phone. For example if you were calling an estate agents it would be helpful to know what other estate agents you're working with currently.
- Location – often referencing customers you work with who are in the same location as your prospect can be the safety blanket for them to have confidence in you.
- Offering – again a credibility builder with any prospect is referencing customers who take advantage of a certain offering of yours. For example if you had a range of offerings but were trying to sell one of them to a customer it would be fruitful to name-drop other customers who take advantage of that specific offering currently and how it would help them.

  Let's use a real-life example again; when I was working with a managed service provider one of the offerings they were trying to sell was IT health checks. We created reference literature for this specific offering of what customers have taken advantage of this as well as a real-life story to create some gravitas. In this instance the story was about how advantageous a health check can be to prevent major issues and ramifications in the future.

  The salespeople would reference a letting agents they carried out a health check for and how they found that they had major security and data protection risks because all of their documents were accessible by their tenants. Something as simple as referencing customers who use the offering and a short story around it can be the difference that enables you to book that meeting or attain that sale.
- Renowned – sometimes a renowned business can be a buzzword which encourages prospects to work with you. If, for example, you were prospecting a business and said that you work with Jim from a one-manned band then this may hold very little substance. Conversely, if you mentioned how your work with the Ministry of Defence, Unilever, Facebook, *The Times* etc. then this

would hold much more weight. On the renowned side it does differ how effective this can be. If you're prospecting the SMB market then telling a prospect that you work with renowned companies may make no odds to them. In my experience I've never seen it do any harm though.

Offerings

- Just breaking down all of your offerings and then sub categorising them in any way you see fit can be great for reference literature. For example you could break down your offerings and sub category offerings that are sold into a certain vertical such as education. Then when you next contact an education customer you have all the information you need, you can say how St. John's school utilises this offering currently and how they benefit. In this case your pitch becomes much more relatable for a prospect. Whereas if you simply call an education prospect and stated how you have this great offering that may interest them, then the pitch will carry much less weight.

Elevator Pitches

- Elevator pitches are always good to have on hand and I recommend having a number of them so that you can mix up your approach and remain invigorated. Most sales icons will have a range of elevator pitches, often categorised by the vertical that they are prospecting. So spend some time generating a number of pitches for each vertical that you're prospecting.

This has all been a bit full on so far, so to make it easy we'll show what we mean visually:

Customer Base

Vertical

Education	Estate agents	Dentists
St. John's school	Estate moves	JJ dental
Fitzpatricks academy	Hampton sales	Cornerstone orthodontists

MK postcode	AL postcode	HP postcode
Jk dental	Luke's timber	Hemel homes
Olivia's restaurant		LK lighting
		Lettings direct
		Samuels solicitors

Offering	MK Postcode	AL Postcode	HP Postcode
Cloud backup	MK shoes, bishop academy		
Server monitoring		Smith's carpentry, lettings direct	
Help desk support		Smith's carpentry, l p financial	HP travel,
Web filtering	MK shoes		

Renowned – IT solutions provider example:

Offering	MK Postcode
Cloud backup	Lucozade
Server monitoring	Mercedes Benz
Help desk support	Frankie & Benny's
Web filtering	Arcadia group

Activity

Spend some time now to put together your reference literature. Start with the basic format which I've depicted above but then as you gain more confidence adapt and change the format to suit you and your business.

Remember that this job is never complete, you should be constantly adding new parts to your reference literature as you add more customers and as your business offerings change.

How do I use this reference literature?

You should use your reference literature every time you make a phone call, irrespective of how experienced you become. That doesn't matter if I'm calling a customer I've worked with for years or a new prospect that I've never spoken to. Our reference literature may hold the key to a sale; it could help us answer that nagging question or build the credibility we need to keep the person on the phone a few minutes longer. Just by having your reference literature there in front of us when we're on the phone we'll be making our lives so much easier and equip us to sell effectively. So if the customer asks a tough question, you won't be riled, whether they ask who else you work with locally or what makes you different from the other competitors who call. Regardless of the questions asked, if your reference literature is prepared correctly it'll help you through the most difficult or simple of questions.

A word of warning here, your reference literature isn't a script, it's supporting material. I hate scripts, they rarely work. That's because they're not free flowing; the nuances to how a person speaks isn't reflected when they read from a script, it's not natural and that's reflected in an individual's delivery. Most customers can tell straightaway when someone's reading from a script so don't be inclined to do so. Your reference literature is supporting material, a quick reference guide. It should be easy to read and scan for information on a question that a customer might ask. But the rest is down to the salesperson, they must use the information and compose their delivery in the right manner in a bid to express things naturally as they would.

Some people have said to me in the past that they don't like working off of notes on a screen and can't they just write this down on a notepad before they start cold calling? The answer is yes, you can, but you won't become a sales icon. The beauty of the electronic form is that it complies with the discipline – time. If on every occasion you were about to make some calls you had to write all this information down then you'd spend about an hour or so writing it all…wasted time, time you could have spent calling, prospecting and closing them sales on your quest to become a sales icon. What I truly love about having this in an electronic form is that it can forever be a working document which can be altered and improved. You'll find that over time your brain will subconsciously think of new great material you can add to these lists to add more and more weight to your pitching.

What else should be in your reference literature?

I've given you a very basic example of what a bare essentials reference literature template should look like but yours will no doubt need to be much more in depth. I can't give you the exact answer as to what else you should include but I can give you some guidance as to what other sales icons have done in the past.

FAQs:

Frequently asked questions would be a great addition to your reference literature. Is there anything that you regularly get asked on the phone from customers? If so, write them down and collate them in this section. Things like:

- What ISO accreditations do you have?
- What qualifications does your team possess?
- What's your environmental policy?

I can't tell you what your frequently asked questions will be, only you'll know that.

Buzz words:

Are there any buzzwords or statements in your industry that you can mention to entice the customer? By entice I mean a statement you can mention to get them to discuss this topic with you and keep them talking. This sounds confusing so let me use some examples.

Regulations – have there been any regulation changes in your industry that you could mention to customers? Just simply asking how's X regulation affecting your business would do the trick. Take my work in IT previously, a new regulation in the UK came into force in 2018 known as general data protection regulation (GDPR) which governed the way businesses used and protected clients' data and enforced a sanction for breaches of the regulation. This would be a buzzword I would have in a list if I was working in IT. So if I was making a call to a prospect or customer I'd see this buzzword and simply ask the question 'so John, how is GDPR affecting the business?'

Market challenges or pressures – are there any in your industry that would be worth mentioning? This could be a range of things, for instance let's say I'm selling machines to automate manufacturing and reduce the need for manufacturing staff. If I came across some information that told me that recruitment of manufacturing staff was at an all-time low for candidate supply then I'd have this as a buzzword. I'd be saying, 'John I know the recruitment of manufacturing staff is difficult lately, how's this been effecting you and the business?' So think about market challenges and pressures, could any of these become a buzzword.

Hot topics – are there any hot topics in your industry that are worth mentioning? Again this could be a range of things but let me use an example to make this clear. In the world of IT in 2017 there was a major outbreak of malware denoted as wanacry. It affected organisations worldwide, most notably taking down many of the UKs national health services (NHS) IT systems. If I was working in this industry then wanacry would be one of my buzzwords. I would just be asking 'what the business has done since the wanacry malware outbreak?'

But this may not be the only hot topic, maybe there are specific things occurring in your industry. Take the airline industry. Not long ago the giant airline known as monarch airlines was in financial uncertainty. If I was working in an industry relating to airlines and speaking to competitors of monarch airlines then I'd be using this as a buzzword, something like 'how has monarch airlines financial uncertainty affected your business?'

Let's use another one, Airbnb, a massive disruptor in the hotels market. A business that has rapidly transformed the market and user experience. If I was working in the hotel sector, maybe selling to hotels then the Airbnb effect would be a buzzword for me. I'd be asking my prospects and customers 'what are you doing to counteract the Airbnb effect?'

Hopefully you get the picture. You can have numerous buzzwords that you can throw into a conversation to get the prospect or customer conversing more with you. Moreover, asking these questions will differentiate you from the average salesperson. You'll learn more about your customers' challenges and be able to cater your offering to aid them in their strategic goals.

Just a short note here, some buzzwords will have a shelf life. Take the example of monarch airlines above, they wouldn't be in financial trouble forever. There's probably only a short period of time that you can use these buzzwords, so be mindful of whether buzzwords do have a shelf life or not. It's not to worry if they do; every market is constantly changing so they'll be new buzzwords that develop overtime. It's your job to brainstorm what they are though.

So within our reference literature, our buzzwords layout should look something like this:

Buzzwords

- GDPR
- Manufacturing recruitment
- Wanacry
- Monarch airlines
- Airbnb

As you can see it's simply bullet points of the buzzword topics. Again all this reference literature should be is support material, a quick reference guide. I want to be able to look at it quickly and see what buzzword might be appropriate to drop into a conversation.

Success Statements:

Are there any success statements about your business or your offering that you can quickly drop into conversation? Has your business or offering won any awards? Is there anything that's differentiated you from your competitors?

I personally think there are many things that you can put into this section so spend some time brainstorming yours. It's important to put yourself in your customers' shoes; what will they care about? I've identified below some great examples of success statements that sales icons have used in the past:

- Named in *The Sunday Times* top one hundred companies to work for
- Customer retention rates of X for the last five years
- All products are made from 100% recycled materials
- Manufactured in the UK
- Source from sustainable sources
- Average call waiting times of X seconds
- Voted product of the year by X body
- Invest X in innovation every year
- Hold X accreditation

You could have many success statements but try not to go overboard with too many. My advice is come up with a few and then test them. See what feedback you get from customers. What interests them? What keeps them on the phone? What statements do they ask questions about and want to know more? If you can identify those which work then you're on to a winner. Just keep using them and you'll be incredibly successful.

Competitor battle cards:

Now I'm not the type of person to focus on competitors too much. I don't think that salespeople should ever discredit competitors' offerings as in most cases it only reflects badly on that salesperson. However, to become a sales icon it'll aid us if we're aware of our competitors' offerings and mindful of their strengths and weaknesses. The reason being is that if I understand the pros and cons to their offering then I can lead my customers in the way I want them to be led.

For instance if I have made a competitor battle card and highlighted some pros and cons of a competitors offering such as the following:

Pros

- Good level of technical resource
- Wide range of offerings

Cons

- Expensive
- Lengthy contracts

Then whenever a conversation verged into the competitors' pros such as technical resource or range of offerings, I'd attempt to steer the conversation to the competitors pricing model or length of contracts. I'm not discrediting the competitor in anyway. I'm using my battle cards on them to work in my favour.

Don't go into copious amounts of depth here. You only need to put battle cards together for your main competitors not all of them, and maybe just for the main offerings that you're commonly going up against. Otherwise you could run the risk of spending all of your time putting together battle cards and never actually selling.

Exercise your reference literature:

The only way we're ever going to get proficient at using our reference literature is if we exercise it. So what I propose is having it open in front of you and making some calls to prospects or customers. Use each section of it, test one of your buzzwords or success statements in five of your calls then move onto another. Name-drop some customers you work with, either renowned or local to the prospect, and see what effect it has.

So far we've explained how your reference literature works. How it should be your quick reference guide for support material detailing all of the key information in front of you when you're making phone calls. If it's put together correctly it should aid you in your phone calls especially cold calling and all in all help you to book more meetings with prospects and customers.

But preparation goes much further than that, the next step to our preparation is that we need to understand the sales process that we should follow. Included in this is some psychology in selling, so let's jump into this now.

4.2 – Sales Process

One thing that I always struggled with early on in my sales career was structure. I'd try loads of approaches such as the puppy dog sale, features benefits selling, solution selling etc. but no matter what I tried it had minimal effect. Then I realised the importance of structure. If I am to control and steer any conversation with a prospect or customer then I must follow a clear structure. Yes I may drift off from a topic at certain points but the structure is always clear and I will always revert to my position in the sales process.

I'm going to introduce the structure we champion for an initial meeting with a buyer. Whilst this is aimed at an initial meeting, it will transpire that following meetings also mimic this structure too. The parts we incorporate into that structure may differ depending on the interaction, but the structure will always remain the same.

Now to reiterate, this sales process should be the blueprint structure for any interaction, but most commonly for face-to-face meetings. The sales process is as follows:

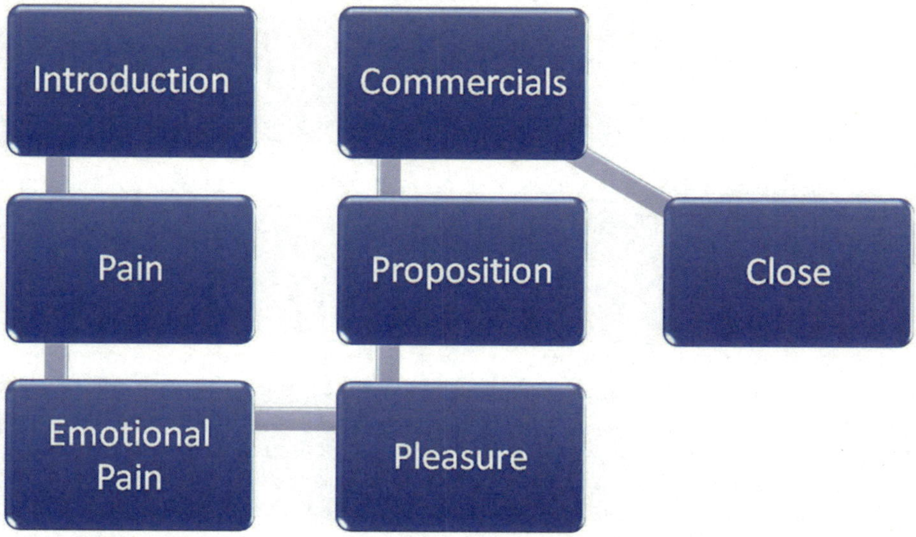

So let's jump into all of these areas to uncover what should be included in each of them.

4.2.1 – Introduction

This has to be the most important part of the interaction process, first impressions. Now I'm going to assume you can take care of the visual first impressions yourself; this book is not here to tell you to tuck your shirt in and look presentable.

What I will help you with, however, is gaining a good first impression with what you do and delivering the best introduction step as you can. The core areas that we will address in the introduction step are:

- Rapport building – focus on the person
- Learn about their business
- Understand their challenges and strategy
- Find out what's important to them
- Power or value statement

Step one – rapport building:

First things first, your number-one focus when introducing yourself to a prospect or customer is them. You should convey that they are the most important person to you in the world at that time. Initially we want to focus on the person behind the suit, who are they? If you can get them talking about themselves from the outset then rapport building is a breeze. So how do we do this?

Well one of the greats in this space is a man called Dale Carnegie who wrote one of the most influential books of all time known as 'How to win friends and influence people.' It's one of my all-time favourite books that I revert to regularly.

In this book Dale identifies some truly profound concepts which I believe would aid any sales icon in their rapport building. I highly recommend you reading this book at some point, but to help you in your rapport building, I have highlighted those which I believe to be integral in this area.

- Become genuinely interested in other people
- Smile
- Remember that a man's name is to him the sweetest and most important sound in the English language
- Be a good listener
- Make the other person feel important and do it sincerely [11]

Just reflect on those points again and ask yourself how you can apply them. I personally had those exact points fixed to my Filofax, therefore every moment of the day when I used this it would be there in front of me as a constant reminder. With every single interaction these points would be filtering through my mind one after another, as I knew if I could apply them I would build a strong rapport.

Dale Carnegie isn't the only person to have this view, Steven Covey muses in his book 'the seven habits of highly effective people' how one of the sweetest words to anyone is their own name [12]. This couldn't be closer to the truth. Deep down everyone you meet is self-involved to some extent, everyone's favourite subject will always be themselves. It's defined as implicit egotism, which is the concept that we all possess, at least at some level, a certain self-centredness. As human beings we have an unconscious preference for things associated with ourselves.

Take a group photo, chances are you look for yourself first, then maybe family then people you know. So use this to your advantage; every meeting shouldn't be solely business and only business. Spend some time to try and find out more about them, be personable, I promise it will pay off tenfold. Ask them about their hobbies, their family, their career history and note it all down. Then for any further interaction you have they'll be some resource in your locker to get their guards down straightaway; if they like football you can ask them if they saw the game on the weekend. Or if they have a young daughter you can enquire how they are? What do they enjoy?

Questions, alike much of sales, are the art to building rapport. If we can ask the right questions, listen and act appropriately then we will be building significant levels of rapport. So to help you in your journey let me give you some great rapport-building questions which you can ask.

Rapport building questions

- How local do you live?
- What brought you to the business?
- When did you join the business?
- Where were you before working here?
- Where did you grow up?
- How did you get into this profession?
- Where did you study?

Note that they're all open questions. My goal is to get the prospect talking and feeling relaxed in my presence. Do bear in mind that some questions are better openers than others. I personally love to start with how local do you live. I find it's a great opening, it normally moves onto their commute or their history living here etc.

So first things first, focus on the person behind the suit in front of you. Learn about them and build rapport. Don't straightaway revert to business, and definitely don't let silence ensue, make them feel comfortable and at ease by talking about them.

Step two – learn about their business:

The second area to address in the introduction step is learning about their business. Now I'm not telling you to go into a meeting blind and simply just say 'tell me about your business?' This won't build much credibility at all. What you should do in your preparation stage is learn a little bit about their business, look into things like:

- What industry they're in
- Their industry trends and challenges
- News on their business
- Successes of their business
- Structure of their business

Then when you go into a meeting you can ask educated questions about their business to build credibility but also understand more about them. Take the following approaches below and deem yourself what you feel would be the best to opt with

Approach one:

"Tell me about your business?"

Approach two:

"I notice from my research a number of things. I can see that you've grown substantially over the past few years, in particular by the acquisition of X. I'm also conscious of the fact that businesses in your industry are being pressured by Y. Now there's only so much I can uncover from your website so can you tell me a bit more about your business and how you operate day to day, please?"

For me that's a no brainier; if this was two competitors vying for my business then I'm opting with the business that uses the second approach. We've only just met yet they're demonstrating to me that they have taken the time to learn about my business and are openly intrigued to learn more.

Step three – understand their challenges and strategy:

Every business is made up of multiple departments and stakeholders, all with their own day-to-day operations. Each departments operations will differ to one another but all are influenced and often affected by the same business challenges and strategy. I like to think of departments as interconnected cogs in a machine, as whilst they turn by themselves if one cog is compromised or slowed, it affects the entire machine.

The challenges and strategy are the things that any prospective supplier must understand in great detail. If any supplier can demonstrate effectively, above any other proposition that their solution enables the cogs in the business to run cohesively and smoothly then they will be successful in their bid. Now the challenges of a business and its strategy are the items that affect at least the majority if not the entirety of the cogs in the system. So that could be a challenge affecting multiple departments, take for instance mobile working. A challenge of a business may be that multiple departments want the ability to work seamlessly from anywhere in the world. In addition, we could have a strategy such as we want to grow the business from £20M turnover to £30M turnover in the next five years.

The things to bear in mind are that businesses will have multiple challenges and multiple strategic plans. So if we can uncover as many as we can and be mindful of them in our sales cycle then we're on the road to making our sale.

Examples of business challenges

- Digital transformation
- Mobile working
- Lack of internal resource
- Market saturation

Examples of business strategy

- Increase turnover to X
- Grow by acquisition to Y headcount
- Standardise our portfolio to Z
- Increase market share

Now I'm conscious that some people you speak to will be slightly reticent to give you this information, so maybe you have to sell the benefit first. I personally would use a story pitch, something such as the following:

'I think one of the more important things to understand about your organisation is the challenges you're experiencing and the strategy that you have in place. Then if I'm mindful of those I can help you to achieve that strategy and work through those challenges. Let me use an example, I was working with X in the Y industry. We had an initial conversion much like we're having today and they identified to me that their challenges were X, Y, Z and their strategy was A and B. We helped them in their journey by implementing C and the result was D. In light of this could you please outline what your strategy and business challenges are, currently?'

This is but an example of how to entice someone to discuss their strategy and business challenges with you. You may find that someone you're speaking to is so open from the outset that you can just ask them the question openly, 'what's your business strategy?' Conversely, others may be very closed and you really need to sell the benefit of them in order to obtain this information. What I'm trying to say is cater for your audience, one approach won't work for all.

Step four – find out what's important to them:

This is such an important step in the process. This information will help you in the entirety of the sale and relationship with the customer. If we can understand what they care about then we can pinpoint on the certain areas that will increase our chances of making the sale. Conversely, we can gauge from the outset whether the business or opportunity is worth pursuing or not.

Let me use an example, if I'm selling a high-end premium product or service, irrespective of what that product or service is. If I am sat in front of a prospect whose sole focus is cost effectiveness or sweating assets or looking at the budget level solution then straightaway we're not suited to one another. Just by finding out what is important to the person I am speaking to will help me gauge this.

So the question is how do you find out what's important to the customer. Well, again, questioning is the key, but it's the right type of questions. You could simply ask, 'what is important to you when assessing your X supplier?' But it's not always that easy, maybe you want to use some discovery questions to uncover what is important to the prospect or customer.

For instance, linking back to my example before of selling a high-end product or service. If I wanted to understand what the prospect or customer values I'd be asking:

- What's your refresh cycle of X products in the business?
- How much value do you associate to X?
- How important is it that…?

The key thing we're trying to uncover here is what's important, so that we can focus on these areas later in our proposition phase.

More on this topic will be discussed later in this book in our section on questioning and pitching.

Step five – power statement:

Now I've put this in as step number five but what I should mention is that it can be put before step two in many circumstances. So after rapport is built a power statement can be used.

So what is a power statement?

Well it's a short captivating blurb. It's a statement you can make to intrigue the person you're in front of, to make them want to know more and give you the time of day in the meeting. Some people call it a power statement, some people call it a value statement. All in all it's a short thirty-second to one-minute statement.

Your power statement must be captivating, as it can make or break the sales process and we'll digress as to why. We champion a power statement within the initial stages of meeting someone because of the primacy effect. Sounds alien but think back to a presentation you've made in the past, maybe in your work life or back at school. Were you ever told that in a presentation it's best to either be first or last to present? You may have thought that this was hearsay but it's true, it's known as the serial-position effect. It states how a person has a tendency to recall the first items and last items best, and those items in the middle worst. The primacy effect is part of the serial-position effect, it relates to the fact that a subject will have cognitive bias to recalling the primary information it takes in. Whereas, the recency effect relates to the cognitive bias to those items at end of a series of information.

So the first reason we use a power statement at the start of the process is because there is a higher chance of the recipient remembering this information due to the primacy effect. The second reason is something known as thin slicing. We all know that first impressions are important, it is reported that when we first meet someone we judge them within one tenth of a second. Now I'm not here to focus on your first impression from a physical appearance, body language or vocal perspective; that bit's down to you to master. The part that you'll need help with is thin slicing.

Thin slicing is the step after first impressions. It's where a person judges something, whether that be a person, item or situation. This judgement has an observation window of around five minutes, to which various information will be absorbed and digested, then a judgement will be made known as thin slicing.

Thin slicing is scarily accurate too. Malcolm Gladwell in his book Blink touches on some of this accuracy in great detail. One such story he talks about is that of the Getty Museum, when they purchased a marble statue called the kouros for $10M. The Getty made sure to validate the authenticity of the kouros with scrupulous checks from renowned geologists and other sources. Throughout the process many stakeholders were sceptical and thought it was a fake, despite its seemingly legitimate legal documents and background history. The scepticism of many of the world's experts on Greek sculpture came from anomalies with the kouros, things like the fingernails were out of character for this period or the colour didn't match that of other alike sculpture. Many experts said it's a fake but science did not, tests showed that it dated back to the correct time period. Long story short, the experts were right, it was a forgery, an expert forgery at that. So much so that the only people who could spot that it was a fake were the experts. Those experts, however, could spot this almost instantaneously and it's all because of thin slicing. A judgement from an observation in a short time window.

So how about the accuracy of thin slicing? Well again I'm going to briefly mention a point from Malcolm Gladwells Blink as it's an authority on the subject of thin slicing. He talks of one behavioural psychologist named John Gottman who through the use of thin slicing can predict with 95% accuracy whether a married couple will still be married in fifteen years' time [13]

Thin slicing is powerful, that's why we need to use it to our advantage. We have a short window before the person we are speaking with makes a judgement on us, therefore we must do our upmost to ensure that thin slice they take on us and our proposition is a positive one.

So reflecting back, power statements are essential at the start of this process as the recipient is more likely to remember it due to the primacy effect. Moreover, at the initial stages they're thin slicing us, so a captivating power statement should ensure that their thin slice is a positive one.

Now you understand that value and purpose of a power statement let's look into the things you can incorporate into your power statement. Those which sales icons use include:

- Stories
- Facts and statistics
- Visionary material

To show you how these can look I'm going to use some examples of power statements.

Story power statement one:

'John, your business reminds me of another I work with namely JJ Hampton. They were in very much the same position as you, struggling with X and wanting to achieve Y. At the beginning of their journey with us I encouraged them to attend our X workshops and then have a trial of Y. They did so, and now experiencing Z. So what I encourage is we talk through some particulars and then see if the same journey would aid you also.'

Story power statement two:

'John, I can understand that in your position you're probably evaluating whether IT can be an enabler for your business or not. All I would encourage you to think about is businesses like Airbnb, Spotify and Uber. All of them are examples of businesses who were major disrupters in their market and now dominate their industries market share. All of them took advantage of IT and the digital transformation. Now I am by no means saying that I can turn you into an Uber overnight. But I can aid you in your journey to making IT a business enabler and meeting your strategic goals.'

Facts and statistics power statement one:

'There a numerous ways I can see us assisting your business in the future, but first of all I need to understand more about the way you work and some particulars. I'm confident that any work we do will be advantageous though. Take for instance my customer namely X. Since working with us over the last five years they have increased employee engagement by 46%, they've won numerous employee satisfaction awards as well as seen annual turnover grow year on year at a rate of 20%. So to uncover whether we can aid you in the same way let's take a deeper dive into your operations.'

Facts and statistics power statement two:

'John, did you know that there is direct correlation between your office environment and productivity. On average offices where employees rated their environment as being good incurred a productivity boost of 10% compared to those of a lower rating. So what I'm trying to say is that if we can work with you effectively you have the potential to increase your staff's productivity by 10%. Just think about what that could mean for your goals and financials.'

Visionary power statement:

'John, the business seems to have been very successful thus far. What I'm proposing is one step further. I could see you expanding to an additional office, increasing your market share and revolutionising your way of working. I've seen this happen with countless customers of mine from taking advantage of the digital age. Take, for instance, X company, they implemented our e-commerce solution, which opened up a new revenue stream for them and now after two years their e commerce accounts for £500k of their annual turnover and that's still set to grow.'

High-level offerings overview:

For those of you who are selling a wide range of solutions you may want to also give them a very high-level overview of your offerings. By high level I mean a short twenty-second description. For instance if I'm selling a range of security solutions I would finish my power statement with some like this. 'We help businesses like yours through security consultancy, supply and install of hardware, maintenance contracts and key holding services.' Conversely, if you're only selling a small group of offerings, for instance one product range then state that. You could say something like 'we strive to remain specialist in our field, for this reason we only provide security key holding services.'

Activity

Put together some power statements of your own. When I put these together I try to think about some success stories. You should try the same, think about the customers you have or customers of your business. What were their journeys? What have the results been? Use your businesses history and customer base to your benefit.

Key aspects of your power statement

- Use multiple power statements – the same as everything in sales, one approach won't work for every meeting. So be flexible, use power statements that will influence the person you sit in front of.
- Believe in the content – above all else you must believe in the content of your power statement. If you don't believe in it, you think it's misconstrued or uninspiring then don't use it. This statement is called a power statement for a reason, it needs a passionate delivery, in that short statement you need to wow the person you're with. In order to do that you must be passionate about the words and meaning of what you're saying as well as its delivery.

We've now concluded on the introduction phase of the sales process. If we follow the steps outlined we should have created a great first impression. Our prospect or customer should feel at ease and be open to an honest conversation. This is where we move to the next phase, known as pain and pleasure selling.

4.2.2 – Pain and Pleasure Selling

All human beings have a certain level of tolerance before we get to the point where we have to change something. It's the boiling point before change. Take one of your previous jobs, why did you leave? The answer is either to gain pleasure or to escape pain. Tony Robbins explains this beautifully in many of his books in that human behaviour all relates back to the principle of trying to gain pleasure or escape pain[14]. Think about that previous job you left, I bet you moved because of some form of pain such as a poor manager, too much stress or workload, lack of career development etc. If it wasn't something of this nature then it was to gain pleasure such as a pay rise elsewhere, more flexibility, better job satisfaction etc. This principle of pain and pleasure is behind every human action and emotion and it's key to understand this driver in order to sell to others, especially if you want to become a sales icon.

As I said, every human action and/or emotion centre around pain and pleasure. Some people can tolerate more pain than others, some people are less concerned with pleasure and more concerned with escaping pain and some people can take a lot of pain as they know it will lead to pleasure. Take for instance an entrepreneur such as Duncan Bannnatyne, when setting up his various business enterprises in care homes, nurseries and health clubs he would have experienced a high level of pain. He was working long days, getting very little rest or downtime and everything revolved around his businesses. I remember one such story where Duncan was so badly in debt trying to raise capital for one of his care homes that he sold almost every asset he had including his ice cream business, his various homes, all the way down to the television set on his wall. Now the question is why did he put up with such pain? The answer is clear, he understood that this short-term pain in the form of stress, workload and debt would lead to immeasurable pleasure. So in Duncan's mind this pain he experienced was worth the pleasure it would lead to.

Let's take another example, say a famous sports person such as Conor McGregor. The majority of the world will know of his stardom, the epicentre of which being a boxing fight between himself and Floyd Mayweather in 2017 which was reportedly worth more than $100M each. But we may not all know his story. Well, Conor had a somewhat insurmountable level of pain. As it turns out it may have been insurmountable to some but not to Conor. He started his career as a plumbing apprentice where he experienced significant financial woes, including having to enlist on the doll and moving into his girlfriend's house when he had nowhere he could afford to stay. He started fighting in mixed martial arts (MMA) on a semi-professional basis earning £85 a fight to supplement his earnings. But all along through this pain he had the pleasure in his mind of becoming a world champion and making millions. Truth be told, in less than half a decade this pleasure had become a reality.

I could go on and on, writing example after example analysing every single successful person on this planet and I'd find the same thing. Behind everyone's actions there are pain and pleasure; either they're fighting to avoid pain, or aspiring for some form of pleasure or a combination of the two. Pain and pleasure are the core principles to all of our human emotions and actions and the better we can understand these the better we can be at selling.

How can we use this?

Now that you understand the principle of pain and pleasure you should use this to your advantage. The majority of salespeople out there will not use this, they'll focus simply on finding a need and trying to fulfil it, or the old feature benefit sale. What we should do, however, is pain and pleasure selling.

What is pain and pleasure selling?

Pain and pleasure selling is twofold, the first part revolves around pain and the second part revolves around pleasure. With every customer and prospect we want to fully understand what their pain is if they have any, and also understand what their pleasure would look like.

Why? Well try this on for size, did you know that:

- 70% of people make purchasing decisions to solve problems
- 30% of people make purchasing decisions to gain something

(Study from impact communications)[15]

Often people don't know they're in pain until they take the time to review things, or until you prise it out of them. The only way you find out what their pain or pleasure might be is by asking intelligent questions, note the term intelligent.

I remember meeting with a prospect years ago when I was selling IT, the guy that I met was very open with me about everything and I started with my pain selling initially. I can recall asking a question like 'tell me what the service is like from your incumbent provider' to which his answer was 'yes, it's pretty good.' So I dug a bit deeper with a more probing question such as 'tell me about an instance where you thought their service fell below your expectations.' At this point he unloaded, he said 'well, there was one occasion that I thought was a bit dodgy, I paid for a project upfront, then when they completed the project they said it took longer than expected so they wanted more money from me.' From this I asked, 'what did that mean to you and the business?' he answered, 'well I was quite angry actually, I had to go to my boss and ask for more money which made me look quite foolish, and we had to cut the budgets elsewhere because of this.' I then asked, 'what other instances did their service fall below your expectations?' He said that 'they often take a while to come back to me when I log an issue with them.' To which my reply was 'how long do they usually take?' He said, 'from a couple of hours to a few days sometimes, actually come to think about it I have an issue with them currently that I logged three weeks ago and still nothing has been done.'

This example goes on much further and I end up uncovering many more pains. The core things I am trying to do are:

1) Identify pains
2) Link to emotional pain
3) Quantify the ramifications where possible
4) Finish by concluding and linking back

Identifying pain:

As I said this is the part where I'm trying to uncover what their pains are, it may take some time and in-depth probing using intelligent questions but the more pain I uncover the better chance I have.

Link to emotional pain:

Again most people are self-involved to a certain extent and that's why linking to emotional pain is so important. You can't link things to emotional pain always, but where you can, do so. The reason being is that emotional pain hits home much greater than just simply pain for the business. Such as say I'm uncovering pain with a prospect, say he's a managing director and I ask him about what pain he has to which he says, 'I've had a big issue with X supplier which caused the factory to stop running.' When I try to link this to emotional pain I could ask something like 'what did this mean to you personally?' To which his answer may be something like 'it infuriated me. I was on holiday with my kids and I had to come back to the office and sacrifice quality time with them just to fix this issue with X supplier.'

The emotional pain resonates with the individual much more powerfully. Finding a pain is great, but if you can find how this links to an emotional pain then you're in a much stronger position.

Quantify ramifications where possible:

When you have identified pain, try to quantify the ramifications where possible. Take the example above of the factory ceasing operations due to manufacturer X. You could quantify this by finding out what the downtime of the factory was, let's say 5 hours. Then ask what the average production rate is per hour and then what they make per unit. They may not give you all of the information for this but if they don't then paint that picture for them. For instance you could say 'the issue with supplier X cost you 5 hours' downtime. I don't know what your production output is but if you manufacture 1,000 widgets an hour worth £10 then that 5 hours of downtime has cost you £50,000!' This quantifies the pain to them, it's something they may not have thought about in context. It is this quantification that helps you at the later stages of the sales process. For instance, if I was pitching to take the business off of supplier X but I was more expensive I would highlight how in reality we're not more expensive because they've cost you £50,000 in downtime, and the question to ask yourself is what if this happens again (rhetorical).

Finish by concluding and linking back:

When you think you have extracted all you can from their pain, emotional pain and quantifying the ramifications, move on to concluding and linking back. Highlight everything you have found out succinctly and then attempt to link back to what they said before. For instance, if they said they're happy with their incumbent you could list off all of this and say, 'would you still say you're happy with your incumbent?' It will add some uncertainty to their thought process and make them question themselves to your way of thinking now that you have highlighted the full picture to them.

So to use an example of this let's say I've asked the prospect about their incumbent, they've said they're happy with them. If I then find out the following pain and emotional pain:

Pain

- Lack of visibility of their suppliers stock, caused them to lose a couple of deals worth around £30k
- Late deliveries every few weeks, lost a contract because of this

Emotional pain

- Wants to grow the business but suppliers service is preventing that growth

Then if I can't find any more pain or emotional pain from the prospect then I would conclude on what I've found and link back. So for this example I might say something such as the following:

'It seems that your supplier is causing you some unrest, you've already highlighted that their lack of stock visibility and late deliveries are costing you money, in excess of £30k loss of business. You highlighted that you want to grow the business but they're inhibiting that growth, now with all this in mind would you still say that you're happy with this supplier?'

This is how we link back everything we want to pose a cloud of uncertainty in our prospect's or customer's mind. If we execute this in the right manner then they'll want to know where you can help.

So this far we've uncovered the power of pain and pleasure selling. We know why it's important and how much of a driver it is for human behaviour. What we now need to understand is how do we uncover this information, what's the best way to find a person's pain and pleasure? Every human being is different, therefore pain for some will just be regular circumstance for someone else. Take for instance people on low wage, for them low income may not be that painful. Whereas if you took a high-earning individual and dropped their pay grade to that of a low wage, you can bet that this would be incredibly painful for them. So now we're going to move onto how we uncover the individual's pain and pleasure, and this is through intelligent questioning.

What is intelligent questioning?

Questioning is often the differentiator between an average salesperson and a sales icon; the art of asking intelligent questions not only uncovers more but distinguishes you from your competition. There are various intelligent questions that you could ask; some questions will suit your sales style or business more than others.

Pain questions

- On a scale of one to ten rate the service from your incumbent?
- Why have you given them this rating?
- What are some specific examples where they have fallen down?
- How much time and money did issue X cost the business?
- What could your incumbent improve upon?

Emotional pain questions

- How did issue X affect you in your role?
- After x, y, z, problems how does the rest of the business view your incumbent?
- How has the service from your incumbent effected your relationship with other people in the business?

Pleasure questions

- What would your ideal service/product look like?
- How impressed would you be if I could offer you x, y, z?
- If you could change anything about your incumbent what would you change?

This is by no means a finite list of intelligent questions for pain, emotional pain and pleasure. These are just a set few example questions that you can try or use as a starting point to develop your own.

The questions are important but what's more important is your reaction to those answers and how you close things off with the prospect or customer. For instance, review the following conversation with my prospect:

Me – tell me where you feel your incumbent has fallen down?

Prospect – well they often do take a long time to come back to me

Note – I don't stop here. I've asked a pain question and uncovered a pain. Now I want to focus on it and intensify it, so I continue.

Me – how long do they usually take then?

Prospect – can be a few hours, sometimes even a few days.

Me – is there any communication within that time?

Prospect – none at all

Me – what do you have to do then?

Prospect – well, I have to contact them again and ask them to hurry up with an answer, at which point my boss or worse my customer is on at me.

Me – how does that make you look in front of your boss or customers?

Prospect – honestly, it makes me look incompetent even though it's not my fault I'm just the middleman.

Me – that must be really tough for you, is that a regular occurrence then?

Prospect – probably happens about once a week

Me – how much time do you lose from this personally then?

Prospect – easily an hour each time chasing the incumbent and then informing others in my business and our customers.

Me – who else in the business does this also affect and in what way?

Prospect – mainly the sales guys. I think John lost a contract last year because of it.

You get the gist of the conversation. I'm identifying pain, intensifying it, making it emotional. My next step would be to quantify ramifications where possible and then focus on their pleasure.

Activity

Take some time now to brainstorm some intelligent questions for pain, emotional pain and pleasure. Try to fit them to work into your sales style and the business that you work for.

What if they don't have pain?

Sometimes a prospect or customer won't have any pain, when this occurs you can do one of two things:

- Focus on pleasure
- Move on

Focus on pleasure – if there is no pain that you can uncover then focus on pleasure. Prospects may change for pleasure, obviously it's an easier proposition if they have pain but pleasure is just as powerful a driver. So find out what their receiving now from their incumbent, what would pleasure look like for them. Once you've got a good understanding of this then position it with them, it could be that they're happy with their incumbent but you could significantly reduce their workload or offer them an additional service that their incumbent can't. There are numerous avenues you can explore, what's integral to find out is what pleasure looks like to them and what they're getting at the moment.

Move on – if there is no pain and you can't offer more pleasure for your prospect or customer then move on. It's a truly uphill battle if you can't defeat pain or provide pleasure; all that will happen is a price war will ensue, or you'll waste drastic amounts of time on what really is a lost cause. A note here however is to keep in touch. Just because a prospect or customer doesn't have pain or a route for pleasure at the current moment in time doesn't mean that this won't change in the future. Move on doesn't mean move on forever, it means move on now but come back at a later time.

So far with this section we should be able to uncover someone's pain and pleasure. Just remember that if we can empower people to escape pain and achieve pleasure then we are delving into their raw human behaviour. If we can understand this and demonstrate astutely how we can achieve it, then we will be successful in making the sale. Now we will move in to the proposition phase, now that we have built rapport and understood what will drive and influence our prospect or customers' behaviour or actions.

4.2.3 – Proposition Phase

So now it's time for the proposition phase, this is your chance to understand your customers' requirements in more detail and then briefly convince them to continue in the sales process with you. That is if you deem the opportunity to be viable and sufficient of course.

The proposition phase consists of the following:

- Fact finding
- Business information
- Current solution in place
- Incumbent supplier
- Requirements
- Road map or plans for development
- Succinct proposition

For every single business and industry your fact-finding will be different, so I can't tell you exactly what to ask. But this proposition phase is your chance to find out the facts that you need. This could be business information; if you work on a per user subscription solution you would want to find out how many people the prospect or customer employs. You may want to find out what solution they use at the moment which is alike to your offering, who their incumbent is and their thoughts on them, their experiences, how long they've used them, why they use them. You may want to uncover more about their specific requirements, especially if you are selling something specialist. What they value and don't care for etc. As I said this part is very bespoke so your fact-finding will be different than others.

Once you've covered off some brief fact-finding that's when I always encourage sales icons to speak to prospects and customers about their roadmap or plans for development. The reason being is that this opens up the opportunity spectrum; it may be the case that the short-term requirements are minimal, but their roadmap looks promising. In such circumstance you would deem the prospect to be worthy to pursue for future long-term gain.

I could go into great depths on the subject of fact-finding but I'm not going to, well at least not at this point in the book. Later on though we're going to dive into meeting preparation sheets which will describe what fact-finding information may look like.

A word of caution is to not overly focus on fact-finding. You can defer additional fact finding to a later stage such as another meeting or phone call. Your time in this initial meeting is precious so use it wisely, sacrifice fact finding for gaining buy-in from the customer. What I mean by this is focus on them, their needs, their pain and pleasure and your proposition to gain their buy in to continue further in the sales process with you.

So next up we move to our succinct proposition.

What should a succinct proposition include?

Bear in mind that we are at the initial meeting part of the process. At this stage we know very little about the person we're in front of and their business. So you should never at this stage make the mistake of a lengthy proposition or a long pitch to a customer.

Sales icons should think of it like this. I've conducted a brief power statement to interest the person I'm in front of, then I've spent a good deal of time focusing on their business and operations, their pain and pleasure and fact finding some key information. The goal of my succinct proposition is to light a fuse in my customers mind through the words that I deliver, this lit fuse leads to an explosion of confidence. I want to take things one step further than my power statement by delivering a proposition that incorporates what they've told me and tying that into where I come in. The goal is not necessarily a sale there and then, but it's willingness to move further in the process with you.

Paint the picture and lead to a close:

In your succinct proposition I want you to paint the picture in the customer's mind and lead to a close. Tell them what you feel the journey is from here, what you can see helping them and where you come in. You could even elaborate on some of the power statement tools, let's review these again:

- Stories
- Facts and statistics
- Visionary material

So why not try using them and link to what they have told you already. Let's make it easy with an example:

Succinct proposition:

Mr Edwards, I thank you for everything you have shared with me today. I'm inspired by both what you've achieved as a business in the last ten years and your goal of doubling your turnover in the next five years. I admire such aspirations. Now I'm conscious of the difficulties that you're facing with your current supplier, we've touched on many including their poor service, lack of communication, and missing key performance indicators that you've set. I can't tell you at this stage that we can fix everything straightaway if you moved over to us. But at a later stage I will be able to state whether we can help you or not.

If I briefly reference a customer of ours, that being J Hammersley Limited, they were in more or less the same predicament as you. They had been using the same X supplier for ten years and suffered from alike poor service which was costing them money. After some deliberation they moved over to using us three years ago and since then they've streamlined their X, we helped install a new Y and changed countless of their processes. We're still early on in the journey with them but they've attributed a cost saving of X year on year since moving to us and have grown their turnover by 15%. In addition they reported a customer satisfaction score of nine out of ten which we're incredibly happy about.

Now there's much more that we need to do in the process, but I envisage you following the same sort of journey as J Hammersley. We could help you achieve your target of doubling your turnover in five years by implementing innovative solutions such as X, Y, Z to increase productivity. So the rest of the process works as follows… (commercials phase).

4.2.4 – Commercials Phase

If you're like me, you've probably made this mistake before and realised where you've gone wrong and rectified it. If you haven't made this mistake then take a look at this real-life example of the mistake I made and see if you can spot the mistake.

I was prospecting a business for weeks, sent various emails and had many positive telephone conversations before the decision maker agreed to an initial meeting. At this stage I was overjoyed as you always are when your hard work starts to pay off.

Step one – the first meeting went really well, great rapport built, qualified the opportunity, seemed like a great potential customer. I agreed with the prospect to have one of our technicians come and analyse his systems as a good will gesture, this was in an attempt to impress him with our skillsets when we came on site and through the detailed report we formulate from our analysis.

Step two – the technical engineer went to site, they spent half a day analysing their systems and half a day writing up a report on their findings.

Step three – I spent between half a day and a day writing up my proposal, adding in the engineers' analysis and preparing for the presentation meeting of my proposal.

Step four – I presented our report findings from the engineers' analysis and my proposal for them. To which I am met with the following statement from my prospect 'how much? There's no way we can afford that, I'm sorry but it's just never going to happen.' Opportunity over!

Now if you haven't spotted where I went wrong yet let me clarify. This was a lesson I had to learn and learn it quick and it was all based around the commercials. Where I fell down was by not clarifying the commercials with the prospect, an estimate of how much I think it will cost them. This is hard to get spot on but I should have at least had the conversation to set their expectations.

Why have this commercial conversation?

The main reason why I should have the commercial conversation with the prospect is because of time. Take the previous example, I wasted easily two to three days' worth of time for zero payoff, what's worse is that not only did I waste my own time, but I wasted others also. If I was very unlucky and this trend continued and I still failed to have the commercial conversation with prospects then my time would be numbered and I would have been out of the job pretty sharpish.

Having the commercial conversation upfront is beneficial in many ways. First of all, it saves you wasted time down the line. You've already invested some of your time pursuing the opportunity but if you know the commercials don't fit then you know not to invest anymore time. Secondly, it enables you to gauge how serious the prospect is, if they're standoffish or uncomfortable with the commercials you state then you know it may not be the right solution for them. At this point it's better to cut your losses then continue any further.

Additionally, the commercial conversation aids you in your chances of success; if you have the conversation and are told that the incumbent's price is X then you have more intelligence to work from. This could even mean better margin for you as you would have pitched at a lower price before.

Finally, having this conversation early on weakens the blow at a later time. Discussing pricing can often be difficult and ideally you don't want to pass on any surprises to your prospect at the later stages of your sales cycle especially not with pricing. By discussing it early they're already conscious of the rough amount it will be, so they focus less on the price and more on the value added which you have positioned.

When should we have the commercial conversation?

For some people it will differ, but ideally you want to have the commercial conversation early on such as in the later stages of your first meeting. At this point you've invested enough time to qualify and also pitch your business and offering. But at the same time you haven't invested too much time that it's a waste of valuable resource.

What should you say?

The core things I would focus on are

- Commercial set up
- What they're paying
- Where your price will be

Commercial set up – here I would try and find out how things work commercially for the prospect such as do they pay monthly or quarterly etc. Are they in any contractual agreements with their incumbent, if so when does the contract expire and is there a notice period?

What they're paying – you can pose this question in many ways, you could simply ask what they pay their incumbent now if you feel it appropriate in the circumstance. I myself prefer to use a testing question such as 'would I be right in saying you pay X per month?' In this I'm testing the water, that X is a rough figure as to what I think they're paying. What I'm keen to do here is notice their reaction, they may just answer saying 'no we pay Y.' But what I want to do is read into their reaction to this number X I've positioned, they may be slightly heated and say, 'no it's not that much,' to which you gain valuable insight once again. It's a good question for testing the water on the commercial side so try it yourself.

What your price will be – what we want to do in initial meeting is make the process as seamless as possible with the highest chance of success. We don't want the prospect to feel uncomfortable at any point and surprises make prospects very uncomfortable. So once you've found out the commercial set up and asked about what they pay now or put a tester out as to what they pay, then position your own price. This helps soften the blow at the later stages when you present your proposal and it's not such a shock when your prospect sees the pricing as you have already forewarned them. But don't simply just say, 'our cost is going to be roughly X.' You need to focus on pushing your value and this is where we link back to the information we have previously found. You want to position it in a way that links back to all the pain they told you about or all of the pleasure they're striving for or both.

Let's use an example to make this process around the commercials as easy to understand as possible.

Prospect – JJ manufacturing

Contact – Mr Smith (contracts manager)

Prospects pain and emotional pain:

- Incumbent takes a long while to come back to us, this costs the business money; we've lost at least one contract worth £10k because of this.
- This poor service makes Mr Smith look stupid in front of his boss as he's always the middleman.
- Mr Smith wastes easily one hour a week chasing the incumbent.

- He often has to work overtime as a result of this loss of working time, which eats into his personal time with his daughter.

Pleasure drivers:

- Wants improved communication channels from a new supplier if they choose to leave their incumbent

Commercial process conversation

Me – thanks for all the insight you've provided so far Mr Smith, on a separate note, what's the commercial setup with your incumbent?

Mr Smith – we pay them on a rolling monthly contract, there's no tie in though so we can leave at any time.

Me – that's great thanks, just gauging the usage amounts you've highlighted to me would I be right in saying that you're paying roughly £3 a unit from your incumbent?

Reaction – Mr Smith seems calm and hasn't changed his demeanour following on from the price I stated

Mr Smith – you're not far off. I think it's £2.80 at general production rates, but in peak periods when we're buying over one thousand units a month it drops to £2.75

Me – okay that's great. Now from our side if we were going to work with you I predict on your usage rate that it's probably going to cost around £3 per unit flat rate. Now I can understand that this is more than you pay, now if you look simply at the tangible aspects but when you look at the wider perspective, we'll most probably end up cheaper or price neutral. In addition to this, we've got in place strict SLAs for response times so the circumstance of taking a long time to get back to you and costing your business should never happen with us. With this in mind you'll keep your boss satisfied, but from a personal perspective you won't have to give up your free time with your daughter. In essence, I'm going to fix all of that pain you mentioned with our much more efficient communication channels. Now before we move forward with any actions, is £3 a unit palatable if we were to fix all of these issues for you?

Mr Smith – yes, I can live with that.

Me – great, let's get our actions agreed then so we can move things forward.

Note that in the commercial conversation I've focused on my three parts which I'll reiterate:

- Commercial set up
- What they're paying
- Where your price will be

This way I've gained everything I need to identify if the prospect is worth pursuing. How to identify if they're worth pursuing further is often a judgement call; to help other sales icons in the past I've put together a matrix which may also help you.

Commercial Analysis Matrix

	Their Commercials are cheaper	Their Commercials are more expensive
Pain only	**Grade C** Worth pursuing, push added value of dismissing pain points	**Grade B** Worth pursuing, push added value of dismissing pain points and cost effectiveness
Pain and pleasure	**Grade B** Worth pursuing, push added value of dismissing pain points and gaining pleasure	**Grade A** Worth pursuing, push added value of dismissing pain points, gaining pleasure and cost effectiveness
Pleasure only	**Grade C** Worth pursuing, push added value of pleasure	**Grade B** Worth pursuing, push added value of pleasure and cost effectiveness
No pain and no pleasure	**Grade E** Judgement call as to worth pursuing, price will be a stumbling block	**Grade D** Judgement call as to worth pursuing, price could be the in roads

The grade analysis is the key point. Grade A is a great opportunity, for this you have pain points, pleasure points and you're also cheaper than the incumbent. This is the dream scenario; it can be rare for this circumstance to occur for some businesses and industries as often when you're fixing pain and building pleasure it costs more. If this circumstance does occur then you have the opportunity to make more margin than usual though as if you have this information you can push your price up if you're feeling confident. Grade D and E are the concern areas, these should be left as a judgement call for you. Honestly, I've won opportunities in the past where there's no pain or pleasure, but it's an uphill struggle, and the majority of the time you will lose them.

Don't worry about remembering this matrix or grading all of your opportunities on the commercial side. Just bear in mind that this matrix is here to use as a tool to come back to if you're ever deliberating over things.

What if they don't want to discuss commercial terms?

If the prospect doesn't want to discuss commercial terms then it's not the worst thing in the world. For certain opportunities or even people they may keep the process completely blind and only provide a set amount of information. If the circumstance arises where your prospect won't discuss the commercials then take a judgement call as to whether it's worth pursuing.

Why not discuss commercials in the call?

Often when conducting sales icon training sessions I've been asked this question, and it's valid, why not discuss the commercials on the phone call. You can discuss the commercials on the call as if you can qualify or disqualify them at this point then you save more time down the line. I personally prefer to meet with the customer to discuss this. The reason being is that you find out more about them, from meeting with them there's a better chance of them remembering you in the future and there may be other opportunities that you uncover just from having a sit-down meeting. The real downside to discussing commercials over the phone is that it might annoy the prospect, to which they can easily get out of the call. Worst case scenario is that they're a valid prospect yet they won't meet with you because you annoyed them over the phone by delving into the commercial conversation. It is for this reason that I don't ask this question over the phone as it can be detrimental to my chances of getting a meeting with the prospect. Moreover, if you have undertaken your prospect attack plan correctly the prospects should be of the right calibre to represent good opportunities for you.

Activity

Take some time now to brainstorm some ways that you can position this commercial conversation with prospects when you're in a meeting. Again the core things I want to discuss are:

- Commercial set up
- What they're paying
- Where your price will be

Personally, I'm rather blunt with these questions but that suits my sales style. You need to brainstorm some questions that work for you to find out the core commercial information that you need to know. It may need to be more extensive than that which I've outlined or maybe you don't need to know too much about the commercials. Nonetheless, take the time now to brainstorm some questions that will work for you and start asking prospects those questions.

4.2.5 – Closing

This is the final and often most important part of the process, the close. Now up until now I can have made mistake after mistake and yet if I close in the right way it'll be all made up for. Conversely, I could have had the most perfect meeting in the world, built rapport, focused on pain and pleasure, nailed my proposition, talked through my commercials and it would be all for nothing if my closing isn't on par.

So what's a close? Well when I say close, most people think ask for the business, things like:

- Are you ready to place the order?
- What would prevent you from placing the order with me?
- When can I expect the order?

Now whilst these are all examples of closing, I would call these closing a sale. Now for you it maybe pertinent to ask these types of questions at this stage, but for most salespeople their sales cycle is much longer, therefore asking for the order here would hinder them more than anything. So when I say close, I mean ask for commitment.

The two parts here to focus on are:

- List of your actions from the meeting
- Gaining commitment for next steps

So the actions part is the easy bit. Here I would list off any actions I've taken on personally in our meeting, it could be things like:

I've noted that you were interested in X so I'll make sure to send you some more information on this is my follow up email

I'll find out some clarity on X and come back to you

I'll email over the contract

I'll speak to X and what their availability is to get a webinar arranged

You get the hint, basically it's anything that you've discussed and said that you would do.

I'd then move into commitment for next steps, which is the point whereby you're asking the prospect or customer to commit to something further in the process. This could be:

- A next meeting
- A conference call
- A webinar
- To send over requested information
- An order
- A trial commitment

It could even be multiple of these or something more specific to your industry or offering.

If you gain this commitment you're one step closer to your sale and you're in the driving seat. It is at this point where countless salespeople fall down, they'll do an amazing job and then their close will be something like, 'I'll call you in a few weeks to follow up.' Don't ever fall into this trap, you're giving the prospect or customer an easy out, there's no commitment at all. Instead, look the customer straight in the eyes and ask them for some form of commitment. The worst that can happen is that they say no and if they do then that's great too, you've just saved yourself from hours of wasted time following up as they're obviously not interested.

Once you have finished all of this, end with rapport once again. Thank them for their time and then focus on some more personable questions. I call them closing rapport questions. Things like:

- What holidays do you have planned this year?
- What's your passion?
- What do you do in your spare time?

So to conclude on this section, we have determined the structure we should follow in the sales process from introduction to close. Remember though that this is but a structure, be as fluid as you can be but always revert to the structure for the best results.

Meeting Time Proportions:

Just a quick note before we move onto the next part of this section. Thus far we've made you aware of the rough process sales icons follow in a meeting, then comes the next dilemma, what part in the process to focus more of your time on? Now every meeting will be different, but wherever possible focus 50% or more of your time on:

- Pain
- Emotional pain
- Pleasure

As I've already highlighted, these are the areas that will motivate any human being to change and ultimately buy from you. So you want to uncover as much as you can here to have everything in your arsenal for later in the sales process.

4.3 – Meeting Preparation Sheets

So we have established the sales process that we are going to follow. Now's the time that we put this process into action by putting together a meeting preparation sheet. Remember that at this stage you've been successful, you've managed to book a meeting with your prospect, half of the battle is won. But this is the point where so many salespeople let themselves down, they put in all this hard work and graft to get a meeting and walk into that meeting almost blind…big mistake.

The sales icon discipline is to prepare for that meeting beforehand. One thing you do not want is to go into that meeting with a blank piece of paper in front of you, which incidentally I see most salespeople do, they are just making life hard for themselves.

Why?

Well think about it. How many times have you come out of a meeting where you thought to yourself, 'oh I should have asked that' or 'bugger, I forgot to find out X, Y, Z.' In order to become a sale icon you need to make this a thing of the past, and that is through preparing appropriately before your meeting.

What you need to prepare:

So start by being mindful of the process we outlined previously, let me reiterate it below:

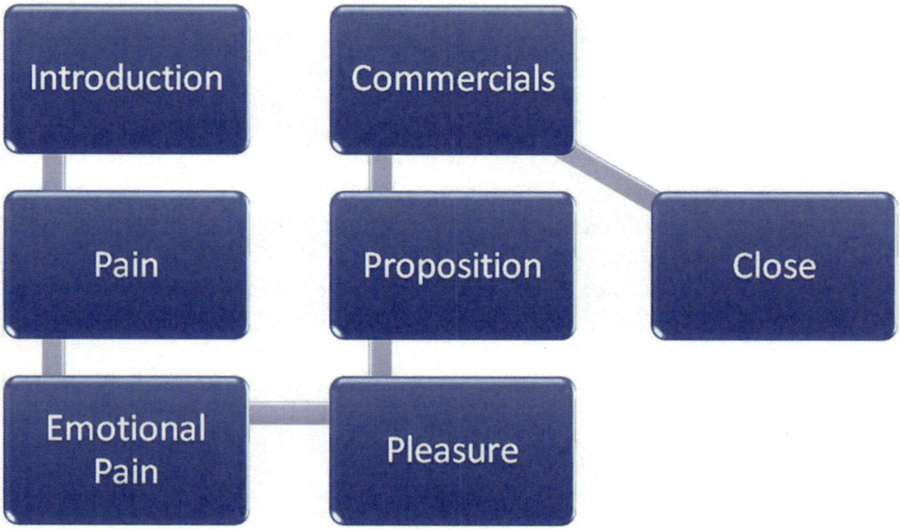

So use this as your blueprint structure, try listing certain subheadings on the notepad you use for taking meeting notes. These subheading should follow the structure as above;

the subheading should be topics or areas you want to discuss (take a note to leave considerable space in between each subheading for parts you'll add).

The subheading and information you prepare before your meeting can be anything you deem appropriate. To help you put yours together I've depicted an example list below, but this is by no means finite, but should help you on your way:

- Company research
- Qualifying criteria you need
- Core information you need
- Insight you want to mention
- Bespoke parts
- Pain and pleasure questions

Company research – spend some time researching the organisation and note down anything that will be useful to mention in passing. If you were going to an interview you wouldn't walk in without knowing anything about the company, you'd want to know what awards they'd won, how large the team are, their core offerings, their customers, their goals, their history. So why should you treat a meeting any different than an interview. Find out all of this core information beforehand and use it to impress your prospect when you go and see them.

On the other side of the fence the prospect wants to work with a business that understands them and is going to add value to them. If in your meeting you say something like 'I saw that your MD John Smith highlighted last June that your goal for the next year is to reduce your environmental footprint, how do you think this effects…' Or 'from researching your financials I can see that you've experiencing major turnover growth of 28% over the last 2 years, how does this affect your strategy for…' Simply by name-dropping a few core facts about the prospects business will differentiate you from the majority of your competitors and make you memorable and credible.

Qualifying criteria – although you're trying to pitch and sell you also need to qualify the prospect at the same time. There are a range of things you may want to find out such as:

- Demand – how often they use your product/offering. If you were a shower manufacturer this may be "how many showers do you fit a year?"
- Decision maker – is the person you are meeting with the only decision maker? Should you ask who else is involved in the decision
- Timescale – if you were to be successful what timescales would they be working on, in terms of when would they order?
- Competition – are they working with other competitors currently? Or are their competitors tendering for the same opportunity? What are their thoughts on them?
- Budget – this topic is always tricky to position with a prospect but it's integral. If you fail to understand the budget and their constraints then you may end up pushing a high-end solution when the prospect was looking for a cost-effective approach or vice versa.

Core information – in the majority of meetings you will need to find out some core information which is integral to you tendering for the opportunity. The complexity of this information will differ from industry to industry. For example, if you're selling ventilation extractor fans the only core info you may need is quantity required, size and performance requirements. Whereas an IT managed service provider may need to know the in-depths of a prospects IT environment from their workstations operating systems to their anti-virus solution. The point is that there are some core criteria you need to find out in any meeting. List these core criteria down beforehand so that you don't forget to find this information out.

Insight – as we said when you get in front of a customer this is your chance to pitch to them, to wow them with your USPs and interesting information about your products/services/business. Most of your insight will come in either the power statement or in the proposition phase. So in your meeting preparation denote some insight that will be good to share with your customer. Try and make this as bespoke to the prospects' needs as possible. It's much better to pitch them insight that will intrigue them rather than generic things they won't value. For instance, if you were pitching to an SMB prospect and one of your insights was that you work with many multi-million-pound businesses it may have little effect. Whereas if you pitched some insight that they can relate to such as we work with X,Y, Z SMBs who are 2 miles away from your office. We provide them with…you get the gist. These are the things you could incorporate into your power statement or maybe your proposition phase.

Examples of insight

- Customer retention rates
- Local customers
- USPs
- Important background of your business
- KPIs
- Etc.

Bespoke parts – there may be some bespoke parts you want to prepare for the meeting whatever that may be. For instance they may have mentioned a hardship they've been experiencing when you spoke to them last on the phone which you may want to probe into further. Or a bespoke aspect may be that you have an offering that you feel will be perfect for their business model. What I'm trying to explain is that you may want to include some bespoke parts in your meeting preparation, no meeting is ever the same therefore your meeting preparation shouldn't be either.

So to summarise, list subheadings in your notebook for items you want to address or find out more about in your meeting. Plan those subheading in the structure we've discussed and list those which are important such as examples you'd like to reference.

Sales Journey Plan

For years, I struggled with being consistent and making regular sales. It's something that puzzled me constantly. I couldn't understand why some opportunities closed and others didn't. Then I looked into the granularities of my sales, why did I win this, why did I win that. What I realised is that there's a pattern, a correlation if you will between interaction steps and a sale. I found that if I timed my interactions steps correctly, if they had sufficient weight and there were multiple of them then my success rates dramatically rose. Conversely, when I reviewed the opportunities I lost, commonly they lacked interaction steps, and/or they weren't timed correctly or they didn't hold sufficient weight to them.

This is where I learnt the power of a sales journey plan, which if executed correctly will propel you to become a sales icon.

Just to start with some background, a sales journey plan can be used at any time in the sale. Most commonly though I encourage sales icons to use this once they have prospected their customer, had a meeting and identified an opportunity in the not-so-distant future.

What are they?

A sales journey plan is a basic outline of how you expect the opportunity to progress. It'll include timescales, actions and transitioners (more on these later).

Why should you do them?

Well the core objective of a sales journey plan is to help you make the sale. For instance, have you or any of your peers had an opportunity before which was maybe far away in the future say six months away, then when you've contacted that person again in six months they've forgotten everything you previously discussed and maybe gone elsewhere? That's exactly what a sales journey plan will defend against. It's there to follow, a plan to stay continuously in the mind of your prospect so that you can secure the sale.

What does it look like?

Your sales journey plan will differ from opportunity to opportunity. Some industries will have more detailed plans that others, some not so much, so it will depend; you need to formulate a sales journey plan structure that works for you but here are some examples to consider. The basic outline for a sales journey plan is much like a timeline, such as:

Date – opportunity X
Date – action 1
Date – transitioner 1
Date – transitioner 2
Date – close

If you're thinking, wait a minute, what is a transitioner? Don't fret, more will be explained on this aspect in due course. To make this basic sales journey plan easier let me use a real-world example for you to consider.

Example
Company – IT solutions provider
Opportunity – IT backup solution
Date of meeting – 25/01/16
Expected close date 29/06/16
The sales journey plan for such an opportunity may look like the following:

25/01/16 – initial meeting
26/01/16 – email actions and notes
01/02/16 – email educational literature
15/02/16 – email customer references
01/03/16 – webinar of platform
01/04/16 – one-month trial
01/06/16 – proposal meeting presentation
15/06/16 – final meeting presentation and close
29/06/16 – close date

Notice how by putting a plan together you're attempting to ration out your contact time and your contact intervals with the prospect. The goal is to keep your prospects in mind, keep them engaged and interested but at the same time not become over persistent and all in all an annoyance to them. Now just taking a short amount of time to put together a sales journey plan will differentiate you from the majority of salespeople out there and put you in the realms of being a sales icon.

Note – you may have multiple sales journey plans for each customer depending on how many opportunities you have with them.

When should I do this?

There is no hard and fast rule for when a sales journey plan should be conducted for an opportunity but usually the earlier the better. Even before an initial meeting with a customer would be ideal. The reason being is that when you have your initial meeting with the customer you can sew this seed with them on the plan of action moving forward between the day you meet and the date when they are looking to move ahead. If we take the previous example again, a good pitch to the customer would be

'The ideal process from here would be for me to demonstrate the offering in more detail before June. The best way for me to do this is through a range of mediums. I'd encourage you coming on a remote webinar to see the user ability of the offering in the flesh. I'd also encourage you trialling the offering so that you have first-hand experience of the platform before you commit. Let's schedule in now to have a remote webinar on the 1st of March and for you to start a month free trial on the 1st of April if that works with you?'

You don't have to get every part of the plan scheduled in there and then, gauge things when you are in the meeting of how receptive the prospect is, or how difficult they may be to tie down if you don't position this and get it booked in today. I've been in meetings with sales icons where they have managed to get every item in the sales journey plan scheduled in the diary in that initial meeting.

From setting out this plan with your prospect, you're going to gain instant credibility. They're going to believe that you're the ultimate professional who they want to work with in the future simply by putting a plan together and voicing it with them.

Note – it's unlikely that any two sales journey plans will ever be the same. More common than not, they will share a rough blueprint and have some common denominators. What I've found is that certain offerings usually follow roughly the same blueprint with maybe a few bespoke aspects. Take our previous example again, one slight tweak may be that when you send through customer references you adapt these to be local references to that prospect or references that are within the same vertical.

Why I love a sales journey plan?

Have you ever done something where you've found the formula for how it works and now you can just replicate it? If you can remember back to when you last undertook a maths equation, if you know the formula it's easy. Or cooking a certain meal, at first you have to think about the process, when to add what ingredients, how long to cook each for etc. Once you've conducted this a few times you master the process and find the formula to make your favourite spaghetti Bolognese or carbonara. The same rings true for a sales journey plan. What you'll find is a formula for success with a certain way of positioning an offering. You'll notice the actions and transitioners you utilised to win the deal the last time you pitched that such offering, you replicate them again and low and behold, you're once again successful. Don't get me wrong you're not going to win every time but this technique in finding a sales journey plan that has the formula for success will aid you in winning many more than you would have.

How often?

My advice is to review sales journey plans regularly, the better the opportunity the more common you may want to review its plan. You may notice something extra you can add to the plan, or a way of doing something differently. At minimum you should review the plan for an individual opportunity whenever you have an action to carry out. Again using the example previously if it came up in your diary on the 01/02/16 that your action outstanding was to email educational literature, then after doing this it would be a good occasion to review that opportunities' sales journey plan. Who knows from simply reviewing it you may see a mistake you made in the plan before or be able to brainstorm a certain action and transitioner that will help to close the deal or bring the deal forward.

Who for?

There's no hard and fast rule as to what opportunities you should create a sales journey plan for. My words of caution are don't do it for every single opportunity otherwise you could spend too much of your time planning and not actually selling. Therefore for the smaller opportunities you may deem them not sizeable enough to warrant a sales journey plan. You have to be the judge, however, it may be that this opportunity is strategic, i.e. a small opportunity initially which will lead to much larger business in the future. In that case you may constitute that the opportunity warrants a sales journey plan despite it being a small opportunity initially. Many sales icons I've worked with like to set a threshold, where basically they stipulate that anything over X amount gross profit I will make a sales journey plan for. Where to put your threshold is down to you. It may be that your sweet spot opportunity is £10k GP per annum, therefore you put a threshold at £6k+ GP per annum for creating sales journey plans. Conversely, you may get so busy that you say you want to raise your threshold for this so that you can free up more time and conduct less sales journey plans or even the opposite if business is declining.

So start using sales journey plans from here on in for opportunities over a certain value. Take some time now and review some of your sales. Ask yourself what was the journey? What did I do? How regular were my interactions? What weight did they hold? What mediums did I use? If you conduct this for multiple opportunities you'll uncover what works and can then replicate the blueprint of the plan for other opportunities, obviously with some bespoke alterations.

So without further ado let's move into the subject of transitioners, which we mentioned but didn't explain so you're probably feeling a bit bemused by this term. What I can say though is that every single salesperson has used transitioners in the past and the majority of your sales journey plans will comprise of transitioners.

Transitioners

If you were to look up the term transition in the dictionary it would say something like the following:

'The process or a period of changing from one state or condition to another.'

Transitioners is a sales term which I created to define the following:

'Actions that help an opportunity move closer towards a sale.'

It may be unclear at the outset what this means in applied form, so I will endeavour to use some examples to explain what this terminology means and how you can use them. But first I feel it's best to explain why transitioners are important and why we should use them.

Why should we use transitioners?

It will probably be the case that you have used transitioners in the past without even knowing, most probably because you never had any terminology for them before. The reason we should use transitioners is to make us more successful, close more sales and in essence become a sales icon. Our studies in sales icon training have proven that the more effectively you can use transitioners, the more likely you are to be more successful than your peers.

We should use transitioners to comply with something known as the familiarity principle or exposure effect which suggests that we as individuals develop greater positive feelings the more we are repeatedly exposed to something. The science behind this is that an individual will feel less threatened by something that they are familiar with. The research into this is proven and that's why many businesses try to take advantage of this fact. Think of advertising, big businesses spend millions on television, radio and written advertisements. They're not doing this to force you to rush out and buy their product or service straight away, sure they'd love it if that was the effect. What they are doing in advertising is applying the exposure effect, they want you to become familiar and comfortable with their product or service so that there's a higher chance you'll buy it over a competitors in the future.

Personal relationships work in the same manner, studies on this familiarity principle in relation to interpersonal attraction have shown that the more often a person is seen by someone the more pleasing and likeable that person appears to be. This explains why back in school the kid you walked to and from school with became your best friend. It also gives a reason as to why work colleagues often become close friends. The more we see, associate and converse with a person, the more our barriers drop, creating a level of familiarity between you both.

This is why activity is so key in sales. It's the reason why the salespeople who conduct the most prospecting often are the top salespeople, they become familiar with their prospects and customers and that leads to sales. We need to be conscious of this familiarity principle in our sales role, we need to make sure that we are conducting ample activity for those prospects and customers to feel less threatened by us and make it easier for us to sell to them. Transitioners are the perfect resource to create familiarity.

Examples of transitioners:

Transitioners will differ from business to business, industry to industry, but the use and effect of them will be the same irrespective of its use case. I have depicted below some examples of transitioners:

- Phone call
- Email
- Meeting
- Trial
- References
- Webinar
- White papers
- Head office visit
- Free trial offer
- Pricing incentive
- Events
- Workshops
- Focus groups
- Training

So let's use some application of these to explain how transitioners could work. I will use a real-world example of an IT solutions provider who I worked with to train their sales force to become sales icons and a specific example of an opportunity they had.

Transitioners example 1:

The IT solutions provider had an opportunity with a customer where they were pitching for them to use their proactive server monitoring service. The crux of the solution was that the IT provider would monitor the health of the customers' servers, and when they discovered an issue they would heighten this to the prospect so they can fix this issue. Thus saving the customer a great deal of time as their manpower can be used for other more innovative tasks than these laborious long-winded checks.

Now usually the IT provider would spend weeks/months prospecting a customer. Normally they would follow the process below:

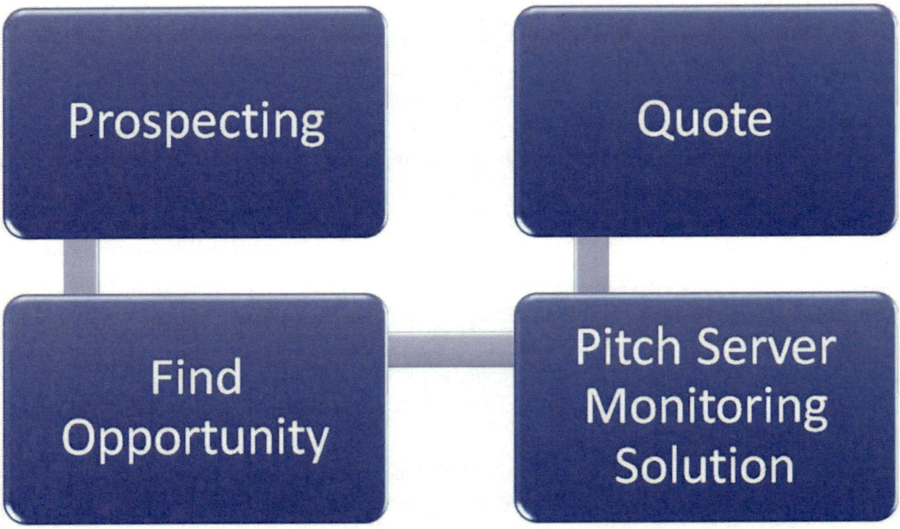

What they were finding here was that they could develop many opportunities but couldn't get enough quotes out nor sales made for this offering. What I informed them to do was to add transitioners into this process, which transformed their approach to the following:

- Prospecting potential customers
- Find need and opportunity
- Pitch server monitoring
- Offer webinar of platform and dashboard
- Quote
- Offer free trial (1 month)
- Send through reporting literature
- Head office visit
- Sale

Transitioner 1 – Webinar:

With this solutions provider what I found is that one of the selling points to this solution was how extensive the server monitoring solution was. The difficulty, however, was its complexity which made it hard to explain thoroughly enough on the phone. However, a webinar platform was perfect for this as it was visual, interactive and the prospect got to see the extremities which would be covered by the solution and how much value this would add.

Transitioner 2 – Trial:

From reviewing current customers of the IT solutions provider I could see that the server monitoring solution was a highly valued service to the customers who had this in place. They had very high retention rates of customers paying for this service year on year and most importantly the service was valuable to customers. There were countless occasions where this server monitoring had found potential issues which lead to the problem being fixed and the prevention of major issues to business continuity. Through pushing for a trial prospects would get first-hand experience of this service in the flesh. It made the sale more simplistic and much more of a necessity. How we made the sale more simplistic was by showing the worth of this service, for instance we would show the prospect that we highlighted X number of issues in this one-month trial. For the average customer of ours we'll highlight X number of issues a year for them to fix. If they didn't have this service and didn't notice the problem themselves then they run the risk of X amount of downtime and the loss of X amount of capital.

Let me explain this further:

If the potential customer in this example had one issue in this month of the trial, we would estimate that on average they'd experience twelve instances like this a year. We could then approximate the amount of downtime an issue like this could incur, let's say for simplicity it could incur one day of downtime. This would total at twelve days of downtime a year, if one day of downtime cost £10k, then they could be looking at £120k of lost capital just because of downtime.

Just take a minute to think about this as a pitch! You can now see how this would simplify a sale quite considerably and how this transitioner gains credibility and a level of gravitas.

Transitioner 3 – Reporting literature:

Now if the other transitioners of a webinar and free trial hadn't given a true representation as to the extent of this server offering then this transitioner would. From my training with them I found that on a monthly basis they would send through a reporting document which demonstrated all of the statistics on the server monitoring, the health of their customers server environment etc. What I was flabbergasted by was that customers were unaware that they would receive this reporting until after they purchased the solution. It was kind of like a perk they didn't know they would receive. I added this in as a transitioner to the process, so the salesperson would send through an example of the reporting literature to paint the picture to the prospect of how valuable a service this is.

Transitioner 4 – Head office visit:

Now the previous three transitioners were there to give the customer confidence in the solution/offering. What they didn't do, however, was give the prospect any additional confidence in the company themselves therefore this could be their reservation later down the line. Therefore, to prevent against this I proposed that the solutions provider add the transitioner of a head office visit to their sales process for this offering. Firstly to prevent this reservation, but secondly that their head office, team and processes were something to shout about and could lead to additional airtime with the prospect and subsequent upscale opportunities.

This brings us to the end of the example, but hopefully you can see the weight that these transitioners added to the process. Now can you just replicate this approach for other offerings? The answer is I don't know, it may work it may not. So what you need to do is try transitioners and see what effect they have, if they help then great, if they'd don't then don't use them.

When should I use transitioners?

Transitioners are a resource to be used. It's not always the case that the more transitioners the better, as sometimes this can be too bombarding for your prospects and actually put them off working with you. There is no rule of thumb for when transitioners should be used, in some circumstances it may be appropriate to use transitioners from the forefront to gain a meeting with a customer. For instance, you may have found an opportunity with a customer and he's dubious about meeting with you, so you use a transitioner such as a webinar as a first port of call. This then impresses him and he grants you the time for a face-to-face meeting.

Commonly transitioners will be used at a later time, such as after an initial meeting. My advice is to use the sales journey plan we discussed earlier, find your success formula for when, what and how you should use transitioners and follow that approach. What's key though is to plan your transitioners into your sales journey plan and then schedule them in, remember 'what gets scheduled gets done' so plan ahead of time and follow it.

Key to a transitioners:

The purpose of a transitioner is to reduce the reservations for why a prospect shouldn't go for a solution and change their perception to why they have to have the solution.

Now the sceptics might disagree with this approach, but I assure you it works, and can only build the professional view that your prospects have of you and your company. Imagine yourself as the buyer here, let's compare two approaches.

Approach one – four-step process:

- Prospect potential customers
- Find need and opportunity
- Pitch server monitoring solution
- Quote

Approach two – using transitioners:

- Prospecting potential customers
- Find need and opportunity
- Pitch server monitoring
- Offer webinar of platform and dashboard
- Quote
- Offer free trial (1 month)
- Send through reporting literature
- Head office visit
- Sale

If you were the buyer which would convince you more, the four-step approach or the nine-step approach? It's an easy decision when you look at it like this.

Activity

Take some time to note down all of your transitioners and at what point they can be ideally used. Please note that your transitioners may be different for each product offering. I.e. for one offering a transitioner may be a trial but for another a trial may be ludicrous and not something you could offer.

Be conscious with any opportunity to ask yourself the question, what transitioners could I use? What activity will give my prospect or customer more confidence in what I am proposing? The more you think like this the more opportunities will close I assure you.

This brings us to an end on the section regarding sales journey plans and transitioners. I encourage you to use them and watch your win ratio increase, your sales and commissions grow and your reputation become that of a sales icon. Think about your sales journey plan before and after a meeting with a prospect or customer and put a formalised plan together to help you win the business. Add transitioners that work for you and the offering you're proposing and follow the plan that you put in place.

Conclusion to Preparation Chapter

This chapter should have given you an insight into the level of preparation that is needed to become a sales icon and the tips you should follow. Starting with reference literature, this topic is something that is so elementary to develop, but so rarely adopted by average salespeople, despite the advantage it offers. Use it as your go-to document, to free up your mind for creativity, to ask those questions or answer those reservations which require a great deal of cognitive thought.

Then we touch on the sales process, which you should use as your structure for any sales meeting that you have. Follow the steps outlined, uncover their pain and pleasure, have that commercial conversation, close them and get commitment for next steps.

Later in the chapter we mention the concept of pain and pleasure selling. Now for many this will be something that subconsciously you already have done, but hopefully through reading this section in more depth it will encourage you to focus heavily on pain and pleasure selling as in psychology terms it is the underlying reason for all human actions.

Staying on the topic of the sales process we also discussed the commercials phase of the process. In my eyes, this is one of those areas which salespeople often miss off as they fear that it'll maybe disgruntle the prospect or customer if they have this conversation. Honestly, though it's a question you must ask, otherwise you face the risk of wasting a great deal of time if your offering is out of their price range.

The two areas that mean the most to me in this chapter and have had the most profound effect on my success in sales are the sales journey plans and transitioners. Which cause prolific results when both used in conjunction with one another. For me, these two things were the missing links in my sales acumen for a long time. But now I can use them to gauge what my ideal plan is for progressing an opportunity to a sale. I can review what transitioners I feel will work best and when and then add them into my plan accordingly.

Key Takeaways – Discipline 4 – Preparation

- Reference Literature
  - Don't simply rely on your brain
  - Write down key information that you can quickly refer to on a call or in a meeting
  - Include items such as
    - Elevator pitches
    - Customer base
    - Offerings
    - FAQs
    - Buzzwords
    - Success statements
    - Competitor battle cards
- Sales Process
  - This is the basic process/structure you should following
  - Introduction – Pain – Emotional Pain – Pleasure – Proposition – Commercials – Closing
- Introduction
  - The core things to focus on here are
    - Rapport building
    - Learning about their business
    - Understanding their challenges and strategy
    - Finding out what's important to them
    - Power statement
- Pain and Pleasure Selling
  - All human emotion and action is influenced by a desire to evade pain and move into a state of pleasure
  - Focus on
    - Identifying pain
    - Linking to emotional pain
    - Quantifying ramifications
    - Concluding and linking back
    - Understanding state of pleasure
- Proposition Phase
  - The key parts are
    - Finding the facts you need (qualification) but not too much
    - Uncovering their plans for development so that we're conscious of future opportunities
    - Delivering a succinct proposition where we want to paint a picture for them leading you towards a close
- Commercials Phase
  - Save yourself a great deal of time and aggravation by understanding their commercial setup
  - Be upfront about your commercial proposition
  - If they can't afford it then move on, don't waste any more time
- Closing
  - Agree the actions from your meeting
  - Get commitment for next steps

- Meeting Preparation Sheets
    - Don't just use a blank piece of paper
    - For every meeting have a meeting preparation sheet
    - This should ensure you follow a structure and get the valuable answers to everything that you desire
- Sales Journey Plan
    - This is a basic outline of how you expect an opportunity to progress
    - The plan will aid you in closing sales, as each part of your plan will add weight to your proposition
- Transitioners
    - Activities that help an opportunity move closer towards a sale
    - These include
        - Webinars
        - Trials
        - Head office visits
        - Pricing incentives

Discipline 5 – Motivation

Motivation is such a powerful thing, yet also so volatile. It's effected by varying factors, which differ from person to person. In order to become a sales icon it is imperative that you master this discipline, and for the high majority of time that you remain motivated.

Simply surviving in a sales environment is very difficult if you lack motivation. I've worked with many salespeople in my time and one area that many often fall down on is their level of motivation, and understandably so. We do a very difficult job which outsiders fail to comprehend. Outsiders just see the perks, the commissions we reap or the corporate hospitality activities, the company cars. What they don't see is all of the rest. We as salespeople are going through days of calling hundreds of people and not getting through or hung up on. We get prospects who waste our time, opportunities that don't fall when we want or not at all. We get continual pressure from targets and through watching our peers bringing in sales. It really is a tough profession and that is why motivation can be so volatile with salespeople.

So I've highlighted some items in this section which will be sure to keep you continually motivated.

5.1 – Recording Our Wins

If you've failed in a sales role in the past or if you feel like you're currently failing then this should be really important for you to take note.

Did you know that:

- The average tenure of a sales representative is 2.6 years[16]

But why is that? Why do so many people fail to be successful in sales and either change role or change career path?

An overriding factor as to why people fail in sales is rejection, and anyone with some experience in sales knows there's a lot of it. Rejection hurts and that's a fact. I read a great article by a psychologist named Guy Winch who talks deeply about rejection. In his piece he talks of the experiments carried out by the psychology department of the University of Michigan. They found something astounding. In the experiments they placed candidates on functional MRI machines and simply asked them to recall a recent circumstance of rejection. They found that the same areas of the brain became activated as when we experience physical pain.[17]

This study is powerful. If rejection creates the same stimulation in our brain as physical pain then there's no wonder why we're all trying to avoid rejection so much. Just think about the human anatomy, we are genetically programmed to try to avoid pain. Think of our primal instincts of fight or flight, we will as human beings try to avoid pain at every chance such as from evading predators in the wild or dangerous situations. Or think of our reflexes. When we touch something hot like a fire or hot stove our reflexes instantly pull us away from that pain.

We're genetically programmed to avoid pain, so it's no wonder why we will do our upmost to avoid rejection.

Now it makes sense why the average tenure of a salesperson is 2.6 years. Rejection isn't the only cause for this, but it is one of the common factors.

So how can we overcome this, how can we fight back against rejection? Well this can all be counteracted by recording our wins.

During pleasurable situations a neurotransmitter called dopamine is released in the brain. Dopamine is often dubbed as the 'feel good' neurotransmitter because it does exactly that, it makes us feel good. There have also been studies that show releases of dopamine helps in improved working memory.

So how is this scientific stuff helpful? Well we know that dopamine makes us feel good when it's released; now we need to use this fact in our sales role. We each have the ability to personally manipulate our own dopamine levels through accomplishments. Think about when you're at home and you say to yourself that I'll empty the dishwasher or vacuum the bedroom, the accomplishment of doing so releases dopamine.

So now we need to use this information to our advantage. It is here that I want to link back to our first point about rejection, how painful it can be and also how many salespeople fail in their role. They fear rejection, and when they get rejected (which as you know is common) they have self-doubts, it effects their output, they're fearful of making calls or meeting people. The pattern, if uninterrupted leads to a salesperson who doesn't prospect, and will either be an average or mediocre salesperson, or leave or lose their job.

We need to counteract this. We need to find a technique to neutralise or counterbalance the effects of rejection. I use these words intentionally as we can't prevent or even reduce the level of rejection you will have, but we can neutralise the effect, and that's through using dopamine.

One of the key reasons salespeople fail with rejection in sales is that they don't record and review their wins. They either focus on that rejection they just had, or a rejection scar from the past. Or they focus on where they're failing, things like how much they are off target or how few meetings they have booked. We need to start by recording and reviewing our wins and then celebrating them.

This is where you're thinking 'what? I know all about the opportunities I win!' Well of course you do, that's not what I mean by a win. In order to become a sales icon you need to adopt the mantra

"I reap what I sow."

In other words whatever I put in I will get out in results. There lies the key…activity. If you have the right activity then the results will follow. It may not be straight away, but in the long-term activity does pay off.

Be mindful of what a win is. I can remember recently I was consulting a telemarketing team. They were disgruntled, finding it really tough. They told me of their difficulty in the market, how competitive it is, how much rejection they get every day and how rude people can be. They also told me about all the pressure, in that they were targeted for how many meetings they booked each week, and this would be published to all the team to see the subsequent week.

I listened to all of their woes and then gave the same advice which I will give to all of you reading. Forget about the macro and focus on the micro and your wins. So for this telemarketing team their macro was booking a meeting. I told them to forget about this as their sole goal, yes aim for it, yes record it and celebrate it when you achieve it but first things first focus on the micro and your wins. If you can celebrate every little win then guess what, you accomplish something. Then your brain releases dopamine, you feel happy and fulfilled and you push some more. When this is happening you counter balance all that rejection. So the key is to focus on the micro and record and review your wins.

So when I say record and review wins I mean the following:

- No. of Calls
- No. of Emails
- No. of Right people
- No. of Meetings
- No. of SQLs
- No. of Quotes or proposals
- No. of Orders
- No. of Drop in calls
- No. of forward appointments

By recording all of this information you'll be able to look back at each hour, each day, each week and notice your progress and your wins. It's a slippery slope when you become disillusioned and demotivated. It's often difficult to get back on track and often becomes a self-fulfilling prophecy. That's why it's so important to highlight and acknowledge your wins to motivate you further.

So next time you make twenty calls in an hour, reflect on it, or when you get through to that decision maker, or when you get a lead or book a meeting. Every one of these wins releases more and more dopamine and that's everything that you need to counteract a million and one rejections no matter how harsh the rejection may be.

So to reiterate, focus on the micro and your wins, not simply the macro. Celebrate what you accomplish and let that dopamine flow!

How to record this?

I personally have a tally book, at the start of each week I take a new page in my tally book and draw five columns. Then for every piece of activity I conduct I mark with a Roman numeral. For instance, my tally document would look a bit like the following:

Day	Cold calls	Calls	Right person	Emails	Meetings
Monday					
Tuesday					
Wednesday					
Thursday					
Friday					

Then for each call I make I mark a line in the calls section, if I get through to the right person I mark in the right person column, and so on for emails and meetings that I attain. Quite easy and quite simple.

For certain activities that aren't as regular, those being SQLs, quotes/proposals and orders. I detail these in my electronic review document in my OneNote which we'll discuss in more depth shortly.

My tally book shows my daily activity on a weekly basis, but this isn't enough just on its own. The question to ask yourself is why does a sales icon do this, what's the purpose? Well the whole purpose of tallying all this activity is for motivation and for review at a later time.

To add an extra dimension to this process, at the end of every week I calculate all of my activity for that week and record it in a more extensive document in my OneNote which I call my review document. This review document looks like the following:

Quarter 1

Week commencing	Cold calls	Calls	Right person	Conversion rate to right person	Emails	SQLs	Meetings booked	Meetings attended	Drop in calls	Forward appointments	Proposals or quotes	Orders

I usually split this into quarters then at the end of every quarter I review my activity.

This sounds like a lot of work, I bet you're asking yourself why this is a good practice. Well for me there are four reasons why a sales icon does this, and those are:

- Motivation
- Goal setting
- Review – feedback to boss or others
- Improvement

1) Motivation – Tallying your activity as you go is a really great practice to adopt if you want to become a sales icon. In your day-to-day operations it's all too easy to become either disillusioned with your success or have the misconception that you're being more active than you thought. I've seen this on countless occasions when training salespeople. I'll come to them at midday and just ask a simple question like 'what's your prospecting activity been today?' To which their answer is usually something like 'I've easily made 50 calls already and about 20 emails.' The reality is somewhat distant to this, as in most circumstances they've probably made more like 10–20 calls and 10 emails. Now by no means do I think they're trying to pull the wool over my eyes or lie to me. The truth is that activity easily becomes a blur and what seems like lots of activity might actually be very little when you write it on paper.

   That is the reason that tallying your activity is a motivating force. You can see for yourself how active you've been, what your successes are so far for the day and it's that insight that pushes you forward and keeps you motivated. In that moment of distress or uncertainty this tally will be your guiding star. So in that moment when you come off of that cold call with a rude prospect, or when you see your sales figures and you're not at the top this tally should be your motivating force. It really is so easy to become demotivated in sales, but your tally should stop this.

   You should use this review document to look back at your wins for the day, week, month or year. It is from doing this that you'll be able to say yes, I'm on the road to success, this week alone I've made X calls, booked Y meetings and undertaken Z proposals. Things aren't actually so bad, I'm doing well let's keep this momentum going.
2) Goal setting – Another aspect that is a single entity in its own right but falls into motivation also is goal setting. Now if you don't record your wins at the moment then it's incredibly hard to set goals. Imagine the circumstance where your boss comes to you and offers you something amazing. Let's say he said to you 'Simon, you've been doing very well, but I want more. Now I'm not asking for more and giving nothing in return, I want to make a deal with you. If you can give me 10% more I'll double your commission for the year.' Wow, imagine that! Now for those of you who don't record your wins this 10% extra is going to be hard to achieve. Whereas for those who record their wins this is quantifiable, so they can review their activity and see how they can give that extra 10% or more.

   Now the likelihood of your boss coming to you and saying this may be rare, but it highlights a point. Where this is most beneficial is for self-motivation as you can use goal setting to push you further. When you track your activity you can use goals to motivate you such as today I'm going to make fifty calls before lunchtime, or this week I want to gain four meetings, or send twenty emails.

When you record your activity this goal setting becomes a new motivating force that you can utilise, and if you do use it well you'll become a sales icon. I will talk about goal setting in greater depth shortly as this is rather important in becoming a sales icon.

3) Review – this is a word that is brandished around quite brazenly and often reviewing things doesn't come of anything. Now because tracking our activity is quantifiable, any review of your activity should be a useful task. How I have taught sales icons to review their activity is to look at the totals of their key activity indications such as how many calls they made, how many meetings they booked etc. This will enable you to be ruthless with yourself, you can review monthly activity with other months, or quarters with quarters etc. From this you can determine how hard you've been working, what's been effective, where you can focus more time. Where it comes in handy is when your boss asks you a question and you need some collateral to back it up. For example he might say 'Simon, your calls have been a lot lower the last two weeks.' From this you can look at your review document and give an accurate answer which might be you're right I need to up my work rate. Your review document may show you that you've had ten meetings and four proposals to write in the last two weeks consequentially you've had limited free time to make your normal dials. Or your boss may say something like 'Simon you're struggling for meetings lately what's going on.' To which again you may put your hands up and accept this is the case. Conversely, your review document may say otherwise such as 'granted I haven't booked as many meetings but I've gained ten SQLs this week for… which are all qualified and will lead to meetings over the next three months.' In essence your review document is there to support you and justify your activity. Do bear in mind though that it will also justify any lack of activity too.
4) Improvement – the word review comes hand in hand with the word improvement. If you can use your activity tracking for review purposes then you can also use this to highlight areas where you can improve. With your review document you'll be in competition with yourself which is my favourite type of competition. I promise you that if you apply the disciplines highlighted in this book then you'll surpass the performance of your peers, it won't be in the short term but in the long term definitely. That's why competing with yourself becomes advantageous as you'll get to the realms of success where no peers are close to you, thus you can only compete with your past self. The way that you do this is improving upon your activity as stated in your review document. I like to improve in unison with my goal setting. I'll list down my personal best activity statistics like the following:

   - Most calls made on a day = X
   - Most SQL made in a week = Y
   - Most meetings attended in a quarter = Z

   And so on and so on. From doing this I have continuous improvement goals to work on, I'll even set challenge days, weeks or months where I try to set new personal bests for myself. I put this in my diary ahead of time, for instance I block out a day in my calendar with PB Calling day with a goal to making more calls in that day then I ever have before.

At some stage in the future you're going to become a high-level performer in sales, you may even become a sales icon. But the same truth will unfold as it does in any field whether that be for white-collar professionals or athletes, if we become complacent our performance will be hindered. One way to prevent against such complacency is by recording our activity. I remember reading a great book by Tim Ferris called *Tools of the Titans*, he mentions in the book an interview he had with Arnold Schwarzenegger who adds some substance to my thoughts here. In the interview, Arnold mentions how he has complete records of every single gym session he has had, every single one for years. Why, might you ask? Well his justification is that it's a recipe for his body. If he had a new movie role that required him to be as big as he was for the commando movie all he has to do is review his gym records to that year and apply the same training. If he needs to slim down and be more toned he'll resort back to another year and month and apply that training.

It sounds so simple, doesn't it? But how does this apply to selling. Well for selling, by recording your activity you can do exactly the same as Arnold does. You can look back at your records and see where you were performing better than before and just replicate your activity.

Let's highlight this is a simple example. Let say I've been selling for five years but I've hit a bit of a rut lately; currently I'm only achieving £5k GP per month. I'm bemused as two years ago I was achieving £15k GP per month; luckily for me, I've recorded all my activity for the last five years. In a bid to improve my performance I set aside some time to compare my activity now to that of my peak two years ago. My findings are as below:

Average per month	Calls	Right person	Emails	Drop in calls	SQLs	Forward appointments	Meetings attended
Two years ago	1,600	160	480	32	16	36	32
Present	700	60	200	0	5	16	18
Difference	-900	-100	-280	-32	-11	-20	-14

After such a comparison the analysis is quite simple. To get back to my previous selling performance I need to:

- Increase my number of calls by 900 per month, with this my right person statistic and SQL will increase too
- Increase my email levels by 280 email per month
- It seems evident that I am no longer conducting drop in calls therefore I need to up this to 32 drop in calls a month
- It's noticeable that I'm failing to forward appoint therefore I need to increase this back to the levels before of 36 forward appointments per month
- We can see that I'm attending far fewer meetings therefore I need to get this back to 32 meetings a month which will be attained by my calling, emailing and drop in calls

Want to deep dive even further? You could even start recording the following to ensure that you're continually improving your performance:

- Number of referrals attained per month
- LinkedIn In Mails sent
- Direct mailers posted
- Number of lead passed to colleagues

I'm sure you'll have some other areas that may be worth recording which are bespoke too.

5.2 – Goal Setting

"The oak sleeps in the acorn. The bird waits in the egg, and in the highest vision of the soul, a waking angel stirs. Dreams are the seedlings of reality." – Napoleon Hill[19]

As I mentioned earlier, goal setting is imperative to your success. If you can be disciplined enough to regularly set goals then not only will you surpass the performance of your peers, but you'll also improve upon your own success, making you a sales icon.

I talk a lot about goal setting in my day-to-day work when coaching salespeople to become sales icons. I've studied it for years and from a range of sources, but it wasn't till recently that I read something profound which enabled me to see a clear distinction in those who set goals and those who do not.

The book I read was 'Mans Search for Meaning' by Victor Frankl[19]

If you haven't read it then I recommend putting it on your list of books to read next. It is based on Victors harrowing experiences in being a prisoner and survivor of numerous concentration camps in World War 2. Honestly read the book, it will change your perception on many things and maybe even your outlook on life.

Anyway back to goal setting. One area, Victor highlights in his book is the clear relation between survivors of such camps and their aspirations. He talks of how many survivors had desires to achieve something should they ever be awarded their freedom. Their desires become their underlying reason for living despite the hardships they were experiencing every day. For instance, Victor himself speaks of his desire to complete a manuscript which he had longed to have published. This manuscript he kept on his person as his single last possession all the way to his first concentration camp before he was stripped of everything. He talks in his book of his battle with typhus fever (reportedly the cause of death for hundreds of thousands of inmates) and how had it not been for his burning desire to publish his manuscript, that this fever probably would have been his downfall.

Victor also describes many other inmates who also shared alike desires too. Whether that be to also publish material, finish scientific works or simply care for their children who at that stage they were unaware of their whereabouts and whether they were even still alive.

Their aspirations for something meaningful and personally associated to them individually were their source of power, they had a goal(s) for such a day when their freedom would be granted.

I hope this shows you how goal setting is powerful, it can shape your destiny. Over time I have come to the conclusion that the most effective way to set goals is to break them down into three parts, those being

- Activity
- Top line business goals
- Personal goals

I will talk about all of these parts in greater depth as we move forward, what's important to remember is that there are three parts. If you can put in place goals for all of these then the likelihood is that your motivation will always remain high, you'll hit your goals and become a sales icon.

The failure of goal setting

The failure that most people make is that they don't set goals for these three parts, and when I say most people I mean most people not just specifically salespeople. So how can I be effective at goal setting, well basically it's the how, what and why, I know it sounds like I've gone crazy but in a minute you'll understand. Goal setting always starts with the what

What = top line business goals

This is where most people commonly fail. Now it's rare for most people to even set a top-line business goal, but when they do this is often where they finish their goal setting. They'll set a goal like 'I want to get promoted and be managing a team in two years' or 'I want to earn £50k a year.' For salespeople, the goal may be alike these mentioned, or it may be something more sales related like 'I want to sell £300k GP this year' or 'I want to sell £5m GP over the next five years.' The failure most people make is that this is as far as their goal setting extends to, they only ever set a 'What' and cross their fingers that it will come true.

Now setting a 'What' is great, but if that is all that you do then it's unlikely to ever come true. I like to describe it in the example of an architect. Imagine an architect becoming intensely excited about a new housing development he's thought up. He spends hours drawing up some beautiful designs for the new development planning every small detail that he can. Then when he's completed his designs he simply leaves them on the side or in a draw and merely hopes that they'll magically be built. Dream on! I know that this seems farfetched and would never happen but it's a good example to highlight how simply setting a 'What' is not enough. It's a good first step but on its own it is merely a pipe dream.

The way that you make the 'What' a reality is through the 'How' and if you haven't guessed it already the 'How' is the activity which will enable you to achieve the 'What.'

How = Activity

Please take note here that the 'How' is not the plan for achieving the 'What,' it's the activity for achieving the 'What.' Plans are great, and they are essential to being successful in anything that you do, in particular for your pursuit to become a sales icon. A lot of this book focuses around a plan for becoming a sales icon and it's very important. But a plan on its own is useless, all plans require execution, the 'How' relates to activity and not simply a plan.

The 'Why' is your most powerful motivation source, it will enable you to meet your goals for both the 'How' and 'What.' The 'Why' is the only goal which is personal, and therefore holds a wealth of emotional power behind it.

Why = personal goals

It's the reason you wake up in the morning, the reason you spend time away from your family, away from your home and away from everything else you love outside of work. No matter who you are, we all have a reason 'Why,' for some of you it may be harder to comprehend than others but we all have one.

I will now explain each of these three parts in greater depth so that you can put together your how, what and why for your goal setting.

5.2.1 – The How

We've already clarified that the 'How' relates to your activity. So if I want to get fitter, then my 'How' would be to go to the gym say four days a week for example. Or if I want to write a book then my 'How' maybe something like write five hundred words a day. You get the point. With sales there's a key point though, and that's to record your activity. So when you make ten calls, or send five emails, note down in your records and do this for all of your activity. If you want to better yourself and strive for your goals you'll notice that it's incredibly hard to improve if you do not record your regular activity. Come to think of it it's actually impossible; sure you can set goals for activity but how will you ever know if you achieve them or surpass them? So use the tally we discussed earlier on in this chapter to record your activity and wins.

When you do start recording your activity and wins, it will open up new realms of motivation within you. I have seen this in myself and with hundreds of other sales icons I have trained. You'll notice as you record your activity that you no longer have any excuses, you can no longer falsify your activity. So as a morning passes and you look down at your tally document and see that you've only made ten calls you'll realise that this is insufficient. You'll push yourself to maximise as much activity as you can and for the first time you'll be able to set activity goals to aspire to and achieve.

One thing to be conscious of is that goal setting is a continuous discipline, there should be no point in time where you're satisfied at what you've achieved. You must be stringent that there is always that next goal to work towards no matter what your previous success has been. This will aid you in your success and discourage from any complacency setting in. To make your goal setting for the 'How' a little bit easier I have depicted below a few of mine that I have set in the past:

- Make 100 phone calls today
- Speak to 50 right people or decision makers this week
- Send 50 emails today

- Obtain 10 SQLs this month
- Develop 5 quotes over £50k this week

The goals that you set need to be in keeping with your success so far, your industry and your knowledge base etc. There is no point setting goals that are completely unachievable as all that will happen is that you waste time setting a goal, it doesn't motivate you and you never use it. You've probably all heard of SMART goals in the past, if you haven't, here is a brief overview:

S = specific
M = measurable
A = achievable
R = realistic
T = timely

Make sure that all of your goals comply with this SMART criteria. What I find interesting is the relation between a goal being realistic and achievable, this is the aspect which is important in goal setting. The achievability of a goal is relative to time and experience. If you've been in a new industry for a few weeks and lack experience then asking you to book loads of meetings would be unachievable. Whereas when you grow in experience it would be very achievable. As you develop in your role and become more successful you need to use the realistic criteria to be critical. Let me explain this in an example to make my point.

Take for example a salesperson who has been in an industry for many years and has a wealth of experience. If he set a goal of booking one meeting a week then contrary to popular opinion this wouldn't constitute as a SMART goal. Yes it's specific, measurable, achievable and timely, but it is not realistic, and this is where realism can work the opposite way to what you thought. The reason for this is that by no means is it realistic to ask an experienced salesperson to book one meeting a week, think about the big picture. If you're an experienced salesperson you'll have a high target to meet, think about it, is one meeting a week really going to be enough? The answer is no!

That's where the realistic criteria comes into its own. It should be used as a way to critique your goals in relation to where you are in your career. Use the realistic criteria to stretch you to be better and it will aid you in your pursuit to becoming a sales icon.

How can I use this?

So how can you use this? From working with many sales icons I have found that the best way you can use goal setting effectively is to look at your previous activity and wins. Let us take the example mentioned previously regarding meetings booked in a week. Now just putting your finger in the air and plucking out a random number will not constitute the realism that we are looking for. Instead it would be more intelligent to look at your review document and see what your previous wins were. You may see from this that on average you're booking three meetings a week and that a goal of booking four meetings a week would be realistic and therefore a SMART goal. Conversely, you may look at your review document and see that you have been booking ten meetings a week. Here your instant reaction may be that you should set a goal to book eleven or twelve meetings a week but have caution. Through further analysis you may see that yes you'd been booking ten meetings a week but in this period you weren't conducting any proposals or some other activity. Conversely, you have ten proposals due which is going to take up a lot of your time therefore your goal needs to be lower than what you had been achieving previously.

Note that this isn't a get-out clause, cheating the system in the way you set your goals only cheats yourself as you'll never become a sales icon. Therefore if you have justification that you'll be busy with other activities and need to reduce your goal for whatever reason then that's fine. If not then challenge yourself to achieve more, and the funny thing you'll find is that eventually you achieve your goals.

5.2.2 – Goal Setting SQL

On first starting my career I made an observation on salespeople which still stands true today, and that is that salespeople are so eager to reach their target and be successful that they want everything to happen at once. They want to make one call, get through to the decision maker, book a meeting and then make a sale. In the real world, it doesn't work like this, believe me I wish it did! This trait, let's call it over-ambition, is a great thing for salespeople, but it can also have a detrimental effect on motivation and subsequent performance.

When we record our wins we will not only see our successes, but we will also see our failures, and believe it or not that is a great thing. As then we can find where we can make ourselves better. Steven Covey calls it 'sharpen the saw', the Japanese call it the kaizen principle and Tony Robbins calls it CANI (constant and never-ending improvement) [18], all of which are the same principle of self-analysis and improvement. By recording our wins we'll see our successes which are great motivation tools, but also our failures which are brilliant to learn from. In my view failure does not exist, it is merely a fruitful learning curve to a successful outcome.

The sales icon solution is to stage your approach as follows:

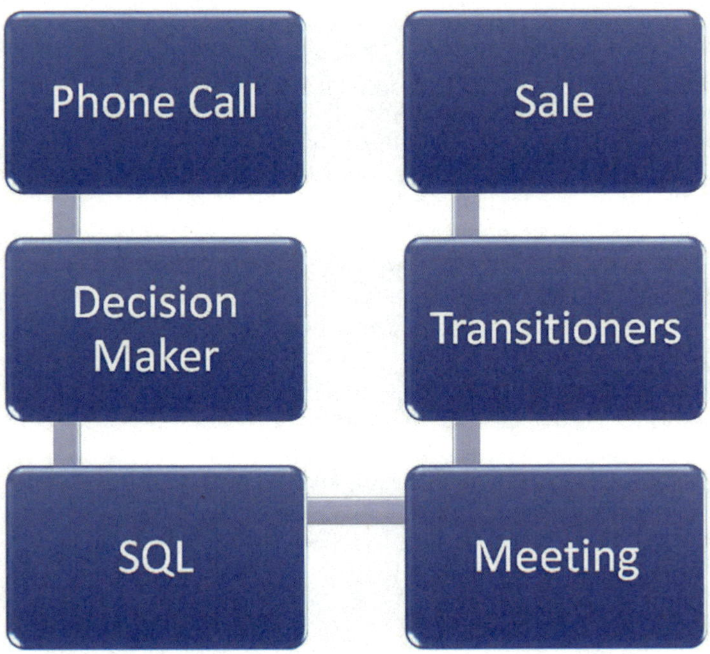

The stages you may be unsure about here are Decision Maker and SQL, so we'll explain these now in greater detail.

5.2.3 – Decision Maker (Right Person)

In this day and age to call and get through to the decision maker you wanted to speak to can sometimes be a tall order. Nowadays most stakeholders are so busy with general business activities that they don't have the time to speak to people even over the phone. Therefore on a call to even get through to a decision maker should be considered a great win in itself. What you need to be conscious of here as I'm sure you're already aware is that the majority of the time you're not going to get through to the decision maker. Most likely you'll get a gatekeeper, or a voicemail. The research we conducted for sales icon found that on average you get through to the decision maker 10%-30% of the time. Obviously this percentage will differ depending on your industry, your company, your rapport with the customer/prospect as well as many other factors. But as a rule of thumb, take it that you will get through to the Decision Maker 10% of the time, at a later stage when you look at your wins more and more you'll see what the exact percentage is for your prospecting. With this you can then plan appropriately as to how many calls you need to make to get through to the number of people that you desire to speak to.

5.2.4 – SQL – Sales Qualified Lead

The feedback we've had from our candidates regarding SQLs is that it was one of the most profound and beneficial changes they made to their approach, so if you're going to incorporate any of the aspects of this book into your sales approach, please do use this one. It will completely change your approach on the phone or in a meeting, as you become much less ruthless and one-sighted on simply just booking a meeting or closing a sale.

So what is a SQL?

A SQL is the abbreviation for a 'Sales Qualified Lead' and it is what you want it to be really. Sales icons have used it in the past to define when interest has been shown by a prospect. For example you call a prospect, pitch to him and he says, 'that's interesting, I was thinking about that for after the summer. I looked at x,y,z but didn't like it because…right now I haven't got any budget, but can you call me back before the summer to discuss this again then please?'

Boom, it's an SQL! A warm lead!

Some sales icons like to be strict on the qualifying criteria for a SQL. It all depends on how busy you are and what industry you are in. If you're very busy then you may want to tighten the qualifying criteria of your SQL, or even add an extra stage, I.e. SQL 1 = stage 1, SQL 2 = stage 2.

Types of qualification criteria:

Many sales icons have used the following qualifying criteria in the past.

1. A lead will be an SQL if it complies with BANT
   B – Budget
   A – Authority
   N – Need
   T – Timescale

This could be the following criteria:

Budget = approved
Authority = stakeholder has the authority to make decision

Need = they need my product or service
Timescale = they desire to purchase within six months

Great Things About SQLs

1. Motivation – making this small change of adding the SQL stage into your sales cycle may sound small and insignificant, but you'll see its effect is dramatic on your motivation. From your review processes at the end of a working day, week and month you'll be able to look back see how much you've achieved. Previously if you had a day of no meetings being booked or no sales being made you would call that a failure. But now you'll be able to review and see the SQLs you've attained and how successful you have been. There is direct correlation between SQLs and your other successes such as meetings and sales. I once spoke to a sales icon of many years and he showed me his review statistics and he found that he was converting 96% of SQLs into the next stage of a meeting. He now couldn't operate without using SQL as a stage in the sales process. By adding this stage you will get a sense of fulfilment that things are going in the right direction, which will give you the motivation you need to push for success.
2. Pipeline – to become a sales icon your thought process needs to extend further than just the here and now. Most salespeople are too short term, looking for quick wins and sales for the day or this month. By adding in this SQL stage you're thinking long term, and by continually following this discipline you'll notice that your pipeline grows and grows. Quick wins will be something of the past which no longer concern you. Most sales managers are constantly on their salespeople's backs regarding prospecting and their pipeline. The SQL stage will help deter any fears they may have and make your life so much easier. You'll be able to identify what opportunities you have now, but also what your future opportunities will be by showing them the SQLs you have generated.
3. Forecasting – SQLs will enable you to forecast your sales better than ever before. You'll be able to determine when you expect a meeting and/or sale to fall and forecast accurately based on this. The more and more SQLs you generate the better your future pipeline will be.

Call Reminders and SQLs

Now you may have a great CRM System where you can schedule call reminders, which if you do great, use it. If you're not this fortunate, however, don't be disheartened, you can simply use your outlook calendar for call reminders.

In the section on core action processes we talked about the term calendar for scheduling an activity such as a call back in your calendar. What I encourage sales icons to do is schedule these calls as individual activities in their outlook calendar, albeit having them scheduled in the early hours of that day, between say 0500 and 0700. Does this mean you're meant to be calling at that time? Of course not, it's just a free slot where the call reminders can sit in your calendar.

It'll make more sense in a minute when I show you a visual example of this, but before I show you this I want to just highlight why I love using my outlook calendar for call reminders:

1. I, like all sales icons live by my outlook calendar, therefore by having it here it never gets missed.

2. If I fail to get through to the person I can just drag and drop that call to another day and time, it's fast and simple to do.
3. I can colour-code my call reminders as a way to prioritise certain calls over others

These are the core three for me but there are many other benefits too.

I just want to focus a bit more on the colour-coding part again, in particular with SQLs. As you become busier you'll notice that you have hundreds of call reminders in your calendar over the upcoming weeks and months. This is where the difficulty occurs, say when you have fifty call reminders on one day how do you distinguish calls? Which do you prioritise? The key thing you want to do is distinguish your SQLs from other leads which are colder. Why I hear you ask? That's because your SQLs are warm leads and should take priority over any other lead. Just think about it, they should take priority because they have a higher chance of success so in turn you ideally need to be calling them more often, a few times a day if you fail to get through to the decision maker. So use colour coding to coordinate your calendar. In your outlook calendar if you look in the tool bar you'll see something known as 'category' which you can use to colour and name your leads.

I personally have three colour codes for call reminders:

Red = Urgent
Amber = SQL
Green = Cold

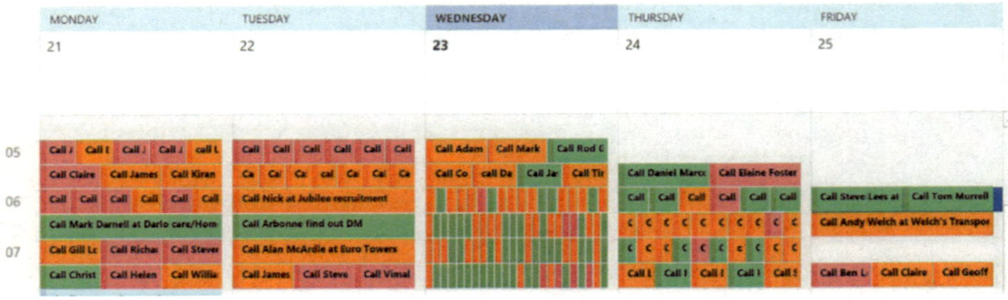

So if you choose to adopt this practice you'll have the ability to turn to a date in your calendar and instantly see which call reminders are say SQLs and therefore take priority. Following on from that you'll see your results fly as an important call will never go missed ever again.

Example of SQLs

What you quantify as an SQL might be different from another salesperson. The important thing to bear in mind is that it's a warm lead, but the timescale isn't immediate, it may be in a couple of months. Just to help you understand this, I've depicted below a few examples:

- Uncovered opportunity with prospect but their budget doesn't come in place until six months
- Prospect informed me that they're unhappy with their incumbent provider but they're in a contract for nine more months, review process starts in six months

- Invitation to tender process will begin in four months

You get the idea. Your SQLs will feed your future pipeline so nurture them closely.

Activity

As an activity try adding this stage into your process and witness first-hand the value that it adds. Focus instead on developing an SQL on a phone call with a prospect or customer instead of going in for the kill for a meeting straightaway. Uncover the SQL, record it as a win and schedule it in your diary for the time period when you can convert it from a SQL to a meeting.

5.2.5 – MQL – Marketing Qualified Leads

This is much alike the SQL stage; however, with a slight twist. For some of you MQLs may not be necessary, it all depends upon the strength of your marketing campaigns and your general marketing approach. For example, if you focus solely on cold calling then the MQL stage wouldn't be useful for you.

Sales icons use MQLs as a stage before SQLs, which works as follows:

So where do MQLs come from? MQLs are marketing qualified leads therefore they can develop from the following sources:

- Email reply
- Survey response
- Lead passed from partner company or marketing
- Exhibition lead
- Web tracking
- Referral

1. Email reply – if a prospect replies to your email with some form of insightful information that shows promise for the future then this may qualify as a MQL. Notice how I said, 'may qualify,' you need to scrutinise these yourself, use your judgement to class whether an email reply justifies becoming an MQL or not. Remember the discipline start with the end in mind. A lead should only be qualified as an MQL if you feel there is potential for it to become a sale at a later time. There really is no point fabricating leads and making them MQLs or SQLs if they're not, you're only cheating yourself.
2. Survey response – if a survey response comes back with some information filled out that eludes to there being an opportunity then this would be classed as an MQL.
3. Lead passed from partner company or marketing – again it's necessary to carry out your due diligence with the lead to determine if it is genuine and if there is a future opportunity. I must say, however, that with leads from partner companies I have often seen them have one of the highest conversion rates. Consequentially, sales icons often use the 'sniff out what sells' discipline to utilise this further. They attempt to encourage leads through this channel

through promotions such as SPIFF campaigns or try to build rapport with partners through corporate hospitality. I have even seen some reps benefit from the 'treat others how you'd like to be treated' concept, thus they have taken it upon themselves to pass leads to partners in the hope that they'll return the favour, and I must say I have seen some fantastic results come from this.

4. Exhibition leads – in my experience these are some of the best leads you'll have. They may not necessarily have the highest conversion rates of your channels but it's usually pretty high nonetheless. If you were to consider the quantity of leads developed as well as the conversion rate then this channel would undoubtedly be the best to utilise. I've seen sales icons gain anywhere from 30–250 warm leads from an exhibition (when it's done right). If you gained 250 leads at and exhibition and had a conversion rate of 30% it would lead to 75 meetings, which would undoubtedly help in surpassing your target. Needless to say an exhibition lead would only qualify as an MQL if you gain some insightful information and seems like there may be an opportunity. A word of warning, someone who only passes you a business card wouldn't constitute as an MQL. You need some really meaty information. But this shouldn't be a problem if you implement the exhibition maximisation principle which we discussed earlier.
5. Web tracking – this is the organic source whereby prospects visit your website. Your business will need some form of software to track this information, to which there are many viable solutions on the market. I've known certain businesses, one in particular in the fashion retail industry to rely on this as their main lead generation channel. Thus for some businesses this can be a great medium, for others, not so much. With certain software you can track the exact pages a prospect visited, how long they stayed on each page, what content they downloaded etc. So you can use this to your advantage, say for instance your business has a substantial amount of web traffic. In such circumstance then registering every visitor as an MQL would be nonsensical. Therefore you may want to be more candid in what qualifies as an MQL. For instance you could set criteria that any prospect who visits our site for longer than two minutes will constitute as an MQL, or anyone who downloads content, or anyone who visited more than five pages etc. The criteria is down to you.
6. Referral – this is a fantastic lead source, and in my opinion is an area that a high percentage of salespeople overlook. For some reason we as salespeople are reticent to ask the simple question of 'who else do you know of that would benefit from working with us?' It's such a simple question and we should ask it of every single customer that we work with, what's the worst that can happen? If only 10% of our customers are willing to give us a name then that's 10% more MQLs from this channel than we had before. What I would also add is that MQLs from this channel often have a higher probability of converting to a sale as you'll be referencing the customer you work with who referred you. Straightaway the prospect who has been referred to you will have much more confidence in you simply by association.

Prioritisation

So we've discussed in depth how goal setting should work for you, with quite a detailed focus on MQLs and SQLs. But in order to become a sales icon you need to take this one step further, and that's through prioritisation. Effective prioritisation will enable you to surpass your target and earn buckets of commission. The way in which we do this is to incorporate the MQL and SQL techniques with our lead generation techniques, in particular the 'sniff out what sells' discipline. What you'll see is that your channels have a percentage conversion rate (as discussed previously) which you can use to prioritise your leads and be efficient with your time. What you need to do is prioritise your leads in the following way:

Priority 1 = highest conversion rate
Priority (last) = lowest conversion rate

Yours may look different than other sales icons' due to your industry and brand etc. For example if your conversion rates looked like the following:

Priority 1 = events with a 34% conversion rate
Priority 6 = …

What you can do now is use this to prioritise your current leads. As we discussed the higher the conversion rate the more you want to concentrate on that lead as it has a higher chance of success. Undoubtedly, all leads are important, but when you get to the stage where you're so busy with meetings, proposals and other activities you'll need to be as efficient as possible with your valuable time. This is where that prioritisation really comes into its own as a valuable tool to use.

Tip

You could denote leads with their priority rating 1 to 6 etc., or even colour-code your leads in your calendar or campaign planner so that it's easy to distinguish between leads of varying priority.

So this brings us to the end of this section of the chapter. From this we should understand the 'how' part of goal setting, what it comprises of and the way to use it effectively. Next we will move onto the 'what' section of goal setting.

5.2.6 – The What

So we've now established what the 'How' aspects are for goal setting which is a step change for many as often people simply set the 'What' goals only. Now we have already cited that the 'What' are your top line business goals that you want to achieve.

Now before I digress into anything more on the 'what' I just want to share something with you, did you know…

You become 42% more likely to achieve your goals by writing them down on a regular basis[20]

This came from a study by a psychology professor called Dr Gail Matthews. 42% can you believe that? Now most of us in our profession when we become successful at anything start to look at the micro aspects, what will make me 1% more productive here, or save me 0.5% of my day there. When you hear a percentage of 42% that's too high to disregard. So before I go any further, just process this, and please at a minimum write down your goals and write them regularly, every day if you have to so that you make sure you're empowered and driven to achieve them.

So yet again with the 'what' we must make sure that these are SMART goals as we mentioned previously, and what is vitally important is that you write them down.

Examples

Now we've all probably set the 'What' goals in the past so this shouldn't be anything revolutionary for you, but just in case you haven't here are a few examples of 'What' goals that you could use:

- To manage a sales team in the next X years
- To become sales director by the time I am X
- To sell £X GP this year
- To bring on board 20 new spending accounts this year
- To be the number 1 salesperson within 2 years
- To win salesman of the year award in the next 2 years
- To make £X commission this year
- To win that business trip this year
- To make the biggest sale in the company's history within 5 years
- To have 100 spending accounts in the next 3 years

Short term and long term

Your 'What' goals can be in any form that you wish, short term or long term, though for some the timescale may have an effect to how motivational the goal is. I myself prefer to have two sets of 'What' goals, the short-term goals and the long-term goals. The short-term goals are usually those which I could achieve within one or two years and the long-term goals are achievable over ten or more years.

It's important to ensure that if you choose to use short-term and long-term goals that they don't contradict each other. For instance, if you worked in your accounts team and your short-term goal was to get promoted but your long-term goal was to become the sales director then these goals would be seen as somewhat contradictory. A more appropriate short-term goal for this long-term goal would be to get transferred into a sales role as a first port of call.

How many goals and how aspirational should they be?

It's tough to say how many goals you should set. You need to be cautious not to have too many as they may become a convoluted message. Personally, I like to have around two or three short-term goals and one or two long-term goals when it comes to 'What' goals.

On the subject of how aspirational your goals should be let me tell you a short story which I have never forgotten from a young age. I was just starting out my career. I had graduated from university with a degree in mathematics. I was feeling on top of the world, on a complete high believing somewhat arrogantly that I'd effortlessly have a great career of my choosing as I had so much to give. Oh how wrong I was, looking back I applaud my confidence, but I can see now how truly naïve I was. After I graduated I had an experience which added to my ego in that I successfully passed through a graduate programme whereby there was an intensive selection process of which only the top twenty percent of graduates made it through. The company that ran this selection process subsequently set me up with a number of promising interviews with businesses for varying sales roles.

It was in one of these interviews that it happened, and I can remember vividly as if I was there today. I was interviewing for a young and upcoming IT firm in central London; they were a small business then, but their growth and expansion plans were formidable. They were, on all accounts, a great business that was going a long way! I met with one of their managing directors a man named Russell; he was a captivating individual, the type of person who speaks with such control and passion that you can't help but be spellbound by every word that he spoke.

It was one of my first interviews. I was nervous obviously, but it went OK as first interviews go. The part that I will never forget is when he asked me the following question, 'tell me what your aspirations are?' Now at this point I was on a bit of a back foot. I had never been asked this question before, not formally at least. More importantly, not only had I never been asked the question but I had never asked the question of myself. I paused for a moment and thought to myself what I want. A few seconds passed and then I said, "I'd like to be a director one day, make a good bit of money, maybe have a house abroad, oh and a mustang. I'd love to own a red mustang." He said okay, "When do you want this?" I replied "Erm, probably by the time I'm forty."

Now if you can't guess the outcome yet then I should say I didn't get the job, and unsurprisingly, I wouldn't employ someone who gave me this answer. The part that hit home with me was what he said next. He said "Simon, you're going to do well for yourself in life, you're a smart lad with your head screwed on. What I'm going to share with you is a small bit of advice, take it or leave it, but take it and you'll achieve more than you ever thought possible. The advice…be more ambitious! None of this by the time I'm forty or wishy-washy goals like maybe owning a house abroad. Set your goals in life and make them as ambitious as can be and if you truly believe in yourself and them goals then they will become a reality. You're the creator of your own destiny!"

Now despite me not getting the job this interview was one of the biggest life lessons I could have, and it happened in the space of a few minutes. I sat in front of a very successful young individual and he told me his secret for success, and the best thing of all was that I was starting out in my career. Thus if I could take on board what he told me and apply it then I would be as, if not more, successful than he was.

I had time to process this life lesson and over the coming weeks I mused over what the true secret to success was. I spoke to my now father-in-law, who is a very successful man in his own right. He started from the bottom, grew up in a working class family in a rough area of Luton. But his environment wasn't his future, from an impoverished background he's gone on to own numerous multimillion-pound businesses and now lives the lifestyle of his wildest desires. So following on from my interview with Russell I asked my father-in-law about what he thought the secrets to success were. It was in this moment that I learnt another life lesson. He told me that he too felt that ambitious goals were the key to success and he recommended an audio book to listen to whilst I drove around in my car on a daily basis.

The book was called *Lead the Field* by Earl Nightingale[21] and it was this book that was the catalyst to shaping my life and my future. It's something I still to this day listen to a number of times a year just to recap how I work and my approach to life. If you need a book to read or an audio book to listen to then this is one I would recommend, and I hope that it changes your life as it did my own.

One of the key takeaways from this book that I recite to myself daily was on the topic of goals, and it is as follows:

"What the mind can conceive and believe, it can achieve" – Napoleon Hill[22]

Take a moment and read this quote a few times to take it in. Now for me this is profound, and when you apply it to real life it all makes sense. Most human beings are natural sceptics, you think about most of the visionaries that have ever lived, Isaac Newton, the Wright brothers, Thomas Edison, Steve Jobs etc. Whoever the visionary is, they've had an idea that they believe in and there have been sceptics who feel that such an idea is foolish or unachievable. Yet in the face of adversity these men have proven them wrong and have succeeded in their goals. These are just the famous names too, I'm certain that you will have heard of family friends who have achieved truly inspirational goals from unlikely positions.

The whole point to this section of the book is that you and only you set your limits. Therefore, be as ambitious with your goals as you can be and if you regularly take action then those goals will be achieved. Once again,

"What the mind can conceive and believe, it can achieve" – Napoleon Hill

Just a quick side note, the second key life lesson I spoke of that I learnt from my father-in-law was the lesson on continual study, in that learning new things and personal development should never have a sell by date. I'll go into this in more depth later on.

How do I set 'What' goals?

The question of how to set your 'What' goals can be more difficult for some than it is for others. To reiterate the 'What' goals are your top line business goals, the statements about your work that you one day wish to say. Now if you don't know in your gut what your top line business goals are then I recommend undertaking the following activity.

Activity – 'What' Brainstorm

Get a piece of blank paper and schedule thirty minutes of free time in your diary where you'll be uninterrupted. All that you need to do is list as many top-line business goals as you can one after another. To help you try thinking about what wakes you up in the morning, do you ever get that burning desire to sit in your boss' chair? Or do you wish for the day when you sit at the top of that leader board as the number one? List as many different things as you can, at this stage the more the better, be as ambitious as you can be and don't have any self-fulfilling prophecies that something can't be achieved. What always helped me in this process is thinking back to conversations with colleagues or friends. We've probably all had them conversations when someone is boasting to you about something they achieved whether it be a great sale or massive commission they won. Use that as your source of power, what did they say, how much better would you like to do?

When you have explored all eventualities review your list and identify the top two or three that you have, those that present the most burning desire to achieve should be your 'What' goals. As we stated before you can have a mixture of short term and long-term goals, whatever is the most motivational for you.

Points to remember are

1) Certain goals are sub goals of others – for instance if you set a goal of making £500k GP in sales this year it may not make sense to have another goal based on commission. The reason for this is that in most circumstances they go hand in hand so either pick a commission as a goal or sales achieved. In this example if you were making 10% commission then these sales would earn you £50k in commission. Therefore having two goals, one being to make £500k GP sales and the other being to make £50k commission, in actuality these are the same goal.
2) Some goals will be more motivational for some people and less so for others. Take for example becoming the number-one salesperson. I've met some salespeople that really don't care for this too much. This may be because their peers are average salespeople so it's not too challenging or maybe because they don't like to compete with people. Whereas a goal that directly relates to them such as to make £50k commission this year lights up their eyes and gives them the fire in their belly to strive to succeed.

5.2.7 – The Why

Now that we understand our 'How' and 'What' it's time to discuss our most powerful motivation tool in the field of goals and that's the 'Why.' Now I really do hope that you adopt all the disciplines I've spoke of in this section, but if you choose to only adopt one facet then make it the 'Why' goals.

To recap the 'Why' relates to your personal goals, they are the reasoning behind everything we do. They are the thoughts in the back of our mind when we wake up before sunrise and on those late nights sitting at our desk. They're what we envision on a tough day when the pressures mounting, or even on a great day when we edge even the slightest bit closer to them. They are the force that determines our work rate, our disciplines, our organisation, our communication our entire working practice. The 'Why' holds within it the power to change anyone's life, no matter their upbringing, class, education or financial circumstance. So now your interest is heightened, let me explain how you can use the 'Why' to change your life.

On every occasion in my career when I have met someone who is an average or below average performer in any field the similarity between them all is the 'Why.' In the vast majority of cases they have no 'Why' at all, or a poor one at that. They are simply going through the motions, doing their job and nothing more.

I like to explain this point in an analogy, we have two sailing yachts, one boat represents an average performer who has no 'Why,' the other sailing yacht represents a person who has a strong 'Why.' In this circumstance they start out together in the same position in the sea, everything is uniform, the conditions, the yachts, the only differentiator is their goal.

Now at the start of the journey both parties hear about a paradise that sits northeast of their location, yet the wind blows north and so does the current, and with that the road of least resistance is north also. The average performer being average has no desire to achieve anything more than sail the yacht, thus in his naivety, and some might say stupidity, he continues with the easiest route, heading north with the current and wind wherever it may take him.

Juxtapose with this the other person with the strong 'Why.' Now the path of least resistance doesn't inspire him, he can envisage those finer shores that sit to the north east, and he's set the goal of finding this paradise no matter how arduous the journey ahead of him might be.

So their journey starts, the average performer sets off happily following the path north with the wind and current. He makes blissful pace with little to no obstacles in front of him, with no plan or goal he moves freely guided solely by the forces that push him.

Conversely, the man with the strong 'Why' has a very different journey. He tacks slightly against the strong wind and current in a bid to head northeast towards his goal of paradise. From the first moment the route presents its challenges. Travelling slightly against the current and wind mean that progress is slow and uncomfortable, wave after wave crash over the bow of the boat which the man must simply deal with. Moreover, navigation is hindered as the forces continually push the boat off course of its goal, thus the man must regularly assess where he is and correct his course accordingly. To make matters worse the man can see dark clouds ahead; it is at this point that he must make the decision of whether to continue on his course or change, maybe to the easier course heading north.

His moment of uncertainty wavers fast as the man with the strong 'Why' once again envisages his goal of that paradise. In his state of determination he stays true to his course of heading north east straight into the dark clouds of the storm.

The journey for the man with the strong 'Why' still doesn't get any easier. As he moves deeper into the storm the wind increases and with it comes the torrential rain. To add to his woes the weather conditions have reduced the visibility completely, now the navigation is even more complex than before. At this point again it would be easier for the man to turn back and change his course, but with his strong will he perseveres and pushes through the storm.

It is at this point that the ordeal takes a turn, the worst of the storm is over, as he progresses further the visibility improves, the rain stops, and the sun begins to shine. The journey becomes even more pleasant as the wind changes direction in the man's favour pushing him north east at a rate of knots. His luck doesn't end there, floating in the water he finds barrels of wine which he hauls onto the boat, in jubilation he gratefully tests the wine as a celebration for making it through the storm. To his elation he sees on the horizon the island of paradise ahead, more determined than ever he adjusts his course and shortly moors up on the island that he had merely dreamed of, the arduous journey paid off.

Cutting back now to the other man, the average performer. His journey couldn't have been more different; he floated away following the current and the wind north, wherever it took him. It was unlikely that he met a storm at any point as his mere nature caused him to avoid any adversity that presented itself. With no true desire he would continue on like this for eternity achieving nothing, simply being moved whatever way the forces took him. It wouldn't be till maybe the end of his journey that he would reflect and wonder what if he'd had a plan? Only to deem at this point that it's too late to change anything and amble on as he had.

So what does this analogy mean? Well let's break it down and identify which parts relate to real life.

1. We have the two men. These represent the groups in society, those average performers and those aspirational beings with a strong 'Why.'
2. The same starting position, circumstance and conditions. This is to signify that often people start in the same place as each other yet their careers take a very different path due to the aspirations that they have.
3. Paradise to the north east – this is a metaphor for a goal, no matter what goal that may be. In real life we all hear of success stories, those where people became very successful from starting with almost nothing. Now these stories aren't kept secret, everyone knows about the likes of Alan Sugar who has grown an empire from nothing. This is true of society too, we all know of people that have achieved their goals (their paradise), yet despite people being aware of what can be achieved it doesn't mean that they will set their goal to achieve it. Much like in this analogy where both men are made aware of the paradise yet only one is determined to get there.
4. Northern wind and current – this is the path of least resistance and the road that average performers will take. They want an easy life, often all they care for is a pay check every month and their work rate will be the bare minimum to get by.
5. Tacking against the strong wind and current – this signifies the path of a person with a strong why. They take the more difficult road away from the average performers. They go the extra mile, they work the longer hours, they put their customers first and do all that they can to satisfy them. They spend hours grafting, and continually improving in a bid to achieve their goal. This tacking slightly against the wind and current signifies the more difficult journey that's not simply smooth sailing.

6. Waves crashing against the bow – this is used to highlight some of the hardship that is experienced along the way. These are the day-to-day issues that effect a person with a strong why.
7. Navigation is hindered, regular course assessments must be made – this couldn't be truer for anyone in their pursuit of success. Granted that obstacles will present themselves from time to time, and it's at those times that we need to take a step back to reflect, review our goals and adjust our approach where needed to achieve those goals.
8. The storm – now in your journey to become successful you're going to experience your fair share of storms, if it's just the one then count yourself lucky. The storm represents a powerful circumstance that forcibly attempts to push you off track. In real life this could be a setback in your job such as you get made redundant or you lose a big customer, whatever it may be. Now it's your strong will to achieving your 'Why' that will give you the perseverance to push through any storm no matter its strength, and no matter how regular such a storm occurs.
9. Post storm, conditions improve – again relating to the real world this is often the case, you'll find that as you come out of the storm things get easier as you progress. It may be the case that you learn from the storm that you know how to avoid it all together in the future, or how to manage the storm better than you have done previously.
10. Barrels of floating wine – this is to represent the fortune that comes with pursuing a worthy 'Why.' For those motivated individuals, you will find that in pursuit of their 'Why' they also achieve other great wins such as they make enough commission to buy a nice new car or treat their family. This may not be their direct 'Why' motivation, but it's a by-product of being determined in achieving their 'Why', and at this point in their journey it's time to reap some of the benefits.
11. Paradise – you can probably predict that this is our ultimate goal, our 'Why,' which in this case was the sole motivation that kept this captain pushing through till the very end.

Personally I feel that this analogy is perfect to explain the power of our 'Why.' Now in real life not everyone falls into these two brackets of an average performer and a man with a strong 'Why.' In reality there are a number of boats that set off, one boat for the average performer with no 'Why,' one boat representing someone with a weak 'Why,' and so on increasing up to the man with the strong 'Why.' Now the journey would follow the same structure, the discrepancy being that some boats would waver as the journey moves on. Such as at the first point of friction some boats would change the course of their journey for the easier path following the current and wind. These first stragglers would be those with a weak 'Why,' they'd fall at the point that the waves start to crash over the bow. As the journey moves forward more boats would steer away from their goal as more adversity presents itself such as the storm. And so on and so on, with every step of the journey more boats would be lost as the hardship increases, until all that is left is those with a strong enough 'Why.'

Each boats achievement can be outlined as follows:

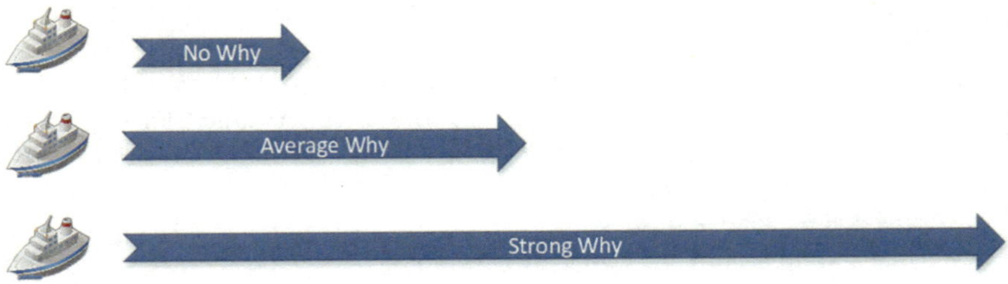

The whole point in this analogy is to identify that the 'Why' is your strongest motivational force, get it right and you can achieve whatever your heart desires. But having a 'Why' is merely not enough. What this analogy highlights so well is that the strength of your 'Why' is paramount to your success. The stronger your 'Why' the further you will persevere, no matter what adversity you experience on your journey.

So the two key points to remember are:

1) Have a 'Why'
2) Make it a strong 'Why'

Strength of Your Why

Now if I have failed to convince you on the value of having a strong 'Why' opposed to simply just a 'Why,' then I hope this following story from Napoleon Hill will bring the point closer to home.

This story comes from his brilliant book called *Think and Grow Rich* a fabulous book that I would strongly recommend. The story is dubbed *Three Feet from Gold.*[23]

The story starts with a man called R. U. Darby and his uncle who both had a thirst to become rich in the days of the American gold rush. They went to work with a shovel in search for their ultimate desire, gold. Weeks of hard labour passed before they were rewarded by the discovery of the lucrative shining ore, it was then that they realised that in order to mine the gold they would need to invest in some machinery. Their will was strong and their goal in sight, their next step was to travel home and gain some investment from family and friends.

After gaining the investment needed the Uncle and Darby went to work on the mine in Colorado, the initial fruits of their labour were very lucrative indeed. Their first goal was to mine enough gold to pay back their family and friends who had invested in them, after that everything would be profit. Success was almost in sight until they lost the vein of gold ore. Desperately they continued to drill, changing locations day after day to try and find the vein once again and meet their first goal. Sullen and discouraged they put down their tools after a long period of arduous labour to admit defeat, and in an attempt to rekindle some of the money to pay back their investors they sold the machinery to a local junk man for a few hundred dollars.

The junk man listened to their woes, and after they left he used some initiative of his own and hired a mining engineer to come and look at the mine which Darby and his Uncle had been working on. After analysing the fault lines the engineer came to the conclusion that the vein of golden ore would be present just three feet from where the Darbys had stopped drilling, which is exactly where it was found. The junk man ended up taking millions of dollars in ore from the mine because he was intelligent enough to seek expert advice before giving up.

This is a story that I love, and I often recite it to myself on a weekly basis. In this case Mr Darby and his uncle had a 'Why' and it was probably stronger than most, yet it wasn't strong enough to persevere through their challenge. If they had only pushed on further or been intelligent enough to do what the junk man did, then they would have achieved their 'Why.'

Now on your road to success there are undoubtedly going to be times of hardship, moments where you question yourself and whether what you're doing is wise. In these moments of uncertainty ask yourself this simple question:

"What if I'm three feet from gold?"

Ask yourself that and I promise you that you will persevere no matter the obstacle in front of you and eventually you will achieve your 'Why.'

Examples of the Why

I can't tell you what your 'Why' should be, as for it to be a powerful 'Why' that influences your every action, it must be something that inspires you as a person. One persons 'Why' won't always work for someone else. So just to get your creative juices flowing, let me highlight a few examples that you could use as inspiration for your 'Why':

- To own a fifty-foot sailing yacht with bright red sails and modern interior
- To own a top-of-the-range jet black Audi R8
- To buy my wife a Harry Winston engagement ring
- To own a five-bedroom beach house in Bermuda
- To put my three children through private education
- To work three days a week
- To run my own charity that helps the homeless get off the streets

The list is endless, but remember it has to relate to something that inspires you, otherwise it's useless. For instance the thought of investing time in philanthropy may be exhilarating to some but discouraging to others. Vice Versa material items such as flash cars and expensive watches may motivate some but not others. So make sure your 'Why' is something that truly motivates you.

5.2.8 – The Power of Your Subconscious

Tapping into our subconscious mind is no easy feat, though here lies any person's most powerful resource. Become empowered in our subconscious and there is nothing we can't achieve. First of all, we must harness our subconscious mind, we do this with unwavering belief that we will achieve those things that we think about. They are our thoughts, our deepest desires that for every minute of every day revolve relentlessly around our subconscious minds like a prophecy waiting to be fulfilled. Napoleon Hill described this beautifully within his masterpiece in literature, *Think and Grow Rich.*

No thought, whether it be negative or positive, can enter the subconscious mind without the aid of the principle of autosuggestion. – Napoleon Hill24

Therein lies the key to harnessing our subconscious mind, that being autosuggestion or programming our mind in such a way as to enter a concept, dream or desire into its powerful engine. So our task is to come up with that autosuggestion or programming, Tony Robbins in his book *Unlimited Power* made the point that:

If you don't provide your mind with the programming of the results you desire, someone else will provide that programming for you. If you don't have your own plan, someone else is going to make you fit into their plan. – Tony Robbins[25]

Tony even talks in his book of his own experiences of this power. He mentions how when he was in a state of underachievement and poverty when living in California that he made the decision to set his own goals. He designed in his mind his perfect life, the outcome, he got everything that he programmed into his mind.

We become what we think about. So now we need to focus on how to programme our subconscious mind.

You can voluntarily plant in your subconscious mind any plan, thought, or purpose which you desire to translate into its physical or monetary equivalent. – Napoleon Hill[26]

On this subject there are hundreds of techniques out there for making your goals a motivational force and engraining them into your subconscious. I've toyed with a few in my time, but the two that I have found to be the most useful are:

1. Regular repetition
2. Scrapbooks

Both of which I use myself and have championed with all of my sales icons. If you have a technique that works for you then great, but if not, why not try these techniques which I will explain in more depth now.

1. Regular Repetition

Another book I would recommend as a fantastic read is 'Outliers' by Malcolm Gladwell[27]. It's a truly awe-inspiring book which opens up your eyes in so many ways. One of the key takeaways from the book is the correlation between expertise and the time invested in that discipline. He states how to become an expert at anything you need to invest around 10,000 hours of time in that discipline to be at the top of your game. Hence to be inspired by our goals, we must invest a great deal of time to regularly review them and believe that they will become a reality.

Now a proven learning technique is repetition, the more a person repeats any activity the better they become at it as is becomes second nature after a while. Take driving a car as an example, when you first start learning how to drive it couldn't feel more alien. You miss the biting point, you over Rev the car, you stall, you grind the gears, you hit curbs etc. But with more time invested, your skill improves until it becomes second nature and you hardly have to think about how to drive; it's just natural.

We want our 'Why' goals to work in the same way, we want them to be so engrained in our subconscious that you don't have to consciously think about them. The answer to how we achieve this is regular repetition. One of the best techniques for engraining this into your subconscious is to start every single day by writing down and visualising your goals and when I say every day I mean every day. By starting every day in this manner you programme your mind into a motivational routine; it sets the mood for the day as from the off you're inspired to achieve your goals. Moreover, the continual repetition slowly drills the point into your subconscious. The beauty of this is the same as driving, after some experience when you get into a car you can drive seamlessly. After you've invested time in the repetition of your goals, you'll subconsciously be focused on them. So when the going gets tough and hardship comes your way so will your perseverance as your strong 'Why' is part of your natural cerebral function.

So start now, every day write down and visualise your goals and make this a regular routine to how you begin your day.

2. Scrapbooks

Regular repetition is a great technique to use, where it falls down for some people though it is on the visualisation point. Some people struggle to visualise what they note down in writing, and if that's you then maybe scrapbooks are a better technique to use. For anyone who doesn't know what a scrapbook is it's pretty simple. In essence a scrapbook is a page of pictures, those pictures are whatever your goals are. So if your 'Why' is to have a big shiny red Range Rover evoke or a beautiful white bungalow on the beach of the French Riviera then you'd have pictures to represent this in your scrapbook.

The process of repetition doesn't change, whether you write your goals down in words or develop a scrapbook. Spend every morning reviewing your scrapbook and visualise yourself living the images that you have chosen.

5.2.9 – Tying Your Goals Together

So we've established our 'How, What and Why,' now comes the next difficult step of tying these all together. One of the most effective ways sales icons have achieved this is through using pyramid goal setting.

What is Pyramid Goal Setting?

If you've ever seen Maslow's hierarchy of needs, then this will make sense as it works in the same way, if you haven't then I'll explain how pyramid goal setting works. Review the diagram below which breaks down a pyramid diagram into tiers.

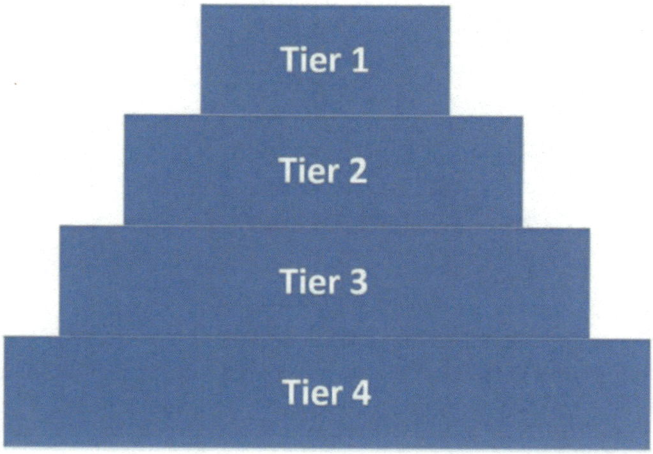

If you take a moment to think about the construction of a pyramid, as with anything you have to start from the ground up, you can't expect to start a later tier until the tier below that is constructed.

Pyramid goal setting is a fantastic tool because your goals work in the same way as building a pyramid. I mentioned earlier how the problem with the majority of people's goal setting is that they set merely a 'What' or a 'Why' and don't think about the 'How.'

What pyramid goal setting does is put a plan or a logical route together for achieving your 'What' and 'Why.' It does this by tying in your 'How.'

How Does Pyramid Goal Setting Work?

Take our diagram above once again, do bear in mind that in this example it is simplistic as it only has four tiers. In reality you may have a goal pyramid that has many more tiers with multiple criteria on each tier.

It works by mapping a plan as to how you will achieve an overall goal instead of just setting a goal and hoping it becomes a reality. Let me show you how this works by firstly outlining the process.

The process:

- Step one – identify your 'What' or 'Why' for the top tier
- Step two – determine what steps will be needed to achieve this top tier goal
- Step three – identify your 'How' to achieving the top tier goal
- Step four – add milestones and timescales
- Step five – replicate this process for your other 'What' and 'Why'

The Steps Explained

Step One

The first step is to determine what your tier one will represent. The top tier in any case will always represent either a 'What' or a 'Why.' So this may be something like to make £50k commission this year or to be promoted to a management position in the next two years. That's the easy part, establishing what your tier one will be.

Step Two

The following tiers below that tier one must all be a 'How'

Tier 2, 3, 4= 'How'

What we need to do in step two is identify what activity will enable you to achieve your top tier goal. What makes this more complicated is that this activity must relate to your top-tier goal in some way, otherwise there is no point in having this as a tier in your goal pyramid. Don't worry if this doesn't make sense yet as we'll explain this in an example shortly.

Step Three

Once you have identified these activities that will aid you in achieving your top tier goal, subsequently write those activities in a 'How' format, remember that they should all be SMART.

Step Four

Add milestones and timescales to your pyramid that relate to your tier one goal. Such as if your tier one goal was to be make £50k commission in twelve months then one of your tiers could be for instance that at the three-month point you expect to have made £10k commission or something of that nature.

Step Five

After steps one to four you will have completed your first goal setting pyramid. The trouble is that this will only aid you in achieving the one top-tier goal you've identified.

To become a true sales icon you'll need to repeat this process for all of the 'What' and 'Why' that you've identified. Not only this but when you achieve a top tier goal you should start on a new venture of another top-tier goal which is harder to achieve.

Example 1

So at the moment this may all sound a bit confusing, so let me explain all of this in a simple example. For the first example we'll make it quite simplistic, and we'll use golf as a topic for a goal setting pyramid.

In this example let us say that we're a young lady who wants to improve our golf game and get a handicap of 20, we currently have a handicap of 25 and play once every two weeks with friends only who are playing off a higher handicap than 25.

Step One

We've identified our 'What' which is to have a handicap of 20 and we'll say that we want to achieve this in 10 months.

Step Two

Now we need to make a judgement call of what activities will enable us to achieve our top tier goal. So we brainstorm what some of these activities could be:

- Have regular coaching
- Play more often
- Practise at the driving range
- Play with people who have handicaps better than 20
- Enter some competitions

Step Three

Here we need to turn these activities into a 'How' that must also be SMART. If we respectively convert our activities into a 'How' they'd look something like this:

- Purchase some golf coaching once a week
- Play at least once a week
- Practise at the driving range for two hours a week
- Play with people of a handicap of 20 or below at least once a month
- Enter six competitions to play in this year at two-month intervals

Step Four

Now we need to add in some milestones and timescales. An appropriate milestone for this may be to reduce our handicap by one shot every two months.

Step Five

Once our top tier goal is achieved then we repeat the process again for our next top tier goal of improving our handicap to the next desired level.

So if we map out what this pyramid would look like we have the following:

The beauty of laying this out in this way is that we can adapt our activity tier if we are not on course to achieve our milestone in the timescale. For instance take our bottom tier here. We may find that this activity is sufficient enough to reduce our handicap from 25 to 24, but we need to up this activity to a new level in order to meet our next milestone of 23. That's where we would apply a phased approach.

Phased Approach

It's also worth noting that certain 'How' activities may be used only on higher tiers, as the lower tiers milestone can be achieved with other 'How' activities initially. So take this example once again, you may be able to move from a handicap of 25 to 24 by just applying the following 'How':

- Play at least once a week
- Practise at the driving range for two hours a week

Whereas when you want to move from the milestone of a 24 handicap to 23 you may need to add some additional 'How' activities. For instance to achieve this milestone your 'How' for this tier might be:

- Play at least once a week
- Practise at the driving range for two hours a week
- Purchase some golf coaching once a week

This may look like the following

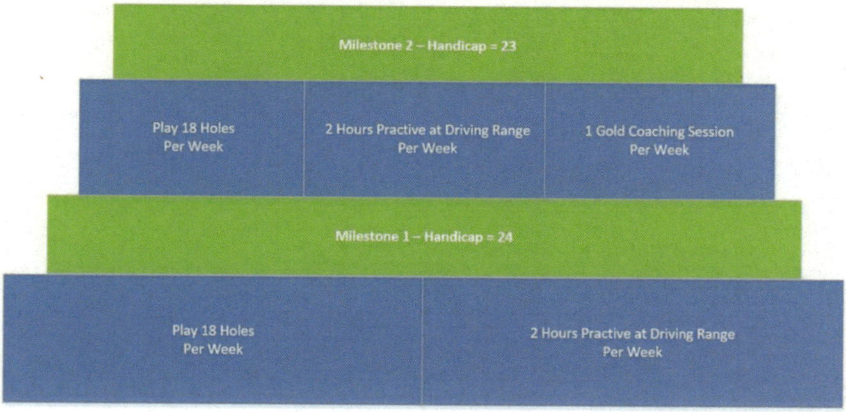

Why Use a Phased Approach?

I often get asked the question from prospective sales icons as to why they should use a phased approach to their pyramid goal setting, surely, it's better off to go all out in order to achieve your goals as quickly as possible! Well the answer is yes you're right, an all-out approach of adopting all the 'How' activities will achieve your goal faster. The danger is the change. Now you may be unique, you may be able to cope with any change to your general day-to-day activities. Most people however are adverse to change. The downside to adopting all of the 'How' activities straightaway instead of a phased approach is that you risk this becoming a fad.

Take dieting for example, how many people do you know who use fad diets. They get the idea in their head that they need to go on a diet and instead of creating incremental changes over time they go the whole hog. They go to the extreme and cut all fat, or carbohydrate or only eat salads for example. Often the result is a fad, they carry on with this approach for a short period of time only to become disillusioned and change back to their previous way of eating.

They say on average that it takes 28 days of continuous action for something to become a habit. That's why I recommend a phased approach. So start with a few 'How' activities and a milestone that is achievable. Then when this has become a habit add a few more to achieve your next milestone and so on and so on. This way you reduce the risk of this change becoming a fad and increase the chances that these 'How' activities become habits.

Comparisons Help

One practice we can adopt is to search out for peers who are the calibre we desire and compare and then match our activities to theirs. Or even better we can try to improve upon their activities to ensure we'll meet our top tier goal. Take this golfing example once again, if we wanted to improve our golf to play off of a handicap of 20 we could find someone who has that handicap. Then we could ask them what they do to maintain this handicap. This may give you your 'How' and aid you in putting your tiers together.

Let's say that you've chatted to Mrs Cooper who has a handicap of 20 and your comparison activities look like as follows:

Activity	You	Mrs Cooper
How regular you play?	Once every two weeks	Every week
How much time weekly do you spend at the driving range?	Zero time	Two hours
How much time a month do you have coaching?	Zero time	Two hours
How many competitions do you play in each year?	Zero	Twelve

Activity

So right now look at one of your 'What' or 'Why' that you're developing a goal setting pyramid for. Take a minute to think about someone you know who has achieved this or something of this magnitude. This could be a work colleague, family friend or even someone you don't know but have heard about. Now take the time to touch base with this person and ask them for five minutes of their time to help you achieve your goals as you idolise what they have achieved. I'm pretty certain that if you position this in the right way with them they'll be more than happy to help.

Then when they do give you some airtime talk them through this pyramid goal setting. Say this is the 'What' or 'Why' I'm looking to achieve, this is what I undertake currently as a 'How.' I know that you've achieved x,y,z and I wanted to pick your brains as to how you did this to aid me in achieving my goals.

Use Reverse-Funnel Planning

Take a minute to think back to our reverse funnel planning, this is where we have an end goal and plan out the activity required in order to achieve this end goal. Reverse funnel planning can tie in perfectly to pyramid goal setting as it will ensure that your activity is sufficient enough to achieve your goal if it's something quantifiable such as to make a certain amount of commission or become the top salesperson etc.

Take the following example of reverse funnel planning:

- Average opportunity size is £20k GP
- Opportunities to sale – 33%
- Warm leads to opportunities – 50%
- Activity to warm lead – 10%

Which means we need:

- To generate 150 opportunities per annum of this size
- To develop 300 warm leads per annum of this size
- To prospect 3,000 organisations per annum of this size

From working out your reverse funnel planning you can use your findings to develop your 'How' activities and thus your tiers. For instance in this example one of your tiers could be to build 13 opportunities per month (equating to 300 opportunities in the year).

Or we could phase this to something like the following:

Top tier – £1m GP
Milestone 9–12 months = £400k GP
Tier 1= 20 opportunities per month
Milestone 6–9 months = £300k GP
Tier 2 = 15 opportunities per month
Milestone 3–6 months = £200k GP
Tier 3 = 10 opportunities per month
Milestone 3 months = £100k GP
Tier 4 = 5 opportunities per month

However, you use this is up to you but your work on reverse funnel planning earlier can be a useful tool for this goal setting pyramid.

Use Transitioners

If you've found a transitioner that dramatically increases your chances of success for an opportunity then you could incorporate these transitioners into your goal setting pyramid. For instance I worked with two businesses in different verticals previously and their transitioners that improved their chances of success dramatically were:

- Trial or proof of concept
- Head office visit

If from analysing your transitioners you find that there is an overriding activity that drastically increases your chances then add it to your goal setting pyramid. Examples include:

- X prospect head office visits per month
- X project trials per month
- X prospect webinars per month
- X pricing promotions per month

Use Previous Activity

The whole point of recording all of our activity and wins is that that we can use it effectively. If we know the input X creates the output of Y then to get an output of 2Y then the input must be 2X, it's simple maths. So use your previous activity to help you set your tiers. If six months ago you were regularly making fifty calls a day and the result of that was say £20k profit a month. Then if I want to grow my profit to £40k a month, I would at least need to be making one hundred calls a day.

I use phone calls as an example here but there's a whole wealth of information in your previous activity that could be used in a tier such as:

- Develop X number of SQLs a month
- Conduct X number of drop in calls a month

- Present X number of proposals a month
- Have at minimum X number of forward appointments

You get the idea. So use your previous activity as a measuring device as to what tiers need to consist of to achieve your top tier.

Sales Icon Example

So thus far we have talked you through what pyramid goal setting is, why you should use it, the approaches to this and a simple example based on golf. Now I want to solidify this concept in your mind using a sales icon example which will be a little bit more complex but directly related to you.

In this example, you're one year into a sales role and could be described as an average performer but you want to change this and have decided to put together a goal setting pyramid to help achieve your goals.

Step 1 – identify our 'What' or 'Why'

For this example let's say that you want to earn £40k commission this year, this is based on you receiving 10% commission for each sale so you know from this you need to sell £400k GP.

Step 2 – find out what activity is required

For this we are going to use our reverse funnel planning as a first port of call which we have the following statistics for:

- Average opportunity size is £40k GP
- Opportunities to sale – 20%
- Warm leads to opportunities – 50%
- Cold calling to warm lead – 2.5%

Thus we require the following high-level activity:

- To have 10 sales of average size (£40k) per annum
- To generate 50 opportunities per annum of this size
- To develop 100 warm leads per annum of this size
- Cold call 4,000 organisations in my sweet spot per annum

So our reverse funnel planning has helped give us some high-level activity we could utilise, in addition to this we also feel the following activity may help:

- Training – in our self-analysis we noted that there are a number of areas where we lack knowledge. Thus to increase our probability of closing sales we could do with undertaking two hours of training a week.
- Networking events – we've attended a few and gained some now loyal customers from these so we feel we should attend more.
- Head office visits – 75% of the time when a prospect has a head office visit they subsequently became a customer
- Referrals – 50% of referrals are converted into customers.
- Drop in visits – a number of drop in visits have converted to customers.
- Prospecting emails – many customers came through this route initially

Step 3 – turning these into SMART 'How' activities

Now we need to look at the activities just identified and convert them into SMART 'How' activities. I'm going to use a phased approach here so increasing my activity by increments each quarter, to help put together my goal setting pyramid I'll use a matrix as a first port of call.

'How'	0-3 months	3-6 months	6-9 months	9-12 months	Total
Cold Calling	500	750	1,250	1,500	4,000
Training	2 hours per week	2 hours per week	2 hours per week	2 hours per week	96 hours
Networking events	2 per month	2 per month	2 per month	2 per month	24
Head office visits	1 per month	2 per month	3 per month	3 per month	27
Referrals	1 per month	2 per month	3 per month	4 per month	30
Drop in visits	10 per month	15 per month	20 per month	20 per month	195
Prospecting emails	50 per month	50 per month	50 per month	50 per month	600

Step 4 – milestones and timescales

I then need to establish my milestones and their timescales to achieving these milestones, for some of this I will again use my reverse funnel planning. My milestones will be as follows:

Milestone 1

- Timescale = zero to three months
- Milestone = £5k commission from £50k GP sales

Milestone 2

- Timescale = three to six months
- Milestone = £7.5k commission from £75k GP sales

Milestone 3

- Timescale = six to nine months
- Milestone = £12.5k commission from £125k GP sales

Milestone 4

- Timescale = nine to twelve months
- Milestone = £15k commission from £150k GP sales

So if I collate all of this I can formulate my goal setting pyramid for this 'What' as depicted below:

Step 5 – repeat

Now we would repeat this process for other 'What' or 'Why' goals which we want to achieve, as well as repeat this process once we attain a goal.

Multiple Pyramids

Stepping back slightly we took some time previously to brainstorm some 'What' and 'Why' goals. Now often you will find that some 'What' or 'Why' goals require a subsequent 'What' or 'Why' to be achieved. This is where multiple pyramids come in.

This sounds confusing but let's explain with an example again.

Example 1

For this example we have a person with the following two 'What' goals

'What 1' – become the top billing salesperson

'What 2' – become a sales manager

Now in this case it's unlikely for 'What 2' to be achieved before 'What 1' and that's where a multiple pyramid would come in. Thus for 'What 2' one of the tiers could be to achieve 'What 1.'

Example 2

For this example we have a person with the following 'What' and 'Why'

- 'What 1' – earn £200k per annum

- 'Why 2' – put my children through private education

Hopefully this solidifies the point as again in this case 'Why 2' requires money therefore 'What 1' would be a prerequisite to this and thus multiple pyramids are required that work in conjunction with one another.

What If It's Not Working?

So you'll know if your goal setting pyramid isn't working if the following happens:

- You fail to hit your tiers
- You fail to hit a milestone in a timeframe

Now failing to hit one of your tiers would be something like having a tier that states to make five hundred calls a month, but you only manage to make four hundred. Now in such a circumstance, you could assess things and potentially deem that you're asking too much of yourself to achieve that tier. Honestly though, that's not the sales icon way, the sales icon approach is to find a way to achieve it. So in this circumstance if you were failing to make enough calls you could look at your other day-to-day activities and see where the root cause is. Where can you buy some extra time to attain those extra one hundred calls a month, could you start early or delegate some tasks to someone else, for example. If this circumstance arises where you fail to hit a tier you need to honestly ask yourself why and how you can hit this moving forward.

The second circumstance is that you've hit all of your tiers, but you've failed to hit a milestone in a timeframe that you've set. If this is the case then you need to analyse how far off you were from hitting your milestone, was it a case of bad luck or an opportunity that has fallen into a later time? Whatever the reason you need to find out why. In the majority of circumstances failing to hit a milestone will be down to your tiers. Although you may have hit your tiers you may not have made your tiers proportional to the milestone and timescale that you're trying to achieve. For instance if your milestone was to make £100k GP this quarter but one of your tiers was something like 'to make ten calls a day' then you may find that this tier is disproportional to the milestone. In such circumstance to mitigate this happening in the future you need to adapt your tiers to be more proportional, such as in this case changing the call tier to make fifty calls a day for example.

Nevertheless if you fail to hit a tier or a milestone in a timescale then all is not lost. You just need to take a step back, review what went wrong and adapt your goal setting pyramid accordingly.

5.3 – Forecasting and Pipeline

Forecasting is often the bane of salespeople's lives as well as their managers. Most of the time salespeople are forecasting on a whim and a prayer, commonly it's very much a finger in the air approach as to whether an opportunity will fall at a certain time, if at all. Now don't get me wrong forecasting will never be 100% accurate, but our goal is to make it as accurate as possible. In this section we will highlight to you why it's important, detail some techniques for accurate forecasting, and tie in some of the previous items we've discussed to aid you also.

Forecast and pipeline – the difference:

Many salespeople amalgamate pipeline and forecast to mean the same thing, when in reality they are very different, and might I add should be kept separate to one another.

Often salespeople make mistakes because they don't keep these two parts separate to one another.

What are they and why are they important?

Basically forecasting is predicting when you expect opportunities to fall in time and the amount they will be worth. For instance, if we were working on a quarterly forecast, and we had three opportunities which we expect to close this quarter worth £10k each then our forecast for this quarter would be £30k.

The reason forecasting is so important is that it gives you an indication of what sales you can expect in a set period of time whether that be this week, month, quarter or year. Without forecasting you cannot take action, it's not possible to judge whether you're in a good position and need to nurture your opportunities or whether you need to up your work rate and bring more opportunities in.

To use an analogy picture two men both in a maze. One man has a map of the maze, he represents the salesperson who forecasts accurately. The other man has no such map, he represents a salesperson who does not forecast. Both men have the same desire and skill level, the only differentiating factor is the man who has the map. Now whilst the man without the map may be fortunate and find his way out of the maze at some point, he'll take wrong turn after wrong turn, and if he's really unlucky his time will run out. Whereas the man with the map, who may even take a wrong turn or two himself has his map to rely on and can follow that to aid in his escape of the maze.

Forecasting gives you an indication of where you currently are with regards to opportunities within a time frame. It's there as an aid to help you achieve your target by measuring where you currently are against target, what you have in your pipeline as well as when you expect opportunities to fall.

Forecasting mainly comes from reviewing your pipeline. Your pipeline is the complete list of all the active opportunities which you have. It may take into consideration timescales, but it won't give you a good indication of how you will fair compared to target. For instance you may have many opportunities in your pipeline which are unlikely to close for whatever reason. That is the big difference between a forecast and a pipeline. Your pipeline is the complete list of opportunities, a forecast is a filtered down pipeline, the filter being expecting the opportunity to close. Therefore your pipeline will at least be the same size as your forecast but the majority of the time it will be larger than your forecast.

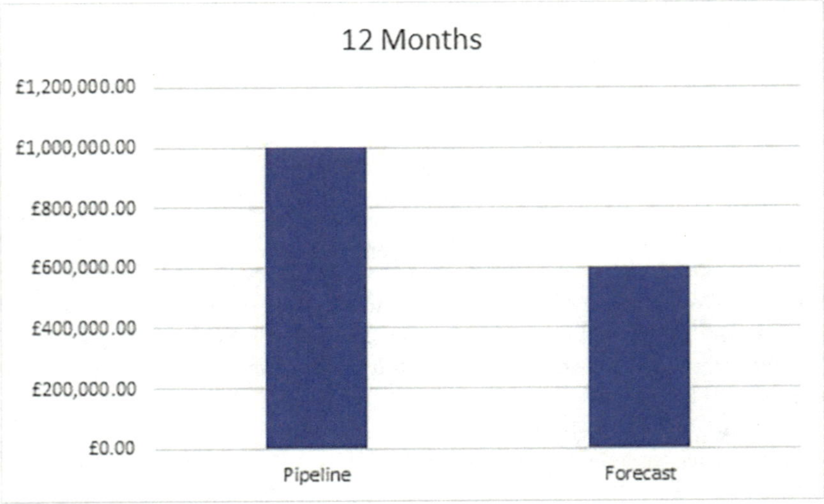

How to forecast?

Now there are many ways to forecast. Most sales icons I work with forecast on a monthly or quarterly approach, really it depends on how you're targeted. For instance, if you're targeted on a weekly model then it may be advantageous to forecast on a weekly approach, if you're targeted on a bi annual or annual model then you could forecast in this way also. Personally, I prefer monthly or quarterly.

The things you will need in order to forecast are:

- Sales target for timespan
- Opportunities in this timespan
- Current sales already achieved in this timespan

Now the average salesperson will forecast in the following way

Month	Target	Sales achieved	Pipeline	Difference to target
January	£20k	£10k	£40k	+£30k
February	£20k	£0	£10k	-£10k
March	£20k	£0	£0	-£20k
Total	£60k	£10k	£50k	Hit

Now there's nothing wrong with forecasting like this, trust me this is better than having no forecast at all. But if you review this forecast again, it states how you're predicting that you will hit your target for the quarter, mainly due to a good pipeline in January. Well experience tells me that the likelihood of this happening is very slim.

Now the pitfalls that most people fall into when forecasting are:

1. They forecast everything with the same chance – what I mean by this is that they don't differentiate opportunities from one another. We've all had the opportunities in the past where we've done a great job, everything's gone to plan, we've used everything in our power that we can, and we have a great feeling that they'll close. Conversely we've also had them opportunities where we just get a bad vibe, the decision maker is very stand off-ish and you're uncertain whether you have a chance or not. Now despite having this insight about two opportunities we'd still forecast them in exactly the same way, sounds ridiculous now right!
2. They fail to take into account conversion rates – salespeople that do this will only look at their pipeline and not take into account their conversion rates. For instance if you have a conversion rate of 50% and a target of say £50k for a month then you know you need to have a pipeline for the month of at least £100k to hit target as only half of this will close.

3. They don't look at natural slippage – for any salesperson there will be a degree of natural slippage for opportunities. That's not to say these opportunities are lost, it's just that they get pushed back due to other factors such as failure to get budget approved or other projects taking priority.

Counteracting these pitfalls:
So how do we counteract these pitfalls? Well try using the following:

> Work out the percentage chance of an opportunity closing, whether that be a 10% chance of being successful or 80% chance of being successful. Later in this chapter we're going to focus on the closing calculator which will help with working out an opportunities percentage chance of closing. If you categorise every opportunity with a percentage chance of closing then you're well on your way to putting together an accurate forecast. There are two simple forecasting methods that I avidly promote, that which is best is dependent on what works for you. The two methods are

Method A – Percentage Value Forecast

- Use total values multiplied by your percentage chance as your forecast

Method B – Likelihood Forecast

- Only forecast opportunities that you deem have a likelihood of X% or higher of closing

So let me explain the Percentage Value Forecast in more depth to show you what I mean. Say for example that I have three opportunities in my pipeline, which I've categorised with their value and percentage chance of closing below:

Opportunity	Value	Percentage chance of closing	Forecast
Opportunity 1	£5k GP	80%	£4k
Opportunity 2	£20k GP	50%	£10k
Opportunity 3	£50k GP	20%	£10k
		Total	£24k

This forecast method would give me a forecast of £24k GP of a pipeline of £75k GP. Now using this for a forecasting method is more accurate if:

- Your percentage chance of closing is calculated honestly
- You have lots of opportunities in your pipeline

So be honest with yourself when you are gauging the likelihood of an opportunity closing, use the closing calculator that we will talk about shortly to aid you in this. If you have minimal opportunities then chances are that this forecast method won't be too accurate for you. However, if you do have multiple opportunities then the law of averages tells you that this will be more or less correct.

If you deem that this method of forecasting isn't for you then maybe try method B, the Likelihood Forecast. In this method, you are once again using your judgement on an opportunity's percentage chance of closing. But instead of forecasting everything in your pipeline you're going to set a threshold for opportunities you deem worthy of forecasting. For instance, you may feel that it's best to only forecast opportunities that you've determined to have a 70% or higher chance of closing. Thus if this was my threshold and I had the following four opportunities in my pipeline:

Opportunity	Value	Percentage chance of closing
Opportunity 1	£5k GP	80%
Opportunity 2	£20k GP	50%
Opportunity 3	£50k GP	20%
Opportunity 4	£30k GP	70%

Then we'd be forecasting the following:

Opportunity 1 = £5k GP
Opportunity 4 = £30k GP
Total forecast = £35k GP

What I've found from sales icons in the past is that this method of forecasting can be more conservative which isn't necessary a bad thing. Often if you use this method you'll under promise and over deliver.

How often should I forecast?

Again the regularity of your forecasting will differ depending on how you're targeted that being monthly, quarterly or annually etc. For sales icons, I recommended reviewing your forecast at least on a weekly basis. When I say review I mean look at all of your forecasted opportunities for this month and distinguish whether they are still likely to close or not. The benefit of constantly reviewing this is that you can assess whether any actions such as transitioners would help to close an opportunity.

Upside to accurate forecasting?

There are countless upsides to accurate forecasting. I'm going to touch on a few key upsides.

Focus your time – this sounds like a peculiar correlation, why would accurate forecasting focus your time? Well think about it like this, let's say that you're buying some stocks, you've done your homework and whittled down your shortlist to just ten prospective stocks to buy. Now in this case you were fortunate to get the inside track from someone in the know who tells you that two of the stocks are guaranteed to rise because of A, B, C. If you knew this then where are you going to invest your time and money? Easy, in them two stocks. Why? Well because you have the information that tells you those two stocks will have the best rate of return.

Your forecast is no different than this. If I have ten opportunities and I analyse them to find that:

- Two have a 70% or higher chance of closing
- Three have a 50–70% chance of closing
- Five have a 50% or less chance of closing

Then my focus is going to be on the top two and then maybe the three after that if I have time to focus on them subsequently. A word of caution here though, take the opportunities size of sale into account too. There's no point focusing on opportunities that don't hold sufficient value. Whereas if there's a blue whale waiting to be landed then focus on improving its chance of closing.

Increases your sales – that brings me to my next point of how accurate forecasting increases sales. If we spend time analysing our pipeline and honestly reviewing our opportunities chance of closing then it will aid us in closing more juicy deals. Take the example of having ten opportunities again, now when you have multiple opportunities such as this it gets difficult to justify where to focus your time. Most salespeople will either focus on closing everything, or just those which have a good chance. By forecasting, you're asking yourself the question of what's the likelihood of this opportunity closing. And with this brings a wealth of other creative questions and answers, as when you ask such a question you'll think to yourself, what can I do to increase the chances? This is where your closing creativity will fire into action, your brain will ask things like what transitioners could I use here? Is there anything I haven't done which I could have? What's going to distinguish me from my competitors here etc. Simply by forecasting, you increase the number of sales you make, as your time spent forecasting is also time spent reflecting on how to close each opportunity.

Increase your work rate – consider Parkinson's Law, which roughly states that work expands so as to fill the time available for its completion. Thereby meaning that if we are under deadlines, somehow we manage to complete our work in compliance with the deadline despite other pressures. In sales my view is that forecasts and targets often work in the same manner as Parkinson's Law. What I mean by this is that when a person forecasts, they spend time analysing what business they expect to close and where that puts them in line with their target. Now on countless occasions I've seen this cause a change in the salespersons work rate, most commonly for the better. They conduct their forecasting and see that they're unlikely to hit target for the month or year, and then this magical change happens. They get a work rate boost, as if someone has just pumped them with adrenaline and caffeine. They up their activity, and guess what, their output increases too. It may not be enough to save the month that they're in, but often they'll make up for it in later months whereby they surpass target.

Regularly spending time to accurately forecast will tell you where you are in relation to expected sales and force you to act. Whereas failing to forecast achieves nothing, you won't know whether you need to up your work rate, close more deals, get more opportunities for next month or next quarter.

What can help us forecast?

Don't get me wrong forecasting can be tricky, but there are two key things that help sales icons in their forecasting that I'll share with you, and they are:

- Conversion rates
- Closing calculator

Conversion rates – as simple as they sound, on average, how often does an opportunity close. Some people will have higher conversion rates and some people will have lower, many people take an approximation that a third of opportunities will close.

Your conversion rates are a great resource to review when looking at your forecast. If you always compensate for your conversion rates then the majority of the time you will hit or surpass your target. Now if you wish to simply use conversion rates to forecast then go right ahead. Personally though, I think they have limitations as its tarnishing everything with the same brush. We're in essence saying that all my opportunities are alike despite some that I will have put immeasurable amounts of activity into, and others that I have hardly focused on at all.

So what I prefer to encourage sales icons to do is use two of the methods I discussed previously in conjunction with the closing calculator.

Closing calculator – when I was relatively new to sales one of my observations when reviewing my own and my peers forecasts was that everything was forecasted in the same way. For instance, if I took two opportunities of the same size, let's say both worth £50k each, in my forecast I had no way of identifying which opportunity was more likely to close than the other. For instance, let's hypothesise that the activity for two opportunities were as follows:

Opportunity 1 – met with the prospect once and quoted

Opportunity 2 – met with the prospect four times, they've bought from me before, I've used five transitioners and they've asked me to hold three dates for them for the project work.

Now my observation was that this seemed ludicrous, the opportunities may be of the same size but there's no way that I should forecast them in the same way. So what I came up with is a classing system, which is a way of classing each opportunity for their likelihood to close. The way that I classed the opportunities was through developing a closing calculator.

The closing calculator:

Now the closing calculator is something that needs to be developed by you as an individual for your business. I can't give you a calculator that will work for everyone as there are many different factors to consider, thus for different industries the calculator may vary.

What is the closing calculator?

The calculator is a set of general questions about an opportunity, each question must be answered and scored. When you have answered all of the questions you then must total your score and turn it into a percentage. This percentage will determine which class the opportunity falls into. Sounds complex at the moment but it will all become clear when I run you through a real-life example.

To demonstrate this simply, let's say I have four questions. I take an individual opportunity and ask these four questions and score them appropriately as follows:

Question	Worth	Score
Question 1	Yes = 10, no = 0	10
Question 2	Yes = 1, no= 0	0
Question 3	Score out of 5	3
Question 4	Score out of 4	3
Total	Max = 20	16

In this very simple outline we scored 16 out of 20, this would equate to 80% therefore, this opportunity would class as a tier-1 opportunity. So that's the rough guide of how it works, the difficult part is developing your questions, giving them a weighting, and gauging which questions are vital to give an accurate judgement.

Example:

For a real-life example I'm going to use one of the technology providers I worked with previously. This is what their closing calculator looked like:

Question	Scoring
Is the prospect a spending customer?	Yes = 5 No = 0
Were we referred to the prospect and they got in touch with us?	Yes = 5 No= 0
Have they had an assessment or trial of the solution?	Yes = 10 No = 0
Has budget been approved?	Yes = 1 No = 0
Does your prospect have the authority to make the decision?	Yes = 1 No = 0
Is there a clear need for your solution?	Yes = 1 No = 0
Have they been to visit us at our head office?	Yes = 5 No= 0
Have we presented our proposal face to face with the decision maker?	Yes = 4 No = 0
How many competitors are there competing for this opportunity?	One = 4 Two-three = 2 Over three = 0
Do we know which competitors we are competing against and their relationship with the prospects?	Yes = 1 No = 0
Have we provided a technical webinar for some of the solution?	Yes = 4 No = 0
How happy is the prospect with their incumbent?	Score between 0 and 5, 0 being very happy and 5 being very unhappy
What do you feel is the likelihood of winning?	Score between 0 and 10, 0 being no chance and 10 being certain it will close

Their classing system was the same as before:

Tier 1 = 75–100%
Tier 2 = 50–74%
Tier 3 = 25–49%
Tier 4 = 0–24%

To show you how this would work I'll give you a short scenario to test yourself.

Opportunity X

- Not a spending customer
- Weren't referred
- They had an assessment
- Budget is approved
- You're speaking to the decision maker with the authority to buy
- They need your solution
- They have visited your head office
- We presented the proposal face to face
- There are three competitors
- We know who those competitors are and their relationship
- We've conducted a technical webinar
- The prospect is unhappy with their incumbent
- You feel the likelihood of successfully closing is 8/10

So try it, what score and therefore tier did you class the opportunity as?

You should have found a score of 40 out of a possible 51, from the scoring respectively 0+0+10+1+1+1+5+4+2+1+4+3+8=40, which as a percentage equates to 78%. Therefore, this opportunity would be classed as a tier 1 opportunity, telling you that it has a high chance of closing.

Let's try one more scenario, again using the closing calculator from earlier. In this scenario let's assume that the following activities have occurred for opportunity Y.

Opportunity Y

- Not a spending customer
- Weren't referred
- They haven't had an assessment
- Budget is approved
- You're speaking to the decision maker with the authority to buy
- They need your solution
- They haven't visited your head office
- We presented the proposal face to face
- There are eight competitors
- We don't know who those competitors are and their relationship
- We've haven't conducted a technical webinar
- The prospect is happy with their incumbent
- You feel the likelihood of successfully closing is 2/10

Again, what score and therefore tier would you class the opportunity as?

You should have found a score of 11 out of a possible 51, from the scoring respectively 0+0+0+1+1+1+0+4+0+0+0+2+2=11, which as a percentage equates to 22%. Therefore, this opportunity would be classed as a tier-4 opportunity, telling you that it has a low chance of closing.

Activity

Spend some time now to create your own closing calculator. This isn't the easiest task by any means, and initially it will probably be a working document, so the first draft of your closing calculator may not be perfect and may require some more adaptation. But keep at it, develop it as much as you can until it is a seamless and efficient tool.

To create your closing calculator you need to come up with some questions which will help you assess an opportunity, plus you will need to assign a scoring to these question. Two important things to consider here are

- Transitioners
- Proportion of scoring

Transitioners – in most cases transitioners will constitute a vast amount of your closing calculator. Why? Well transitioners as a concept are simply actions which move an opportunity closer to becoming a sale. Therefore, the use of transitioners will only help to strengthen your chances of successfully making a sale. Thus to aid you in developing your closing calculator take some time to look at your transitioners and decide which would be useful in your closing calculator.

Proportion of scoring – take the previous real-life closing calculator. Did you notice how the scoring was proportioned more for some questions and less for others? Take the assessment question, this attributed to 10 points, that's almost a fifth of all of the points available. Now this is no mistake, for this technology provider, in the vast majority of cases when an assessment was conducted they were successful in winning the opportunity. Therefore, this is why this question carried so much weight. Proportioning the scoring is a tricky thing to do, but you need to look at your past opportunities that you have won and review the transitioners which you used. For instance if you had say ten opportunities, six you had won and four you had lost. You could look at whether there were any common transitioners to those which you won in comparison to those which were lost. This may provide you with key transitioners and help you to proportion a value to the transitioner in your closing calculator.

Test It

Once you have developed your closing calculator, you should test it. Take some of the opportunities you have won or lost and use your closing calculator to determine what tier the opportunity would have fallen in. This is how you'll know if your closing calculator works or not. If you use it and all of your won opportunities sit in a tier 3 or 4 category then the calculator is wrong, and you better go back to the drawing board and redesign it. If, however, they show them as tier-1 or 2 opportunities then great it's a working tool.

Classification

A word of caution around the classification, just because an opportunity is classified as a tier-1 or 2 opportunity doesn't mean that it's a dead certainty. The classification is there to aid you, both in your closing and forecasting. From a closing perspective you can use the calculator to gauge where an opportunity is classed at the moment. Though you can also get a better understanding of how you can increase the chances of the opportunity closing. Take the previous example again, say for instance that you have an opportunity that is a tier four, you could look at which areas that the scores were low or not at all. For instance, this tier four opportunity may not have had a 'technical webinar on the solution,' so from using your closing calculator you'd see this and realise that this transitioner would be good to use to increase your chances of being successful.

Forecasting will benefit from using this classification too. If you remember earlier we spoke about pipeline and forecasting, and how often salespeople come into trouble from forecasting all of the pipeline for a set period of time. Well the calculator can make that a thing of the past. This is all through the classification as now you have a way of differentiating your pipeline. For instance, if I wanted to forecast accurately for this quarter I would look at all of my opportunities for this quarter in my pipeline, then I would only forecast those opportunities that fall in tier one or two. That doesn't mean to say a tier three or four opportunity in that timespan won't close because they could, but it'll just be an add-on; I won't forecast it. In addition, I wouldn't just cast aside those tier three and four opportunities, they can still be worked and nurtured to becoming a tier one or two opportunity, though your tier one and two opportunities should take priority.

Conclusion to Motivation Chapter

To accomplish anything in this book you must have overarching levels of motivation. Whether you're a seasoned veteran of selling or a novice, you're going to all experience ups and downs. You'll win deals of course, but often you're going to lose them too. You'll have days where you question what you're doing, whether you'll ever get to where you want to be and if the ordeal is worth it. But with the tools highlighted in this chapter you'll maintain motivation throughout, to ensure that no rut is forever.

The key aspect is recording your activity, do this and you'll notice what your micro wins are from day to day. With that you can strive for more and challenge yourself, you can set that goal of making one hundred calls today or getting through to thirty decision makers this week. When we record our activity we can be candid with ourselves. When we see what our activity is we can honestly say to ourselves whether we are doing enough or not. Remember too that this isn't in comparison to our peers, they're not sales icons. When I say doing enough I mean doing enough to achieve our goals, doing enough to become a sales icon, doing enough to set records in our business.

Goal setting and using the 'How', 'What', 'Why' should be instrumental in your motivation. I can remember back in my early career when I set goals I always seemed to be missing something. I'd set a business goal for myself like become number one salesperson or something more materialistic like own an Audi R8. Whilst it was great to have goals (which differentiated me from the masses) they didn't hold as much power to them as 'How', 'What', 'Why' goal setting. The reason being is that 'How', 'What', 'Why' goal setting covers all motivational factors, the 'How' covers my activity, the things that are the micro parts to achieving my wider goals. The 'What' covers my business goals, those things that hold esteem in my field which I hope to achieve one day. Then the 'Why' covers those things that are personal to me, those things that my heart desires that one day I'll look back on with absolute pride in my achievement. With 'How', 'What', 'Why' goal setting no stone is left unturned when it comes to motivation as you have the driving force of motivation for your activity, business and personal goals.

To help you in your pursuit to achieve your goals try using pyramid goal setting to break up your goals into achievable milestones with deadlines attached to those milestones. Use this in conjunction with a scrapbook or regular repetition of writing down your goals and watch what happens. What you'll find is that before long you'll have to redo all your goal setting as you've already met those which you originally set. Remember that you're 42% more likely to achieve a goal if it's written down, 42%!

Myself, I've got to a stage where I'm looking for improvements of 0.5% or 1% with things that I adopt. If someone came to me and said X will increase your chances by 42% then I'd be biting their hand off for X. So please take it on board, if you're only going to do one thing in this chapter then make it writing down your goals.

Finally, we ventured into forecasting and pipeline. In my view, it's integral to understand the difference between the two, get them mixed up and you're in a sticky situation. You could argue the point as to why this is included in the chapter on motivation. Well for me your pipeline and forecast are massive motivational areas. Either they'll give you a kick up the arse because you haven't got enough in there. Or they'll tell you what a great job you're doing and to keep up the hard work.

Key Takeaways – Discipline Five – Motivation

- Recording Our Wins
  - Note down all of our activity
  - This will help to give an indication of day to day wins, our work rate and areas we could improve upon
- Goal Setting

  There are three main categories for our goals, those are:
  - The 'How' – activity goals
  - The 'What' – top line business goals
  - The 'Why' – personal goals
- The How

  These are your activity goals, for instance
  - To make 100 calls today
  - To develop 5 quotes over £50k this week

  ➢ Decision Maker
  - Getting through to a decision maker should be considered a win

  ➢ SQL
  - Stands for sales qualified lead
  - A SQL would be a future opportunity that you've qualified but the time scale is further afield

  ➢ MQL
  - Stands for marketing qualified lead
  - A MQL is a less qualified lead than a SQL, but is still warm and worth pursuing at the due time
- The What

  These are your top line business goals such as
  - To sell X GP this year
  - To be the number one salesperson within two years
- The Why

  These are your personal goals such as
  - To own a 30-foot yacht in the next three years
  - To buy my girlfriend a £10k engagement ring by next year
  - Remember R.U. Darby – what if I'm three feet from gold?

  ➢ The Power of Your Subconscious
  - Use regular repetition of writing your goals down
  - Try putting together a visual scrapbook for your goals

  ➢ Tying Your Goal Together

- Use pyramid goal setting to break a goal into achievable steps
- Set milestones and timescales to meet

➢ Forecasting and Pipeline

- Forecasting is predicting when you expect opportunities will fall in time and the amount they will be worth
- Pipeline is a complete list of all active opportunities you have
- Try the percentage value forecast or the likelihood forecast
- Develop a closing calculator to aid you in
    - Closing sales
    - Prioritising opportunities over one another
    - Identifying what more you can do to turn an opportunity into a sale

Discipline 6 – Success Formula

If you can't tell by now, I work in a very logical and analytical manner, which personally I feel has helped me immensely in sales. Now I'm a firm believer that with more or less anything in life there are success formulas. Those little secrets that people hide or keep close to their chest which are responsible for their success. In this section, I'm going to unlock the drawer to all of them things that equate to the success formula for selling. Some are simple, some are not, some you'll have heard of already, some you won't have. These are the gems that when applied will turn you into a sales icon, so let's begin…

6.1 – Forward Appointments

So far we've talked in depth about the numbers game of sales and statistics to ensure your success. The things like reverse-funnel planning which will give you an estimate of sales success based on activity, and looking at your average closing rates etc.

What holds true in sales no matter what you're selling is the fact that:

'The more people we meet, the more successful we will be!'

Just think about it, my closing statistics will be more or less always the same, let's take an example. If I have a closing rate of 30% of a pipeline of £100k, if I change my focus on improving my closing rate then at maximum I can probably grow this to 50%. In this example I would close £50k in comparison to £30k, so my focus has reaped a £20k additional reward.

Whereas if we change our focus to getting more in the pipeline juxtaposed to focusing on improving our closing rate we could most probably double our pipeline or more. Let's use this example again yet in this case my closing rate is 30% and my pipeline is £200k. For this I would close £60k business, reaping an extra £30k reward.

This of course isn't an exact science, but a more proficient strategy is to focus on increasing our pipeline as much as we can. The secret to dramatically increasing your pipeline is forward appointments.

What are forward appointments?

Forward appointments for those not in the know are appointments booked in your diary in the future. So if you have three customer meetings booked in the diary for each of the next three weeks then you have a total of nine forward appointments.

Why forward appoint?

The key reasons to forward appoint are as follows:

- Interaction steps
- Relationships
- Competition
- Account maximisation

Interaction Steps – You've probably heard before that on average it takes seven separate interactions with a prospect before they have enough confidence to buy something from you. Seven! If that's the case then we cannot afford to simply meet with a person once, we need as many interaction steps as possible. We also know that face-to-face meetings are one of the most powerful forms of interaction that we have as it's more personable and the majority of the time we get more airtime with a buyer. Take your competition, now irrespective of product if you've met with a prospect four times and had three phone calls compared to your competition who's met with them once and had six phone calls it's clear and easy. I could state with almost full certainty that your prospect will be more compelled by your offering and they will understand it in far more depth than that of your competitor. Thus the more appointments we can have with a buyer as our interaction steps the more likely we are to become a sales icon.

Relationships – Even the most charming person in the world cannot develop a strong relationship with somebody after simply one meeting. Therefore in order to develop a strong and fruitful relationship we must meet with people regularly. People buy from people, it has and always will be the case! You want to get to the stage where you have such a strong relationship that your customers come to you first, they ask for your expert advice and when they need something that you can offer that you're the first name that pops into their mind.

Competition – I like to think of relationships as brick walls, every meeting I have with a prospect or customer adds a layer of bricks to my brick wall. My first meeting starts with one layer and every additional meeting adds onto that wall one by one. Now when my relationship is in its infancy with the prospect or customer, my wall will be small and weak so much so that a competitor could jump over the wall or even knock it down. However, with every meeting comes a new layer of bricks, the wall grows taller and stronger until it's impenetrable from any competition. This is the honest truth, the more meetings you have with a prospect or customer the stronger your relationship will be. You'll get to the stage where they stop thinking of you as that person from X company that sells their products and you'll become Karen or John who they love meeting with regularly.

Account Maximisation – I'm yet to work for or with a business that doesn't have a number of offerings. The more offerings that you have the more complexity involved in a sale. Now for ease let's say that you have ten main offerings and your customer has bought one of them, what about the other nine? The stumbling block is that your customer meets with you and your competitors, for simplicity let's say there are five competitors all with ten offerings too. Already we have fifty offerings that are bamboozling the customer. To add another curve ball what about the suppliers in the other business areas they look after, there are probably a few hundred more. Basically it's a minefield for customers, they're going to struggle to understand everything there is to know about your offerings. That is unless you maximise your contact time with a customer, and a great way is through forward appointments. The more contact time you have with a customer, the better they will understand the complete range of your offerings and the better chance you have of selling more to them.

How I Learnt This Lesson of Forward Appointments

Earlier on in my career I was working in IT, I had become disillusioned with the business I was working for, so I applied elsewhere for other positions. The managing director of this other firm contacted me, so I agreed to come in and have a coffee with him for a conversation. They were a company I already held in high regard, they had a brilliant brand in the market, loyal customers and treated their staff incredibly well. More importantly for me was that both the managing directors there were visionaries and well-established salesmen who had started the business some twenty years prior. From the forefront I could tell that I had a lot I could learn from them both.

It was in this interview where I first heard the concept of forward appointments. It was one of their key performance indicators for their sales staff. I had somewhat of an epiphany in this interview, it all made sense, in the past I had focused on activity such as phone calls or opportunities in my pipeline, but never before had I looked at forward appointments as a focal point. It was a revelation, I realised how simple it was, the more forward appointments I have the more people I see and the more business I close, simple. As I discussed things further with the managing director, he told me that their KPI was to have twenty forward appointments booked in your diary at any one time. Now at this point in my career I thought that twenty forward appointments were absurd. I had never achieved that up until now. In my head he might as well have said one hundred as I had no clue how twenty could be achieved. Nonetheless, I took the job and started to think about how I could achieve this.

Low and behold, I achieved my twenty after a few weeks and continued at this rate and hitting that KPI. It was at this point that my managing director set a challenge for me and a few of my peers who were relatively new at this. The challenge was that we had one month to set forty forward appointments, something nobody had ever managed in the business. He said that if we wanted to be earning six-figure salaries then that was the number of meetings we needed to have in our diaries.

Now my first response to this was that it's madness; it wasn't long ago that I thought twenty meetings were unachievable. I honestly thought that I had no chance. I was in a poor mental state and I knew that if I wasn't careful this would become a self-fulfilling prophecy and I would never achieve the goal. It was then that I thought of one of my favourite quotes of all time as below:

'If you think you can, or think you can't, you're right!' – Henry Ford[28]

I absolutely love this quote and try my best to live by it. It's all psychology which is why I love it, if you think you're going to fail at something then chances are you will, but if you think you're going to succeed at something then you'll find a way. So in my moment of stupor I reflected on the quote and decided that I would live up to the challenge, book forty forward appointments and be the first person to do so in the history of my company. It was at this point I asked myself the question 'how am I going to book forty appointments?' This got the creative juices flowing and helped me put together three strategies which were:

- Strategy one – low hanging fruit
- Strategy two – forward appoint
- Strategy three – cross selling

Strategy one – low hanging fruit

The first thing I started with was low hanging fruit. I thought that to boost my confidence if I first focused on booking the easy meetings then I'd be motivated from the outset, and the challenge wouldn't look so daunting. So I began by putting a list together, this list consisted of all of the people who I thought I could easily book an appointment with. This might be because they were already a customer, or I had met with them in the past, or I previously had qualified conversations with them. Whatever the reason was I created a list, this would be my low hanging fruit list. From undertaking this I found that I had thirty-six potentials on my list, this made me feel a thousand times more confident. Though to be realistic I thought that chances are I'll only book eighty percent of these meetings, this gave me around twenty-nine meetings, a deficit of eleven, very doable in my opinion.

Strategy two – forward appoint

This is something I will talk about in greater depth shortly; this technique was incredibly effective. In the past I had been having qualified meetings and then my follow up would have usually been to call them in a few weeks or months to book another meeting. I decided to scrap this approach wherever possible, and instead make this part of my meeting process. In every meeting I would assertively request another meeting and agree dates and times there and then in the meeting. Take note of the word assertive as this part is key. The result was that the majority of the time I would successfully forward appoint in the meeting there and then. So for all of the meetings I had already booked within that month I focused on forward appointing with them. Consequentially from this approach I become much closer to my goal of forty forward appointments.

Strategy three – cross selling

One mistake I had been making up until this point was limiting my options. The business that I worked for had a number of other offerings too that colleagues looked after and specialised in. Up until this point my approach would have been rather blinkered. I would solely focus on my area and offerings I could sell to customers. Whereas to obtain my extra forward appointments I looked to cross selling. So at this time I sold IT solutions, my other divisions included software licensing, cloud, telecoms, cabling and furniture. When I would speak to a prospect on the phone, if they closed the door on IT solutions I'd simply ask about the other areas such as how's your telephony solution? Or have you got any building projects planned in the future? The result of this was substantial, not only did I find other opportunities for cross selling, but I'd book meetings for colleagues which I'd attend also, then after all of that I would end up identifying IT solution opportunities just from getting a face to face meeting with them and telling them more about how we can help.

These were the three core strategies I used, combined with some ferocious prospecting from cold calling to door knocking and networking. So at the end of the month I and my colleagues who were set the challenge had a meeting to review our progress. We went around the room one by one as my managing director asked us how we did. One colleague replied six meetings, another replied twelve and so on and so forth. Then he turned to me and asked me the question, and in sheer jubilation I spoke the words forty-four. Forty-four, I had gone from thinking that twenty meetings was an extortionate goal, to achieving and surpassing a goal of forty meetings by ten percent.

This was a massive achievement in my career, not only had I surprised myself but I had set a record in that business that hadn't been achieved in twenty-two years. Though the true lesson here was in the aftermath. It was those forty meetings that lead to a substantial amount of sales and commission which paved my way to a successful future in sales. The true lesson is that sales is all in the activity – the more prospects I meet with the more opportunities I will have and the more business that will close. All in all, activity is what creates a sales icon.

How to forward-appoint?

We've given you my story as to how I discovered the importance of forward appointments. The vital question to ask is how do we forward appoint?

Forward-appoint at meetings – this is one of the best times to forward appoint, as when you're face to face with a customer or prospect it's harder for them to say no, whereas over the phone it's easy for them to refuse. Whether you forward appoint from the outset of a meeting with someone or at the end, make sure that you do at least. One distinctive reason why is to save you time, as time is one of our sales icon disciplines. Let's say that I have twenty meetings booked in my diary, I attend all of these meetings and instead of forward appointing with the customer in that meeting I choose to call them at a later date to reappoint. Now that's twenty calls that I have to make, all that will take around five minutes of admin, that's a total of one hundred minutes of time wasted just in reappointing previous meetings, and that's on the grounds that I get through to the person on the first phone call. If we extrapolate this over a whole year, it becomes rather scary; for instance if we had two hundred meetings in a year, that's at least one thousand minutes, almost seventeen hours spent just reappointing those meetings. Time that could be spent on other selling activities to make us more money.

Be assertive – get rid of the term 'or' as soon as you can! Feeling slightly bemused by this? Let me put it into context. 'Do you want me to place this order for you now or shall I leave it till when we speak in two weeks?' 'Shall we book our next meeting now or shall we leave it a while?' Sound familiar? Well we've all fallen into that trap. We're overly conscious about being too controlling that we give customers and easy out option, and most of the time they'll take it. So be assertive, get rid of giving the customer next step options and state your authority. I used to at the end of each meeting say something like this 'it would be really great if we could get another meeting in the diary, what do you think?' The most common response was 'yea, give me a call in a few months and we'll book something in.' Not the outcome I wanted. So in light of this I changed things, converse with asking in an open and overly polite manner I became assertive and phrased my question in a more authoritative way, such as something like the following 'it's best that we get another meeting in the diary, when works for you the week commencing X?'

Sell the benefit – why should they meet with you again? Time is valuable to everyone so why should they invest more of their time in you? You need to sell the benefit, be assertive and state with clarity the benefit to meeting with you again. Benefits I've pushed include:

- Because by that time X will be higher on your priority list
- I'll make sure that I present some innovation in the market that you might be unaware of
- I'll bring one of my colleagues to introduce to you who specialises in X
- Because it's integral that we develop a strong relationship so that we can work in partnership with you

Test what works for you and make sure to use it.

Agree to lengthy timescales if need be – how many times are you told by a prospect or customer that they're too busy at the moment or next month to meet with you? Most of the time our response is that we'll get back in touch when things quiet down, maybe in two months' time. Instead of that approach try to book in a meeting further afield, ask them if this month is too busy then how about the next? No, okay how about the month after that? For some strange reason people are more receptive to meetings being booked further away, so try it. My diary now commonly will have scheduled meetings that aren't until three, six or nine months away.

How to gain the motivation to forward appoint?

I'm under no disillusions, booking meetings is a difficult task. But who said becoming a sales icon would be easy anyway. The easy road is to just look after your accounts, or maybe be fed leads by your telemarketing team. Honestly though, that's not going to be enough to earn the commissions you dream of and live the lifestyle you long for.

In light of this I recommend a practice which helped me and in more ways than one. This practice gave me the motivation to keep picking up that phone as well as forward appointing with decision makers that I was meeting with. The best thing about it all is that it's so simple, all you have to do is work out your billables.

Now if you've ever worked with a solicitor or maybe even an accountant they'll have billables for their time, commonly in fifteen-minute increments. Now before you get carried away I'm not saying that you should charge customers for the pleasure of your time to sell to them; that would be madness. What I mean is to work out your billables on a meeting-by-meeting basis.

Let me use a simple example, if I made £100,000 sales in a year I could quite easily work out my billables for meetings. In this example let's say that I had two hundred and forty meetings in that year. From this I could work out what each meeting equates to in relation to my sales, in this case:

£100,000 / 240 = £417

I don't know about you but when I worked this out for myself it was incredible. The motivation it gave me was fantastic; every time I booked a meeting or attended a meeting I would think Cha-Ching just cashed X. The great thing is that it uses the law of averages too. So going back to that last example, out of them two hundred and forty meetings, most of them probably didn't make a sale but some of them did. Therefore, if you can just focus on being motivated to book more meetings then your sales figures will naturally increase. Again let's look at my example from before, what if I had pushed myself a bit harder and booked twenty more meetings. Well the outcome would be:

20 X £417 = £8,340

That's eight thousand pounds more sales with only the adjustment of booking more meetings, why wouldn't you book more?

I don't have meetings!

But what if you don't have meetings, what if you sit in an internal sales role, how can you gain the motivation to pick up that phone? I know this section and a good part of this book is based around booking meetings, but the concept is the exact same you just need to alter the output. So instead of focusing on booking meetings, how about focusing on quotes? What are my billables for quotes? Or maybe focus on booking conference calls, pre-planned and scheduled conference calls. The medium is not of concern, what's important is the end result of sales and having the motivation to be persistent and motivated through thick and thin.

Increasing your billables:

I take on board the point about time here, there are only so many meetings you can attend in the time constraints that you have. If you're already attending forty plus meetings a month and you can't see how you can squeeze in any more than a strategy of going to more meetings isn't reasonable. In this circumstance when you're at your maximum capacity of meetings you can attend, then there is only one thing you can do, and that's to increase your billables.

Strategies for increasing your billables:

- Sales analysis – sweet spot
- Gap analysis – account maximisation
- Cut away deadwood

Sales analysis – the first strategy is to look at your sales analysis. Are we working within our sweet spot? If we're not then adapt our approach and cut away those we are prospecting who are outside of our sweet spot. If you're under massive constraints of time and you can't fit any more prospecting in then those who sit outside your sweet spot will have to go. Take vertical for instance, if you're meeting with and avidly prospecting education but that vertical isn't in your sweet spot then cut them loose. You should only work outside your sweet spot if:

A. You have the time to, i.e. your workload isn't jam-packed.

B. If the prospect is an exception such as they represent a substantial opportunity for you.

So take some time to review your approach with your sweet spot analysis that you conducted before. If you need to free up time then scrap those which sit outside your sweet spot.

Gap Analysis – we talked about this previously in account maximisation in identifying what are the offerings which we do and do not sell to our account base. Those offerings we don't sell are a massive opportunity, we've already highlighted that it's easier to sell to existing customers than it is to focus on net new business. Thus a sure-fire way to increase your billables is to sell more of your offerings to your customer base, the old upselling.

Cut away deadwood – the final approach is to cut away the deadwood. We all have deadwood in our prospect lists, you know the prospects I mean. They sit within your sweet spot, on paper they may seem perfect. You could have even met with them multiple times and used various transitioners, yet sales have been minimal if at all. These are the ones that you may need to cut away as deadwood as chances are that they'll waste more time than they're worth. I use my billables as a good indicator of this, how much time have I invested in them? What have they bought from me? If this is substantially disproportionate from the rest of my customer base then I know to cut this prospect or customer away as deadwood and focus my time elsewhere.

There are other strategies for increasing your billables of course. But these are the three that we have found to be most effective.

Activity

A valuable activity is to review your historic billables. Look at your old sales figures over the last few years and work out your billables whether that be for meetings or other mediums. How have your billables changed? A really important question to ask, but an even more important question to ask yourself is why have your billables changed? If you can pinpoint the reasons as to why then you've found your success formula.

6.2 – Initial Meeting Goals

When I began my career in sales my expectations from an initial meeting with a prospect were unrealistic. I made the mistake that most salespeople make, which is usually one of, or a combination of the following:

- Expecting a sale
- Overly fact finding
- Pushing my company or offering

Now there is a fine balancing in selling, and don't get this misconstrued as all of these points highlighted above are important at any stage of the sales process. However, in your initial meeting with a prospect you need to be wary as to how much focus is on each of these aspects. Let me explain the mistakes I and many others also make.

Expecting a sale

Being the young and ambitious man I was when I started in sales, I often expected a one meeting one sale turnaround. It was just part of my nature, I set high expectations of myself and thought it could be achieved. Now undoubtedly I have accomplished this in my time (though it has been rare), but it's a mistake that I had to learn from quickly. In some industries this may not apply as a one meeting sale might be the norm; however, for most a one-meeting sale is out of the question. If you focus on making a sale the first time you meet with a prospect then the chances are some of the following may happen:

- You'll be too pushy
- You may offer the wrong solution (causing a detrimental effect to the longevity of the customer relationship)
- You may miss the big picture i.e. focus on the small short-term sale instead of the long term large sale
- You may miss vital information on the customer
- You may miss the chance to build rapport
- The customer might be disillusioned with you and never want to meet with you again

There are a whole host of other drawbacks to such an approach. Moreover, this is just from a customer perspective, what does this do to your motivation, if you expect a sale after each initial meeting then you're going to become demotivated pretty darn quick when most of the time it doesn't happen.

Overly fact-finding – the other mistake I made, and the majority of salespeople do too is to focus too much on fact-finding. We get so bogged down with trying to find out as much information as we can that we miss the big picture. What's this setup, how many of them do you have, how many did you grow by last year etc. Let's face it, the thing that matters is the sale; if I had the choice between:

- Finding out all of the facts and information and building little rapport
- Compared with building rapport and finding out few facts

Then I would always choose the latter. The long game is the sale; now if I focus on rapport, chances are that the prospect and I will build up a relationship and they'll agree to meet with me again. If so I can find out more facts later. The ideal scenario is that we build rapport and find out all the facts, but time is limited, so always prioritise rapport over fact-finding. If this is your approach you will find out all the facts you'll need but it will take longer, although your chances of the sale will be greater as you've focused on the relationship with the prospect.

Pushing my company or offering – this is a very easy mistake to make. I can't tell you the right amount of time to spend pushing your company or offering but as always there is a balance. In any initial meeting, we need to be cautious not to bamboozle the prospect, provide them with enough insight to intrigue them but do not spend the majority of your meeting pushing your company and offering.

So we've spoken about what not to do in our initial meeting, but how about our goal for an initial meeting, what should that be? For me it's simple, I want one thing and one thing only as my goal from my initial meeting and that's a reappointment.

Reappointment

It's simple, all I want from that first meeting with a prospect is to come and meet with them again, irrespective of whether they are a small prospect or large. The only variant that may change is the timescale. Take a small prospect for example, it may not be worth reappointing with them in the short term, but in three months it may make sense. Or you may uncover from the meeting that irrespective of size their buying cycle won't begin for nine months so you reappoint for six months. If you focus your goal on reappointing with a prospect in an initial meeting then you're on the road to becoming a sales icon.

Keys to reappointing

The key focus points in order to reappoint will be the following

- Rapport
- Invoke interest

Rapport

If you would win a man to your cause, first convince him that you are his sincere friend. – Abraham Lincoln[29]

If I like you and have got on with you then irrespective of products and solutions I will give you the time of day again and would be happy to meet with you again. We've always got time for our friends; however, we haven't always got time for salespeople. So focus almost completely on building rapport – a relationship will win you not only one deal but a lifetime of deals if you do it right. Whereas if you've come to me with the most interesting proposition ever, yet you're rude, self-involved and not a person I want to converse with then this will be the last conversation that we ever have.

Invoke interest

Most of the time if you get on with the person that you're meeting then there's a high chance that they'll agree to meet with you again. To aid your chances, if you can build rapport in conjunction with invoking interest then it's incredibly likely that you'll successfully reappoint. The key to invoking interest is their pain and pleasure point, find out what these are as we discussed earlier and very briefly tell them how you can help them prevent that pain or achieve that pleasure. Remember no war and peace though, be succinct, you only need to invoke interest enough for them to see you again. The key is the pain or pleasure points, just generic features benefits won't always work as they don't carry as much emotional weight with the prospect.

When I have trained people on the sales icon disciplines this is one point they've struggled with. They question why we should only invoke interest instead of telling them as much about the solution as possible to get them to buy. Well the answer to this is simple, longevity and partnerships. We're not looking for the quick sale, our goal is another meeting. As from obtaining that additional meeting we gain more airtime, build more rapport, find out more about the prospect, open up more opportunities and break down reservations. Like a poker player, keep your cards close to your chest, give enough information to invoke interest, just enough to reappoint.

Examples of Invoking Interest

Let's show you some examples of invoking interest.

Example 1

Pain – I met with a prospect and one of their pain points is that their workload is so intensive at the moment that they're having to work overtime every night.

Invoke interest – 'you mentioned about having to work overtime every night with how intensive your workload is. I think it's best that we get another appointment in the diary for three weeks' time to delve into this in greater depth. The reason being is that I have a number of customers who were in the same situation, we implemented some schemes to help reduce their workload and now overtime is a thing of the past. I think to do it justice we need another meeting for me to present what these schemes are and how they would look like for your business, when's best for you the week commencing…?'

See how simplistic that is? I haven't even mentioned the schemes, but it will interest him. The reason, well that's because it's a major pain of the prospects. If they have a chance to get rid of that pain simply from another meeting then they'll be asking where to sign.

Example 2

Pain – in this meeting their pain point is that their current supplier lacks the professional resource to be able to help them in times of urgency.

Invoke interest – 'it's not the first time that a prospective customer has highlighted to me that their current supplier lacks professional resource. What I think would be best is for me to arrange a head office meeting for you, this way you can meet the team and see first-hand the level of professional resource that we have, then you can determine for yourself how we could sufficiently cope with requests in a timely manner. What would be the ideal date to arrange a head office visit for you?'

Example 3

Pleasure – in this meeting the customer wants a certain feature of a software product so that they can start to monitor their sales team's activity to increase sales.

Invoke interest – 'I'm glad you're interested in that feature you mentioned, but what you should be aware of is that there are a host of other features to enable seamless monitoring too. I believe that an ample next step would be for me to bring our technical consultant in to provide a live demo for you. In this you can have a deep dive into the feature set and answer any in-depth questions you might have. When is a good time to arrange this for?'

Activity

Spend some time brainstorming a couple of statements that will invoke interest. It may be a good exercise to look over some meeting notes from a previous initial meeting and explore what statements you could have used to invoke interest. If you want to test them out then try using them in a phone call. Call that prospect who you met two months ago, invoke interest from one of their pain or pleasure points and book that next meeting.

6.3 – Exercising Core Sales Icon Stages

Imagine for a minute that you're an arable farmer, you have a small area of land which you wish to grow crops on to make money and feed your family. Your end goal as a farmer is to sell your crop and to make money, but you know that in order to do this there are a number of stages beforehand that you must undertake.

The farming stages would roughly be something as follows:

- Sew your seed
- Nurture your land
- Harvest your crops
- Sell your crops
- Start again

The actions of each stage determine the outcome, fail to sew your seed and no crop can be sold, fail to sew enough seed and less crop can be sold. Fail to nurture your crop and the crop will die and nothing can be sold etc. Again, the actions of each stage determine the outcome.

'My actions now, determine my outcome later.'

But what does this have to do with selling and becoming a sales icon? Well alike farming, sales too has stages just the same and the correlation between them is the same too. We get out what we put in at each stage, we can't expect an outcome that doesn't relate to what we put in at the earlier stages.

Core SI stages

Most salespeople group selling into three stages, those being:

- Prospecting
- Selling
- Account management

Prospecting – this encompasses all of those new business-prospecting actions, from emailing prospects, to cold calling to new business meetings.

Selling – this consists of all selling activities, for new business this is usually for prospects who you've met with more than once and are proposing some form of solution. Selling activities to accounts could be included in this group also.

Account management – this comprises of all the activities focused on keeping clients happy.

In sales icon training we like to add one more stage, that being profiling. Profiling comes before prospecting, we have talked about this briefly before. Profiling in essence is any activity to determine whether a business is of the sufficient calibre to be worthy of prospecting. This could be activities such as finding businesses of the right size, turnover, location etc.

So to clarify, the core SI stages are:

1. Profiling
2. Prospecting
3. Selling
4. Account management

Allocating time for these core SI stages:

Now whether you're a seasoned veteran of sales or a newbie, you'll always have to spend some time in each SI stage. I'm yet to meet a business that doesn't want even their best salespeople to get some new business sales regularly. Now the time weighting you give to each stage depends completely on where you are in your sales career, your account base, your industry trends etc.

Say for instance that you're a seasoned sales veteran with lots of accounts to look after. In this case you wouldn't want to spend most of your time profiling and prospecting, most of your time would be for account management. Though I'll reflect, my actions now determine my outcome later. Even as a veteran, if I fail to profile and prospect, then I'll fail with new business too. No matter where you are in your career you must religiously set aside some time for profiling and prospecting, if not you'll stay the exact same. And guess what, chances are you'll lose an account for an unforeseen reason you couldn't control. Something like the business went bust or was bought by another business and now they don't need your services. When this happens you'll be in a world of pain as you haven't put in the new business groundwork to fill that gap, so you've got a large sales void to deal with.

Taking it to the other extreme, let's look at someone who is new to sales. Well this person will have few, if any accounts, so their focus should predominantly be on the profiling and prospecting stages. A word of caution here is start in this way, but as you pick up steam and become more successful you'll have to alter where you allocate your time. The thing is the more profiling and prospecting you do, means the more selling and consequentially more account management you do also as you become more successful. Just be mindful to change your allocation as you become more successful, but don't ever neglect a stage, otherwise complacency will set in.

That's as much depth as I need to go into for the core sales icon stages. Just remember to always exercise every stage, no matter where you are in your sales career.

6.4 – Questions and Pitching

Questioning is often said to be the art of the sale, which I agree with completely. Quality questioning is the difference between being average and being a sales icon. Now there are a million and one sales books which revolve around questioning and I believe them to be exceptional. Thus I'm not going to go into masses of detail here, but I will talk through a few core concepts on questioning.

The aspects I'm going to address are

- Questioning about what's important
- Pain and pleasure questioning
- Questioning in a logical and sequential manner
- Benefit buffer
- Leading questioning
- Pitching

Questioning About What's Important

This is sales 101, first and foremost find out what's important to them, know your audience. This applies later to the pitching section but unless we know what's important to the person we're in front of we're going to fail. Plus guess what, it's different for everyone. If a business fails to understand what their audience wants then they fail, and there are countless examples of this.

Take a favourite place of mine that I often frequent, Starbucks. They've had a business model that they've rolled out to thousands of coffee shops, globally. More or less their model has been replicated everywhere, being uniform irrespective of the coffee shop and where it lies in the world. But this approach didn't work in Australia though, here Starbucks failed miserably! They tried to compete with the coffee giants in Australia the likes of Gloria Jeans who occupy 450+ branches and coffee club who operate 350+ outlets. Why did they fail? Well it wasn't because they entered the market half-heartedly, from their inception in Australia in 2000 to 2002 they opened near to 100 stores. They failed so badly that they racked up losses of $143m and had to make over 700 staff redundant. The reason for their failure was that they didn't know their audience here, they didn't cater to this individual market, and thus the market didn't adopt the chain.

Let's use another example, this time of a business that understood their market originally, then the market changed, and they failed to adapt. Take Kodak, they were the world's largest film company spanning over 130 years. In the days of camera film, they dominated, being the largest known brand and boasting financials to suit their dominance in the market. They at one point had almost a complete monopoly, in 1976 they were responsible for selling 90% of photographic film in the US. But come the digital age they failed to adapt. Instead of adopting and investing in the digital camera sector they vied for an alternate option. Their view was that if they went down this route that it would damage the all-important film part of their business, thus they attempted to steer the market away from digital cameras. The result? Well we all know the rest of the story, Kodak missed the point of what's important to the customer. The industry hence adopted the digital camera and Kodak filed for bankruptcy in 2012.

The point I'm making here is that finding out what's important to the prospect is essential, so focus your questioning on finding this out. Don't be like Starbucks entering Australia, start by finding out what's going to interest that prospect as an individual and cater for it. The Kodak example is important too as it highlights that the world changes and so should you. You may have a customer that values one thing for a couple of years then radically changes what they value at a later point in time. So always focus first on questioning about what's important to them, if you fail to do so then you won't make the sale.

Pain and Pleasure Questioning

In chapter four on preparation we talked in depth about the power of pain and pleasure selling and how human actions are influenced by either escaping pain or gaining pleasure. So focus your questioning in this way too. The vast majority of your questioning should be around pain and pleasure, uncover as much pain and pleasure as you can. Once you've unearthed this you can then start to demonstrate how you can get rid of their pain and push them into a state of pleasure. Then guess what, you make the sale. So when you're questioning, focus most of your time and efforts on uncovering as much pain and pleasure as you can.

Questioning in a Logical and Sequential Manner

I almost left this part out of the book, but actually it's such a common mistake that people make, so let me explain more. Let's start with logical manner, well if something is logical then it makes sense. So when I say question in a logical manner I mean the structure of your questioning makes sense, it has a logical flow. We don't want to be reverting from one thing to another then back to the first thing. An easy way to question in a logical manner is to highlight a brief agenda with a customer, something like, "John,

I want to venture into three key areas today, those being some background on your operations, your strategy and then your challenges. If we start first with your operations tell me about X?" So to question logically focus on a subject say their business, find out all you need to know, then move on to the next subject.

Sequential questioning is the next part. So to explain this let's use an example, let's say we've just met and all we've said is hello. If my next set of questions are 'what's your address?' 'What wage do you take home?' 'How much debt are you in?' Well the likelihood is that you're going to tell me to piss off and that'll be the end of our conversation. The reason is that I've jumped straight into incredibly personal questions from the outset, there's been zero build-up of trust. I've used no sequential questioning. So what is sequential questioning? Well think about the term sequence, a sequence is a particular order in which related things follow each other. Take the alphabet, this follows a sequential order, ABCD. If I was to recite the alphabet as DABC then it's not following its sequential order.

Sequential questioning is questioning in an order that follows on from the previous question. Like any sequence, you can't just jump to the end too soon. I need to start and follow through the sequence. Sequential questioning starts with the low level, low trust questions. As time passes you build up more rapport and trust and then your questioning can move up the sequential order. Thus you can ask things and get answers to questions that initially you couldn't ask. For instance, take the wage question I used before, a financial advisor for instance may desperately need to know the answer to this question. If they ask it from the outset the chances are they'll get shown the door. But if they use sequential questioning and build up to this question then they're more likely to find out the information that they desire.

The pattern of questioning could resemble something like the following?

- How's business?
- What type of work do you do?
- How long have you been doing this?
- What does your daily work consist of?
- What do you love about the role?
- What personal goals have you set for the next few years?
- What financial goals have you set for the next few years?
- What does your investment portfolio makeup of?
- What do you take home as a wage per annum?

This is but an example of a sequential questioning pattern. What you should notice is that as we move down the list the questions are of a more sensitive nature. These are the questions you can't ask from the outset and need to build up to through using sequential questioning.

Use the Benefit Buffer

A tip with questioning is to use a benefit buffer. Asking questions on topics that are sensitive, personal or taboo are never easy if you just come out with them bluntly, so use a benefit buffer just before those questions. A benefit buffer is your brief sales pitch for why you want the answer to the next question. Take the wage question again and let's say I'm a financial advisor. I wouldn't just be so blatant to say what wage do you take home per annum. I'd use a benefit buffer and say something like this:

'Now John, I'm about to ask you a personal question. By no means do you need to answer it if you don't feel comfortable but believe me this information will stay between us and has a valuable purpose. The purpose is that it will give me an indication of what level of risk would be palatable for you in the future and what lucrative investments would be worth your while. So John, if you wouldn't mind sharing with me in confidence, what wage do you take home per annum?'

The benefit buffer can be used for any question. Need to find out someone's budget? Well ask the question with a benefit buffer. 'John I don't want to propose a solution that's all singing and dancing but stupidly outside of your budget. So to ensure I provide a solution that's the right fit but at the right price, how much budget had you set aside for this project?'

Use the benefit buffer in conjunction with sequential questioning and you'll obtain answers to questions that before you would have never even imagined asking.

Leading Questioning

Begin with the end in mind is habit two of Steven Covey's Seven Habits of Highly Effective People. It applies just the same to questioning, but it's important to ask yourself what's our end goal from our questioning? Well really our end goal is to make a sale, and our questioning is going to help us get there. Ideally we want to focus our questions around the business, their drivers, their pain and pleasure, the commercials and qualification questions. These are just the standard questions though, what questions are going to help us make the sale? Those we denote as leading questions.

I see too many salespeople questioning for no gain, maybe in the hope that'll build rapport. They ask questions that are off topic or add no weight to their position in the future which realistically is just wasting both parties time. Instead we should be asking questions that help us make the sale. Leading questions are those which lead the prospect or customer down the path towards the sale. So what are leading questions? Well they are questions that revolve around your strengths; that could be yourself personally, your business or your offering.

We put together leading questions using a three-step process which is:

1. Strengths
2. Leading question
3. Strength statement

So first start with defining what your strengths are, then you can develop leading questions. As I said strengths could be yourself personally, what your skills are in and what that would mean for a customer. For instance if you've got 18 years' experience in a field then that's a massive strength. Business strengths can be a number of things, maybe that you've won awards, or that you have a certain sized team etc. An offerings strength are those of the offering in question, it could be statistics, or reference customers, customer satisfaction of that offering etc.

Once we are sure of our strengths then we can create leading questions that relate to that strength. For instance if your offering won an award, a leading question for this strength would be something like 'how important is it for you that you use a solution which is deemed best in class?' Or separately if you noticed a strength was that your business had a high level of resource in your team a leading question would be something like 'what value do you put on speed of response when you contact your current supplier?'

Then we move to the strength statement, this is a statement that you could use (and I emphasise the word could) subsequent to the prospect or customer answering your leading question. Note that you'd only ever use a strength statement if their answer is positive, if they answer negative towards your question then move on to another question or topic.

The point of leading questions is to find out where your strengths are going to apply most. You don't need to use a strength statement every time, you can keep some for a later occasion maybe in the proposal stage or for subsequent meetings. What we're trying to do is lead them down the path towards a sale by focusing on our strengths rather than our weaknesses. So if I'm a small business, instead of going down the route of asking questions down the lines of resource, I'll instead focus on leading questions of personal relationships, or agility etc.

Pitching

The mistake I see countless salespeople makes revolves around their pitch. Now there are hundreds of pitching methods you can use, I could literally write another book just based on pitching techniques. But in my honest opinion you can't go too wrong by just using one simple technique. There are two techniques I want to discuss briefly those are:

- Scatter gun pitching technique
- Sniper pitching technique

Scatter gun approach:

Now this is the mistake that I see the majority of salespeople make in their pitch, they use the scattergun approach. The approach consists of throwing literally everything you have at the prospect or customer in the hope that something will interest them. To explain it simply if I was selling a product that had ten features and a range of benefits I would straight away just blindly rattle them off.

Now I completely understand why salespeople use this approach, they have the best intentions at heart, they are so eager to win over the customer that they do all that they can. They think that quantity is better than quality. Now I'll put my hands up, I've been a culprit, and if you're honest you probably have too at some point in the past, if not still are. The trouble with this scattergun approach is that it's just verbal diarrhoea, and it causes the prospect or customer to switch off and not listen. This approach follows the mantra of talk first ask questions later, this is the complete opposite as to what we desire.

It's funny because as I write this I can recall an instance just two weeks ago. I was out on a sales appointment with a young man who was trying to sell telecoms. Now he had all the right attributes and intentions, but where he fell down was his pitching approach. As soon as he met the customer he started his pitch and spiel about how fantastic the platform is that he sells. I can recall him saying 'it's an amazing phone system, you can track all call data to see where you're losing calls, you can even leave marketing messages for when people are left on hold to improve your marketing message.' This is just a snapshot of his verbal diarrhoea, it went on for about ten minutes. I could see with every passing second the customer was getting more bored and agitated as his time was so valuable. It was at this point I wanted to pause time, take the young salesman away for a few seconds and say, 'calm down, find out what they care about and then focus your pitch to that.' What he needed to do was to use the sniper pitching technique.

Sniper pitching technique:

So what is the sniper pitching technique? Well I explain it simply like this, imagine we're at a rifle range. Our target sits a mile away, barely visible to the naked eye. The target represents our customer's interest; if we hit the target with a bullet we've managed to interest our customer. The more bullets we hit on the target the more interested our customer becomes, sounds easy.

Now I don't know about you but I'm not the best shot, especially not from a mile off. Now using the scattergun approach I could spray a few hundred shots off and I may get lucky with one, but realistically with that approach I have no hope. However, there's a secret at the rifle range in that every question I ask brings the target one hundred metres closer. So instead of trying to make a shot that I can never achieve I try and make my life easier, so I ask a question and witness the target move one hundred metres closer. Again I think to myself this shot is too hard I need it closer, so I ask question after question after question in a hope to bring my target as close as possible and increase my chances of hitting the target.

Now in this analogy the term taking the shot represents a pitch. My goal is to hit the target with a many shots (pitches) as I can to interest the customer, that is, without verging into verbal diarrhoea. For this I take my shots tactically, I ask questions, find out what may interest the customer, what's their pain, their pleasure etc. These questions help me to understand what shots will hit my target and invite some interest from my customer.

It really is simple. What I encourage is next time you're in front of a customer or prospect, picture this in your mind both before and during the meeting. Then with every question you ask imagine that target getting closer and closer and closer.

So let's make this clear and simple with an example. Let's imagine we're selling something we all use, in this case a pen. Now with any product or service you sell they'll be loads of key features you can push, but for this example to make it simple let's just imagine that the pen we're selling only has five key benefits, those being:

1) Ink lasts two times longer than the average pen
2) Cartridges are recyclable
3) It can be personalised with the initials of the owner
4) Leak-proof cartridge
5) Sleek executive design

Now if I was using the scattergun approach it would be something like this. 'Hi Mr Customer, I'm here to tell you about this fantastic pen. It's a pen like no other, gone are the days of getting through loads of pens as this pen lasts twice as long as your average pen. Not only that but you get a big green tick as the cartridges are recyclable, and it's completely leak-proof so no more mishaps with ink leaking. Sounds great doesn't it, but here's the best thing, it looks so cool, not only is the executive design really attractive but also you can personalise it with your initials. What do you think? I bet you like it!'

Now the chances are that the customer switched off and I won't be making a sale. Whereas the sniper approach is completely different. As I said we ask questions first, we find out what's important then we take our shot with a pitch. First and foremost though we ask the right questions and probe. I'm going to use an example for the sniper approach below, in this I'll only focus on just one feature, in reality I'd focus on them all.

I'd start with focusing on my first feature where the ink lasts twice as long as your average pen.

Me – "Hi Mr Customer, I'm here to talk to you about your stationary requirements. Now what I'm keen to find out is what's important to you by asking just a few questions. Before I start are you happy for me to ask a few questions?"

Mr Customer – "Go right ahead."

Me – "Brilliant thanks, so in regard to your stationary, how often do you and your team use a pen?"

Mr Customer – "We use a pen all day every day."

Me – "How many of you are there using pens every day?"

Mr Customer – "Around one hundred people."

Me – "Wow you must get through a lot of pens then, if you could take a guess how many pens do you get through as a business a year?"

Mr Customer – "It's got to be around ten pens per person so probably about one thousand a year minimum."

Me – "How valuable would it be if we could save you money here and reduce the number of pens you use?"

Mr Customer – "Incredibly valuable, budgets are being squeezed everyday so if I can free some up and reallocate it somewhere else I'd be very happy."

Get the gist? Now I could probe more here if I wanted to, it all depends on the feeling I get from the customer. I may want to find out more info or even uncover more pain or pleasure. It is at this point I ask questions about my next feature.

For instance if I moved onto to the feature that the cartridges are recyclable. I may open with a question such as:

Me – "How often do you recycle here?"

Mr Customer – "No we don't recycle at all, we don't see the point as it's just more hassle."

In this scenario the customer has closed off the avenue to this question. Thereby I know that pushing that the pen I'm selling has recyclable cartridges is going to go nowhere. Thus I cease this line of questioning and move onto to my next feature. I note that when I decide to pitch that I can leave out this feature.

The point of the sniper pitching technique is to drill down into what selling points are going to interest the prospect or customer. We drill down by asking questions and listening for their response, this helps us aim our pitch to the areas of most influence. So next time you're with a customer don't just aimlessly pitch with the scattergun approach. Use the sniper-pitching technique, ask questions, as many as you need to, then you can give a focused pitch.

6.5 – Compound Work Rate

If you've ever looked at investing before then you understand what compound interest is, for those of you that don't let me explain. Compound interest is what makes long-term investments so appealing, things like mutual funds, stocks and bonds. The theory works like this, whatever I invest reaps the reward of interest for every time period that I invest that sum. The longer the sum is invested the greater the return should be as year after year you'll have interest on top of the previous value plus interest, and that continues year after year.

Let me show you the power of compound interest. Let's imagine that we have two brothers. The first brother finds out about compound interest early, and thus starts his investment portfolio in 1991 investing £5k every year. The second brother is late to the party, he doesn't learn of compound interest until the fifteen years later, he then starts investing in 2016. Let's say for ease sake that both brothers invested till the year 2040, and both of them received an interest on their portfolio of 10% each year. But to even up the total investment say that the second brother in a bid to make up for lost time decided to invest double what the first brother was investing year on year. This would mean that after the year 2040 they have both invested quarter of a million pounds.

So let's take a guess at the outcome. You can probably already assume that the first brother will make more money than brother two, but how much more? Maybe a couple of thousand pounds? Let's face it that fifteen-year head start only accounted for seventy-five thousand pounds' investment anyway. Or maybe we're betting slightly higher, say a couple of hundred thousand pounds more.

Well you might be staggered by the result. Brother one after the year 2040 made over five million pounds more than brother two! In total he made over six million pounds, that's six times what brother two made. Have a look at the summarised tables of their portfolios performance over time below.

First Brother's Portfolio:

Year	Portfolio Value	Investment	Total after 10% Interest
1991	£0	£5,000	£5,500
1995	£25,526	£5,000	£33,578
2000	£74,687	£5,000	£87,656
2005	£153,862	£5,000	£174,749
2010	£281,375	£5,000	£315,012
2015	£486,735	£5,000	£540,909
2020	£817,470	£5,000	£904,717
2025	£1,350,122	£5,000	£1,490,634
2030	£2,207,963	£5,000	£2,434,259
2035	£3,589,524	£5,000	£3,953,977
2040	£5,814,543	£5,000	£6,401,497

Second Brother's Portfolio:

Year	Portfolio Value	Investment	Total after 10% Interest
2016	£0	£10,000	£11,000
2020	£51,051	£10,000	£67,156
2025	£149,374	£10,000	£175,312
2030	£307,725	£10,000	£349,497
2035	£562,750	£10,000	£630,025
2040	£973,471	£10,000	£1,081,818

How incredible is this? They've both invested the same amount, and received exactly the same level of interest. The only difference is that the first brother started his journey much earlier, and that was the clear differentiator. He reaps the rewards of interest on interest for a longer period of time causing his portfolio to grow exponentially.

So what's the point here, I thought this book was about selling, not investing? Well the point I'm trying to make between investing and selling is that compound work rate can work the same as compound interest.

What is compound work rate?

I define compound work rate as long-term continual actions, as opposed to short-term binge actions. Think of it in terms of our investment portfolio earlier, the first brother started his investment portfolio early and he invested little and often. This is the approach we want to follow. To become a sales icon we need to have regular continual exercise of our sales disciplines, basically everything highlighted in this book.

We must make our cold calls no matter if we have a customer base, we must put in the training hours no matter our knowledge base. We must plan our approach despite how many times we've done this before, we must set our goals no matter how many we've already achieved. Every discipline we have discussed in this book should be exercised continually and regularly.

Think of this book as your different investment portfolios and invest your time into each one of them. If you do that then you will become a sales icon.

"Genius is 1 percent inspiration and 99 percent perspiration" – Thomas Edison[31]

Compound Work Rate tips

So let me discuss some tips to ensure that you reap the benefits of compound work rate:

1. Skill depreciation and compound work rate

The negative to becoming successful is that often we neglect the activities that made us successful which can cause skill depreciation. Think about how a car loses its value the older it gets, it depreciates. Well, it's possible for your level of skill to depreciate also. When salespeople become successful often they start to drop core activities that made them successful, commonly cold calling is dropped. Skill depreciation will happen with any skill, but to make my point let's use cold calling as an example. Now cold calling is a skill, an art if you will. The more practice you put in the better you become at it. The more cold calling you do the better your pitch becomes to hook in the prospect on the phone, the better you deal with reservations on a call and the better you deal with being rejected, brushing it off and moving to the next one. But like any skill, if it goes unexercised you'll lose your talent for it. Take sports or playing an instrument, how many people do you know who could play fluently as a child if you put the instrument or ball in their hand. However, if you did so now they'd struggle as they've lost that talent that was once there. If you're good at anything in life you need to exercise it, not just to get better but to maintain that skill level. Let your practice slip and so will your proficiency in that area.

This point is highlighted in a study named the Swedish International Adult Literacy Survey which tested participants on a broad set of information processing competencies[30]. The study tested 622 individuals in both 1994 and 1998.

They were given tasks which related to three areas:

- Prose literacy – the ability to understand and use information from texts
- Document literacy – the ability to understand and locate information contained in various formats, including maps, tables, graphics
- Quantitative literacy – the ability to apply arithmetic operations to numbers embedded in printed materials

The literacy ability of participants was measured on a scale from 0 to 500 based on findings of both tests that were four years apart.

The study took particular focus on work interruptions, which were defined as time off work, whether that be through unemployment, long-term illness, childcare etc. The study concluded that there was statistically strong evidence of a negative relationship between work interruptions and skills. Their estimates implied that one year out of work would move an individual 5 percentile points down the skills distribution. In addition the wage reduction would account for between 16 and 29 percent.

This information is staggering; it shows that there is direct correlation between work interruptions and a person's skill level. So let's apply this to our sales role. The moment I stop cold calling for a month, a quarter or a year the more skill level I will lose in this area. We must use the skill or lose it and what a waste it would be to lose it. Think of the countless hours you have spent grafting, dial after dial all to throw that skill set away just because you've developed a customer base. So exercise your cold calling, even if it's just a few calls every week, as the saying goes, every little helps.

2. Don't let peers compromise work rate

This is most common for salespeople starting out either in selling or in a new role. They hammer away at their selling activities, making the gruelling cold calls, doing networking events, dropping in at customers, making sales pitch after sales pitch and winning some business but losing others on their way. They get to a stage of slight discontent thinking 'is this going to work out in the end?' As they plug away with veracious work rate they look around at some of their peers and see many of the top salespeople in the business working in a rather contradictory manner. Their work rate couldn't be further removed, they're not proactive, they're not conducting any of the selling activities like cold calling, they're simply waiting at the end of a phone for a call or an email from their customer base to place more orders.

The effect this has is what psychologists call deindividuation. Psychologist David G. Myers defined this as 'doing together what you would not do alone.'[32]

Deindividuation happens when an individual is seduced to follow a group's behaviour or actions. It can work both positively and negatively, for instance on a positive front take a fitness class such as spinning. Deindividuation can lead to an individual pushing themselves harder within a group who are working hard than they would without them. But there's a negative side too. What deindividuation in essence does is take away your inhibitions, sometimes morals, and even fear of accountability. It's the reason why bad or good behaviour within a group can spread like a virus. If you walk into an office and everyone is procrastinating then you'll have to fight with the unconscious stimuli to procrastinate too. Conversely, if you walk into an office and every salesperson is hitting the phones dial after dial then deindividuation is going to push you to follow their lead.

This is one of the reasons why in my coaching I talk to individuals about their self-control and compound work rate, making them aware of deindividuation and how to avoid it. Additionally when I talk to businesses, I'm trying to promote practices to encourage positive collective behaviour. As with deindividuation if we can get a group conducting positive activities like cold calling then that behaviour will snowball to other individuals and unconsciously push them to do the same.

The tip here is don't be influenced by your peers. You don't know what their goals are, they might be happy with the number that they sell, if so good for them but that's not you. The pitfall many new salespeople make is that they justify this type of attitude as the norm, but all they're seeing is the here and now. That lazy salesperson who is at the top can't have always had this attitude, at some point in the past he must have put in the grind and now he's taking it easy. You may have not seen the years of grind he put in to get where he is now. What I can assure you of though is that if you stay true to your cause, keep putting in the work then the benefits of compound work rate will pay off and you'll soon surpass your peers

3. Out on the road excuse

Here's an excuse I get commonly, 'well I had lots of meetings that day, so I couldn't make any phone calls.' Does that sound like something a sales icon would say? Not at all! We need to overcome excuses like this. I understand that if you have a couple of meetings in the day that you're not going to make an abundance of phone calls, but why not make some. Set a minimum threshold with yourself, set something like for every meeting I attend I will make five phone calls either before or after my meeting. To enable that I'm going to collate a list of say fifty prospects, on a piece of paper or on my device to use as my list for when I'm out on the road. This way if you have three meetings in a day you've promised yourself that you'll make at least fifteen phone calls too. Let's be honest, we can all spare the odd few minutes before or after a meeting to make a few calls so hold yourself to a higher standard, set a minimum requirement and stick to it.

4. Set your minimum drop in calls

Alike the point above why not set a minimum number of drop in calls too. Say that for every day that you have a meeting you will at minimum conduct two drop in calls. Then if I have five days of meetings I know that I will at least conduct ten drop in calls. Set such a standard with yourself and stick to it, that way you will religiously conduct drop in calls no matter what the circumstance.

5. Start early

I see so many salespeople who will work the odd day of overtime but to an extreme extent. They allow their tasks to build up to an unmanageable level and then work till late one night to get everything completed. Now whilst I champion this commitment, I truly think it's unnecessary, consistency will always win in the long term. That's why I propose starting early every day. Instead of having one day a week where you work two or three hours extra instead start every working day half an hour or an hour earlier. The consistency will pay off. If you simply put in thirty more minutes extra every day that would give you an extra one hundred and thirty hours work a year; that amounts to fifteen extra days per year. Getting in thirty minutes early every day is hardly a big commitment, but the productivity increase of fifteen extra days a year could be massive. It could be the difference between being an average salesperson and being a sales icon. Plus what I've found is that this can be your most productive time. In my experience most people will only work for the hours they're contracted to in most instances. So if an office begins work at 0830 then the majority of people will walk in just before that time. Those who choose to start at 0800 have a workplace Mecca, a silent space for sheer concentration. This is the reason why that thirty minutes can often be your most productive time of the day. No distractions just complete concentration on the tasks at hand.

6. Networking

Why not try setting a minimum number of networking events that you must attend on a monthly basis? This may not be in everyone's comfort zone but it's often a great resource for developing business as where else do you get from ten to one hundred influencers or decision makers in one room as a captive audience. But take the compound approach here, network regularly and network often to have the most dramatic effect. Set your minimum criteria such as I'll do one breakfast networking session and one evening networking session a week. Then if you begin to see results then undertake more networking. The point here is don't be the person who half-heartedly networks. If you're going to do it commit to it, be there for every regular session and for the longevity, don't be that person that attends on the odd occasion and then after six months never comes again.

7. Make that extra phone call

If I walked into a typical sales floor at three periods in the day I can predict what I would see in terms of activity from the salespeople on the floor. The first period would be at the start of the day, let's say that a sales team start at 0900 hrs. I can predict that when I walk onto that floor that the vast majority would be chatting about something, making a coffee or checking their emails.

The second period I'd assess would be ten minutes before a lunch break, again I think I could predict that most of the floor would be looking at the clock waiting for lunch, maybe finishing off a few tasks.

The third period I'd assess is before the end of the day, say the last hour of the working day. Again I could predict that most of the floor would be sorting some quotes or sending some emails.

The crux of this point is that I can't predict exactly what the salespeople would be doing but a can predict what the majority wouldn't be doing in these times, and that's calling. That's our big differentiator. If I walked in to that sales floor at these three times and on each occasion there was a salesperson hitting the phones then I could say categorically that that person has the potential to be a sales icon.

So my point here is pick up the phone. No matter what the time is, no matter what your peers are doing your focus should be on picking up that phone and making calls. The customers are outside of the office you sit in, they're not going to come to you. So build that path to your future, with every phone call you make you lay down more of the pathway that's directed towards your success.

Use what we discussed already, think about your reverse funnel planning. What's the minimum number of calls you need to make a day to achieve your goal? Break that down into its daily activity and make sure you never miss that goal of phone calls for a day. If in the worst-case scenario you miss that target for whatever reason say meetings get in the way or a crisis happens then don't let it slide, add the deficit to the next day. If you ensure that every single week you surpass your minimum activity then you will succeed. So whether it's first thing in the morning or last thing in the day, pick up that phone and make your goals a reality!

These are just some tips you can take on board, but I recommend developing some of your own. If you ensure that your work rate and productivity is always high then you will become a sales icon. It may not happen tomorrow, it may not happen in six months, but it will happen just have faith. Compound work rate is just the same as compound interest. The more work rate you put in the more customers you'll develop and more sales you'll make. The higher your work rate the more you'll get out of your customers by maximising their account spend and keeping them satisfied to remain a customer for a long time. Then the more customers you have the more the number grows in an exponential fashion. Success breeds success, they'll talk to friends of theirs and refer you to them. So ten customers will grow to fifteen, then fifteen to twenty, then twenty to thirty and so on and so on. Most probably your business will recognise you too. The better you become at closing the more leads your business will pass to you, they'll consider you as the closer and pass you bigger and better leads the more that you continue to close. All in all the harder you work the easier it will get so persevere, push through the pain, the rejection and the frustration, just focus on applying compound work rate and it will pay off!

If you can't produce quality, then you must provide quantity, then in time the quality will come.

6.6 – Communication

Quality of communication differentiates the average salespeople from the sales icons. It is key throughout the sales cycle, whether it be for prospects, new business customers or accounts, if you fail to communicate effectively then you're unlikely to bring on board new customers, and if you manage to its unlikely that you'll be able to keep them.

Brainstorm if you will for a minute some circumstances where you as a consumer were on the receiving end of both good and bad communication. What made those experiences good or bad?

Let me share with you some of my own, let's start with a good experience.

Communication – good experience:

As a consumer I had a small issue with a mobile phone I had purchased, no major pain but a slight annoyance. I decided to contact the manufacturer (a well-known brand that I won't name) to ask for support. Initially, I went on their website to look through their frequently asked questions (FAQ) to see whether I could fix the issue myself. Unfortunately, I couldn't which didn't upset me, but I saw on their webpage that I could undertake a live chat with a support engineer who could help me with any queries.

Straightaway I'm thinking that's brilliant, simple, easy communication, therefore I put a big tick in the box for ease of communication.

I conducted a live chat with a support engineer and it took less than one minute for a support engineer to come online to help me with my issue. Tick number two, a great experience for speed of response.

On the live chat they undertook a live diagnostic of my mobile, the support engineer talked me through everything as he worked through the diagnostics and he couldn't have been more knowledgeable if he tried. Third tick, communication demonstrated their in-depth expertise.

The diagnostics found the problem and they fixed it remotely from the live chat which was great, but it doesn't end there. Their follow up was of the highest calibre too; the first point of follow up was that they emailed me directly with comments of our conversation and how it had been resolved. In addition they scheduled a call back for a week later to check that the fix had worked and that I was satisfied, and then that I was happy for them to close the ticket logged in my name. Yet another tick in the box, this time for follow up.

So on reflection a great service, the communication was exemplary, in particular the areas they ticked off were:

- Simple and easy communication channel
- Speed of response
- Expertise communicated
- Follow up

Communication – bad experience

Now let me tell you about a bad experience I had, in this circumstance I was a partial customer. I was working in IT and one of my customers had a requirement for something that we couldn't offer but I could outsource to a partner of ours. I thought that this was great, I had an additional area where I could aid my customer despite it being a solution outsourced to a partner through my business.

The experience started OK, I called them and told them of my customers' requirements, my account manager said that she'd put some things together and then get back to me. I left the call more or less happy, eagerly awaiting their response. A few days passed, and I became slightly fretful, I had heard nothing from my account manager, no email or quick courtesy call or anything. So I decided to be more proactive and get in touch with them and ask what's happening with my request. At this stage I'm already slightly peeved as I'm having to chase them when in this scenario I am their customer.

I call my account manager and I am told that she is off on holiday for two weeks. I say okay well can you tell me what's going on with the request I made a few days ago. The representative I speak to knows nothing of my request as they have no CRM system and thus I have to explain the whole situation and requirement again to them. At this stage I'm slightly disgruntled, then the representative says that they'd have to pass me onto someone else who specialises in this area. I say okay that's fine, the representative says that the specialist, let's call him John, will call me today at two o'clock when he's free.

Two o'clock comes and goes, I feel myself getting more and more frustrated. Not only am I frustrated at the way they're treating me, but I'm concerned as to how this will affect my reputation with my customer as he is waiting for me to action this for him. It gets to four o'clock and enough is enough, I call them again and ask for John. Outraged as to why he missed his deadline with me I ask what happened, he defensively explains that the message hadn't been passed onto him. To make matters worse he wasn't aware of the situation and requirement therefore for the third time I have to explain it all again.

This hopefully demonstrates to you a pertinent example for bad communication, the conclusion to this circumstance is that the partner let me down on numerous occasions to follow and I vowed never to work with them again. The point of these examples though was to highlight good practices we can follow with regards to communication.

Practices we can follow:

There are numerous practices that you can follow to provide customers with good communication, some key practices I have highlighted below:

- Acknowledgement of communication
- Regular updates
- Keep to your deadlines
- Follow up

Acknowledgement of Communication – this is so important and often an area where salespeople fail in their communication. If a customer gets in contact with you through any medium, it is important that you acknowledge their communication in a timely manner. In sales icon training we set a maximum time of half a day for acknowledgement of communication, this is a maximum threshold and not a goal remembers. The reason we need to acknowledge communication is to prevent uncertainty for our customers, they've taken the time out of their day to ask us for advice, at this point in time we're important to them and it's our chance to prove that we can help them.

Now the reason that most salespeople fail here is not through lack of intent, most commonly it's through omission of communication. Take this scenario and see if this has ever happened to you in some form. Your customer emails you asking a question, you're not sure of the answer so you forward the email on to the relevant person in your company and ask them to contact your customer to answer them. Sound familiar? Now you might be fortunate in the fact that your colleague gets in touch in a timely manner, but you shouldn't rely on this. As if the circumstance arises where your colleague can't respond quickly enough, then uncertainty will develop in your customers mind. At this point they will either contact you again and ask if you have actioned their previous request, or the worst-case scenario happens where they ask the question of a competitor and they respond much faster. Either way your lack of acknowledgement of communication creates uncertainty for the customer which could lead to you losing their business.

How can we acknowledge communication?

Take the previous example, all that would be needed is one small step to prevent any uncertainty in the first instance. That step is simply acknowledgement, either an email or a call (email has traceability) to say you've received their message, then give them the answer or course of action such as 'I've passed your request to my colleague John, he will be in touch in the next few days to answer your request.' Simple acknowledgement of communication and the customer will be satisfied, even though you haven't been able to answer their question straight away you're doing all you can to help.

Note – don't rely on others, acknowledge the communication, delegate if necessary and chase up. So if I passed an email onto John to contact my customer regarding a request I would call John the next day to see if he's got back to the customer. If he hadn't I would find out when he would be in contact, if necessary explain that to the customer, and again chase up at that later time or date to ensure it has been undertaken.

Regular Updates – here's a comment you will never hear, 'I decided to move to a competitor because you were over communicating.' It cannot happen, you cannot over communicate to a customer in relation to a request so don't worry about it. If you have to email them every day saying sorry no update yet then do so, just keep them in the loop with what you've explored, what hasn't worked, what may work etc. With that approach you'll gain much more confidence from the customer as they know that you're taking ownership and doing everything in your arsenal to help them.

Deadlines – in order to become a sales icon we must always meet our deadlines. Therefore if you agree with a customer that you'll call them back at four o'clock today when they're free then make sure that you do so, set a reminder in your calendar and call them at four. If they don't pick up leave a voicemail and state how you've called back at the time you had agreed, straight away you'll gain credibility. Or if you've said to a customer that you'll come back to them with an answer or outcome by a certain time make sure you do come back before that time. Where salespeople often fall foul is that they don't communicate because they haven't got the right answer yet. This is a terrible practice to follow as you don't know when you will get the answer you require and your customer is none the wiser.

This sounds slightly confusing so let's use a quick example. A prospect or customer of mine calls or emails me, they ask me a specific technical query about my product or offering. The query is more technical than my knowledge base spans, so I inform the customer that I will converse with my technical team and come back to him by close of play tomorrow with an update. I then contact my technical team and ask the question, most probably they can't answer my query straight away, so it sits in a queue. My next step is that I add a calendar reminder in my diary to get back to my customer, I schedule it for midday tomorrow, so I have some leeway before my close of play deadline.

If I've heard back before that time then great I can inform my customer, if not my calendar will remind me to chase this up with my technical team. If my technical team still doesn't have an answer for me and won't have one by close of play then I inform my customer by simply updating him before the deadline that I don't have his answer yet but we're working on it, I will come back to him within two days with another update. Then the process starts again, I may escalate my request with my technical team if necessary and I'll be sure to set another calendar reminder in my diary with the deadline agreed with the customer. This way your customer is confident that we're working on his query. The key here is to hit your deadlines and update your customer even if you don't have the answer yet, communication will give the customer peace of mind.

Follow up – the more interaction you have with a customer the better your relationship will be, fact! Make sure you follow up, take the example we had above of the query I had to pass to my technical team. In this case once I've provided my customer with the answer to their query that's not the end of the process, I must follow up. How do I know that my customer is satisfied with this answer, they might have other queries that follow on from that. Also it's a good reason to interact with the customer, you can simply call and say I was just following up from your query a few days ago, were you satisfied with the answer? Were there any other questions that you had? Separate to that query let's catch up about…? Rest assured they'll be impressed by your intent to help them by following up.

How will I know if I'm failing?

There are so many signs that will highlight if you're failing to communicate with customers effectively. One noticeable sign that I use as a good indicator is customers chasing you. If a customer has to chase you as a follow up to a query they have made then you're failing. If we're honest with ourselves we have all done it, we're in our busy working day dealing with tasks of high priority when an email from a customer comes in asking a question. We see the email, read it but we've got too much work on to respond to it straight away, so we leave it. That left email waits and waits without any acknowledgement of its acceptance, until our customer emails or calls us saying, "Are you dealing with this?" this is the beginning of the failure; our customer will already be slightly dissatisfied by the fact that they've had to ask twice and now we're on the back foot.

As I said this is a key tell-tale sign that we're failing, there are many other signs such as the most dramatic of losing a customer. If however we follow the disciplines highlighted in the section we will always have effective communication. Remember, you can't over communicate!

6.7 – Nurturing

A parent nurtures a child through infancy to adulthood with food, warmth and shelter moving up to education, hygiene, manners, ethics etc. This nurturing to some extent never ends it just changes form, often from being quite basic nurturing to more complex with time. In sales both your prospects and customers should be nurtured in the same manner, they're your baby. Effective nurturing is the way that we ensure those prospects and customers will flourish with us and not our competition. But how do we nurture effectively?

Well let's reflect on what an average salesperson does. It may sound familiar to you, it definitely does for me as I've been a culprit until I knew better. An average salesperson will call a prospect or customer, then they may follow up with an email or two, but what're the traps they fall into? Well let me highlight them:

- Calling lacks purpose
- They use generic marketing emails that shout mass production flyer
- There's no plan, structure or focus to their activity
- Little to nothing is recorded
- They give up early
- Irregularity of contact time

So let me explain these traps in more depth.

Calling Lacks Purpose

"Hi John, I'm just calling

- For a catch up?

  Or
- To see if there is anything I can help with or quote you on?"

Whilst some of the time this will work, it's not the most effective. Instead we want to create purposeful calling.

Purposeful Calling

Some things we can do to create purposeful calling are:

- Outline from the outset of a call the key things you want to understand such as 'John there are three things I wanted to bring up with you, those are X, Y, Z, now regarding X did you…?'
- Provide a brief synopsis of previous interactions such as 'John we spoke in April and June regarding X, and I've since sent you some material via email to demonstrate Y, what were your thoughts on…?'
- Refer to collateral you sent through via email such as 'John I sent you an email detailing X and how Y became more efficient by 20%. I have some more insights to share with you but first I wanted to ask what your thoughts were on…?'

Try these three techniques on for size and I assure you that you'll keep people on the phone for longer and open more opportunities. What will strengthen your position is your nurturing as it'll give you an additional touch point and a reason to call the prospect or customer again. We'll touch on this next, but prior to that we'll discuss the pitfall.

Generic Marketing Emails

We've all seen them, they're big and bold, they have links on and can't be created simply through your outlook alone. Let me ask you a question, you receive emails all the time, what do you do in your personal and work life with these emails? That's right, more often than not you click delete without even looking over the email as you know it's just mass marketing spiel. It's not personal, it's not bespoke so why would you care for it. Now most salespeople do the same, they'll use their CRM and send a generic marketing email like this to prospects and customers thinking that it'll help, chances are that it won't. It may be simple for you to do, just click a button for it to self-formulate and then click send but honestly, it's wasted time. Instead try using nurturing emails.

Nurturing Emails

So what are nurturing emails? Well, first let me focus on the fact that it's a plural, alike any nurturing a singular activity is unlikely to have an effect if any. A nurturing email should be written personally and never be overly formal, conversational is usually the ideal. The key aspects to nurturing emails are

- Hand written
- Personal, yet can be used on mass
- Focused to a particular topic such as:
    - Your offering
    - Market trends
    - A new solution
- Captivating subject line
- Record the use of topics
- Nurture – have regular touch points

Handwritten is the first key part, think back to what most people are doing, most people are sending generic marketing material. How do you differentiate yourself? Well why not write it yourself or at least make it appear that you've written it yourself.

Personal is the next point, though these email topics are likely to be used on mass, make them seem personal, maybe even bespoke the odd part if it'll help. Use their name, use conversational language, make the customer feel like this email was directly written to them. Maybe even put their name or company name into the email once or twice, if they feel that someone has taken the time out of their day to write to them then they're much more likely to give it a gloss over. The balance here is we want material that we can use on mass, but yet is written in such a way that the reader feels it's been written for them. Even with bespoke parts we're talking maybe thirty seconds of adaptation, not rewriting whole passages for them.

Focus on topics and see what effect they have. I've highlighted above how some topics may revolve around your offering, market trends or a new solution but there are countless possibilities for you to explore. Don't get overly hung up on this yet as we'll be using some examples shortly which will show you what I mean. The point I want to stipulate is to use different topics, try things and see what works for you. For me I always find that a reservation of salespeople and cold calling is that they need a reason to talk to the prospect, or they run out of things to say. This is where most salespeople revert to the calling that lacks purpose as above, "Oh Hi john, I just called for a catch up." Conversely, if you're using nurturing emails then you've got focal points to your calling and something to talk about.

Example

Let me give you an insight into how an IT solutions provider put together their email nurturing campaigns when I worked with them. They developed two categories for their email nurturing, the subjects of a nurturing email would relate to either category. Those two categories were

- Vendor emails – this consisted of any email campaigns that revolved around a vendors solutions such as Microsoft or HPE
- Offering emails – this consisted of any email campaigns that were centred around their own business and their offering

The email campaigns that fell within each of these categories were plentiful, I don't expect you to understand what the campaigns stand for just the concept that each campaign has a name. Some of their campaign list included the below:

- Vendor offerings
    - Office 365
    - Nimble Storage
    - Azure Information Protection
    - VMware vSan
- Offerings emails
    - Outsource
    - Introduction
    - ITIL accreditation
    - Legal credibility
    - SMB backup
    - Sole IT manager etc.

Hopefully you get the point here how there were two categories of nurturing emails, then a plethora of campaigns that fell within those categories that all had a name, the name part is important later.

Just for some ideas of content let me share with you the content of one of these email campaigns, let's pick Outsource email, have a look at the content of this below:

Outsource email:

Hi Phil,

I know that you receive a million and one emails but I was hoping to be the one that slips through the net. I work for a company called X, we work with many organisations of your size who outsource part or all of their IT management to us.

We at X are an award-winning IT Solution provider who can help with any IT needs you may have, we work with small one-man band organisations to multinational corporations like A, B, C to name a few.

Why Us?

The biggest statement I can make for why you should consider us is the following:

- *We're at the forefront of IT innovation, for example our Managing Director sits on Microsoft international advisory board*
- *We have 94% client retention rate on our managed service contracts which is some feat when you consider that we have hundreds of customers throughout the UK*

How Would This Work?

We design support solutions to your exact needs. Whether you'd simply need a person to be on the end of the phone who you can call for assistance with an IT issue, to a more proactive service whereby we would install agents onto your workstations or servers to monitor and prevent issues before they occur. Our focus truly is finding the right solution for your business to assist you in your strategic goals.

Range of Offerings

We have a wide range of offerings, such as:

- *Helpdesk support*
- *Proactive Monitoring and break/fix of desktop and server environments*
- *Cloud Backup*
- *Managed Anti-virus*
- *Spam protection*
- *Web filtering*
- *Solution consultancy, design, supply and implementation*

I'd love to come in and meet with you to learn more about how you operate and give you an overview of X and how we may be able to assist you in the future. Whether this is used to benchmark us against your current IT outsourcing partner or even simply so that you have an alternative option should anything go wrong with your current partner.

If I can help with anything then please do get in contact with me.
I look forward to speaking to you again soon.
Kind Regards

Hopefully, this example demonstrates what I mean by a personal yet mass production email. What a business uses as content is down to them, or down to the individual salesperson.

Captivating Subject Line

Most of the time a buyer will read a subject line and decide whether an email is even worth opening, hence your subject of an email is powerful. So don't be drawn in by the typical marketing spiel that everyone does, you know what I mean, things like 'top 10 tips for...' Or 'Expert Advice on...'

Try things that are more personal, that have a better chance of the recipient opening, here's a few subjects I've seen that have had great success:

- Now Your Back From Ibiza (if they were away on holiday to Ibiza of course)
- You don't know me, but I'd like to say Hi
- John have you considered this? (Insert appropriate name of course)

Be creative with the subject line, yes sometimes you'll have to be more formal depending on the recipient but try and be creative and stand out from the rest. If you find out a prospects favourite sport or sporting team maybe use that i.e. 'insight to a fellow X fan' alternatively use topical news, or humour. The point here is be different and get noticed, make the subject look intriguing enough for someone to at least open the email.

Recording Email Topic Activity

One thing we don't want to do is cover the same ground twice. I see countless salespeople emailing content to prospects multiple times in the hope that on the third occasion it'll make a difference, it honestly won't. All it does is waste your time and make you look unprofessional if a prospect realises you've sent them the same content on three separate occasions. Therefore it's important to record when you emailed a prospect or customers and what the topic was. Hence why earlier I emphasised the point of naming each campaign with a unique topic.

So basically if I followed this practice I would keep a record of my email nurturing activity. Let's say that I work for that IT solutions provider I mentioned earlier, and I had emailed a prospect called Port Enterprises five times already in an email nurturing campaign. Then for each nurture email I send I would add it to the list denoting the topic and date of the email. It would look something like the following:

Company = Port Enterprises

Emailed
01/02/17 – introduction **15/02/17 – outsource** **01/03/17 – office 365** **15/03/17 – SMB backup** **01/04/17 – ITIL accreditation**

Do take note that date stamping the activity is key, later in the book we talk about the sales icon lever concept, so I won't go into too much depth here. But the point of date stamping our activity is that it provides us with a record of when we've been in touch. We want to balance our activity, enough to stay in our prospects minds but not so much that we bombard and constantly pester them. So if we record and date stamp our emails we know when is best to call in between that time, and when sufficient time has passed to constitute emailing them again but with a different topic.

The time lapse between one nurture email to the next is down to you, I would advise as a rule of thumb don't let the time lapse longer than a month with any prospect.

Nurturing – Not Giving Up

Again let's spend some time just to think about the average salesperson. Just process the following findings:

Finding One – 44% of salespeople give up after one follow up (the marketing donut)[33]

Finding Two – the average salesperson only makes two attempts to reach a prospect (Sirius decisions)[34]

Just reflect on this for a second, just to be above average I need to follow up three times with a prospect, when you look at it like that it's easy to be better than average. What will take us from above average to a sales icon is effective nurturing, regular touch points with a prospect, that's what leads to sales.

So don't be that salesperson who just sends two emails, tries to call twice and then concludes that the prospect obviously is not interested. Persevere! Keep nurturing them, keep calling them, send them emails on different topics and you'll notice more and more that prospects become more receptive, longer conversations start happening, more meetings get booked, more opportunities come your way and more sales get made. Effective nurturing is the secret, use it wisely and effective to lay your path to become a sales icon.

Nurturing Medium

I've touched upon email nurturing in great depth and I expect it will be a medium that you use regularly and thus the concept of nurturing in this manner is simple to understand. But honestly, email nurturing isn't the only form you can use, there are multiple mediums at your disposal.

Let's think about some, for instance the following:

- LinkedIn – The concept would be almost exactly the same as emails in direct messaging people but instead through this platform. Or maybe you could focus more on blog posts and writing content.

- Direct mail – often an overlooked route, but powerful. Everyone loves a letter with their name handwritten on it, it makes them feel important. Why not try a direct mail nurturing campaign on various topics alike you used for email. You could even use the exact same content if it was easier.
- Webinars – an incredibly powerful source that can be utilised. I can remember working with an IT security company who used this very well. They would run nurturing webinars on cybersecurity in blocks of four, one session a week for four weeks. Week ones session would be the basics, with every session becoming more and more complex.
- Workshops/seminars – how about educational workshops or seminars, each one nurturing and building the content more and more.

I could continue with ideas, but I won't as it's your job to surmise what's best for you. But on that subject I want to leave you with a thought from this piece. Just imagine the scenario whereby you're my prospect and I'm selling to you. Over a three-month period we've had a couple of calls from a cold background, you've read a handful of emails on different content that I've sent across. To strengthen my cause you've also seen two direct mail letters on additional content. You've been so impressed that you've jumped on the first of three interesting webinars and have a seminar booked in your diary from us to attend next week. How bowled over would you be by me and my business. Would you definitely buy, well I can't say, but you'll be much more likely to. So to conclude here, the point I'm trying to make is use multiple mediums in conjunction with one another to really strengthen your proposition.

6.8 – The Sales Icon Lever Concept

'Give me a lever long enough and a fulcrum on which to place it, and I shall move the world.' – Archimedes[35]

This is exactly what we're doing, in our profession all we're ever trying to create is enough leverage to make a sale. Have you ever looked up the definition of leverage, if you haven't then here it is:

Leverage – use something to maximum advantage

So basically this entire book is based on leverage, it's all based on optimising and maximising an advantage. Where can we use our time best? What businesses are best suited to our offering? Where can we get the greatest results for the least amount of effort? Everything is leverage!

Take a power lifter for example, they'll need to eat right, train hard and in the right manner. Challenge themselves continually until they have enough strength to lift that personal best deadlift or squat or bench press whatever it is. For them all of their endeavour is for leverage, tiny minute efficiencies to maximise an advantage. Our selling is the same, we need to maximise certain advantages to make the sale, we need to create leverage.

We've covered a vast amount of content on the mastery of certain concepts and disciplines to become a sales icon. The sales icon lever concept is such that it compromises the majority of items we discussed from our sweet spot to transitioners.

So let me first start with the concept. Picture in your mind a lever, such as the below:

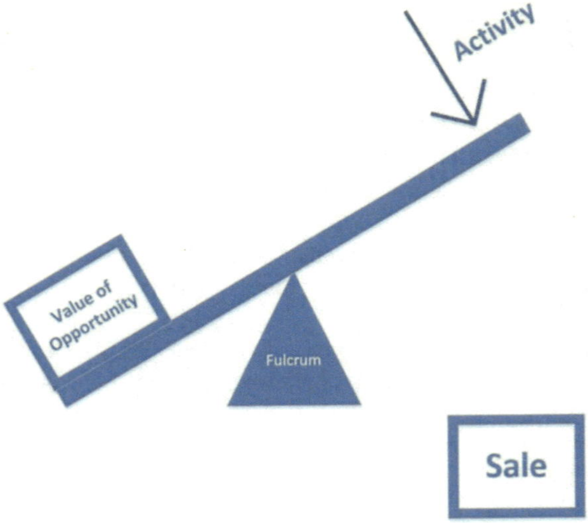

Now don't let me lose you here, we're definitely not about to verge into any Archimedean proofs of the equilibrium of levers. What we are going to do though is position this concept of a lever in our mind for every single opportunity we ever will or have had. So the starting point is think of an opportunity that you have and picture this as a lever. On the left-hand side of the lever is a large load, this represents the size or value of the opportunity.

The right-hand side of the lever represents the activity. Every single piece of activity is represented by a certain weight in sand which will be added to the load value on the right-hand side.

The SI lever concept simply works like this, if we add enough weight to the lever to move it from a fully locked downward position to a fully locked upward position then we make the sale:

- Fully locked downward position = no sale
- Fully locked upward position = sale

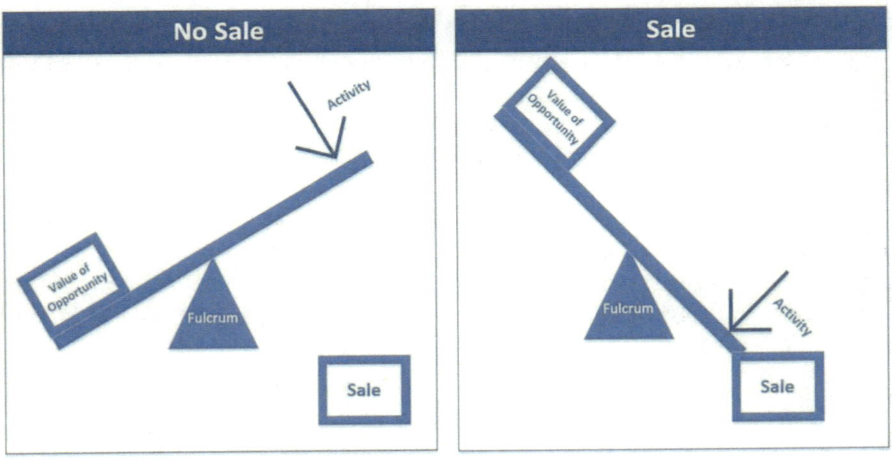

How to add weight?

We add weight to the winning side of the lever by using any form of activity. Every single piece of activity holds some weight in sand; however; some activities will be heavier than others. Let me explain this. So if I email a prospect, that activity on its own will add let's say 5kg of weight to the winning side of my lever. But if I was to use a transitioner with more of a substantial effect, let's say we get a prospect to trial a solution, then this would be worth more weight, say 500kg. So what this concept should be creating in your mind is the view that all activity is positive in that it will push you towards your goal of winning a sale. Yet certain activity will hold such weight that merely by itself it can be more valuable than ten other activities put together.

So here's the next question you'll be asking, what makes one activity hold more weight than another? Well an activity will hold more weight if it offers greater influence towards making a sales. Thus some activities are more compelling on this front than others. For instance a meeting will hold more weight than a phone call, or a trial will hold more weight than a demo. What do them weights equate to? Well I can't tell you that and there is no exact formula as it will differ from sale to sale, but more commonly than not, certain activities will add more weight than others. Therefore if we can grasp which activities are most compelling, we can refine our approach by using less activities that hold greater weight and consequentially make individual sales with less activity. This would mean we have more time free to open up further opportunities.

Key concepts on adding weight:

- Every activity adds weight
- Some activities will add more weight than others
- If we can determine the most compelling activities we can reduce our activity per opportunity, bring in more opportunities and make more sales

Opportunity Value:

The value of the opportunity is the size of the load on the left-hand side. This value will differ depending on the opportunity, if it's a £10k opportunity then this will reside on the left-hand side, and the same for a £50k opportunity or a £1m opportunity. There's no correlation between the weight added in activity and the value of the opportunity. What I'm saying is that a £1m deal isn't necessarily any harder to win than a £10k deal, sometimes it might be, but sometimes the smaller ones can be just as hard to win if not harder. So don't be fooled into thinking the larger the value the more weight that's needed on the lever. But if you're fooled into thinking this then it's not the worst thing.

Example:

So just to strengthen this concept in your mind let's touch on a simplistic example before we add some more complexity to the concept. I have a £50k opportunity and so far I have conducted the following activity:

- Five phone calls
- Three emails
- Two meetings
- One trial

Then my lever would look something like this visually:

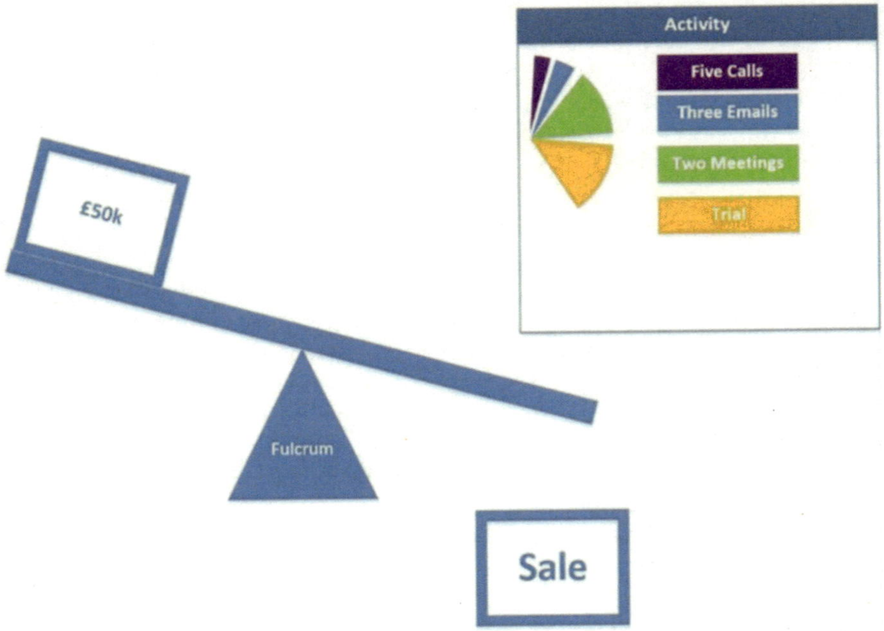

The Hourglass Activity Cradle:

So thus far you get the basic concept, now we'll add a bit more complexity. So looking at the various diagrams previously, I want you to focus on the right-hand side of the lever, the activity side. Now with any sale one thing that will apply is the fact that

"Time kills all deals!"

So what do we mean by this? Well it's simple really, the longer a proposition is mulled over, assessed, adapted etc., the more chance it has of being lost. The same is true for our activity for any opportunity; if there are months between one activity and another then the chances are the weight that we added from the previous activity has all dissipated as so much time has passed. Momentum is very important, more on this later. This is where we incorporate the hourglass activity cradle. So picture in your mind an hourglass, one side of the hourglass is full of sand, then you tip the hourglass upside down and the sand slowly seeps to the other side until it is empty of all its sand.

So now look back to our SI Lever, on the right-hand side they'll be a cradle. With every piece of activity you conduct a certain weight of sand will be placed into that cradle proportionate to the influence that the activity had. The drawback is that this cradle has a small hole in the bottom, just like an hourglass, therefore the weight of any activity will decrease as time moves by (as momentum slows) .

So this should tell you that in order to successfully win an opportunity we must be constantly filling up our hourglass activity cradle to counteract the weight being lost and adding more weight to reach our goal of a sale.

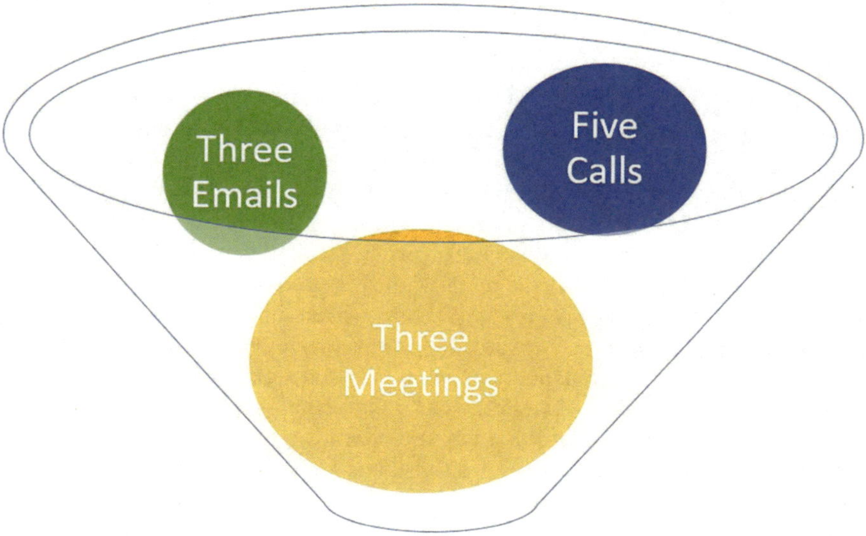

Typically the best salespeople are those that are fanatical prospectors. Those individuals who have the highest amount of activity on a consistent basis. Whether that be through phone calls, emails, meetings, networking events, social selling activities etc.

We put the correlation down to the familiarity principle which we talked about earlier. Basically the more familiar we become with anyone the more their barriers dissipate, "we develop greater positive feelings the more we are repeatedly exposed to something." So the more familiar we are to a buyer the higher the chances of them buying from you.

The power and consistency of our activity has a correlated effect on the buyers likelihood to buy from us. We explain this using the activity cradle concept because it creates a powerful and lasting image in your mind for every activity that you conduct. If you but visualise every activity adding some weight to your proposition then you'll be more inclined to

- Want to conduct activity
- Be conscious of what activities have greater weight behind them

It's a simple mentality change. Instead of aimlessly calling or emailing customers or prospects, take a step back. Think about what activities you have already used and the weight you have added to your proposition. Try to change your mind-set to think of activities as adding weight to our proposition, then we will be enthralled to conduct more and more activity and thus become a fanatical prospector.

Remember though that time kills all deals. Momentum influences the entire sales process. Whether you are cold calling and trying to get a prospect to give you air time on the phone or if you're attempting to close a sale with a new business prospect or even a customer. If you don't have momentum, then chances are you won't achieve the desirable output. Whether that be the opportunity to meet with the buyer, or opportunity to quote or fundamentally the ability to sell to them.

It's a funny thing momentum, because it's incredibly hard to develop, but also it dissipates incredibly fast. The moment we lose momentum in the sale is the moment where that sale is lost. Momentum is like a truck pull, if anyone reading has ever seen world strongest man, think about when the strongmen compete in the truck or aeroplane pull. For those who haven't seen it it's quite self-explanatory. It's a man with a truck or aeroplane strapped to a harness which he needs to pull ferociously until he crosses the finish line.

For any strongman pulling this, the initial stages of getting the object moving are so challenging, it almost takes all of their might just to get the tyres to slowly begin to turn. Though the hardest challenge presents itself when their momentum falters. As soon as they lose momentum they'll struggle to move the object again.

Sales is the same as this. It's all about momentum. To gain the sale we're metaphorically pulling the buyer towards the sales finish line. Every piece of activity that we conduct adds to our momentum or weight to our activity cradle, but over time momentum will slowly start to fall. The law of momentum has the same effect in sales, as soon as we lose it, chances are that the sale won't be attained. The other thing to be mindful of is as we get closer to the sales finish line we should be ramping up the

- Number of activities
- Medium of activities
- Power of activities

Build and build your momentum. Do this effectively and you'll notice that you close more sales.

Activity

Picture in your mind all of your opportunities as levers all in a row. They all hold a certain value at one end, and all of them will be at a different point of elevation depending on the activity that's been conducted.

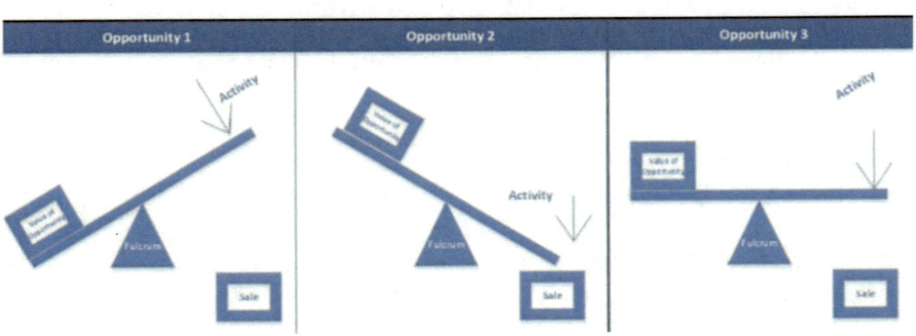

Competitive Levers:

It's been simple up until now, undertaking activity to add weight to your activity cradle isn't the only thing to be considerate of. There's always competition sniffing around any opportunity that you'll need to fight off, and guess what? They have a lever too.

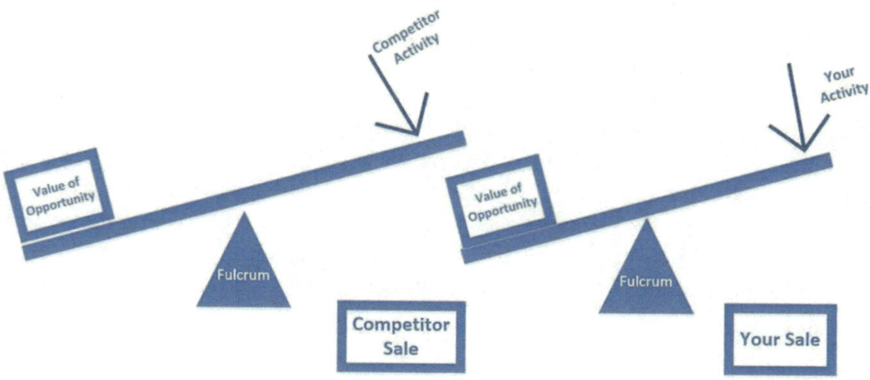

Take the image above, this shows a simple concept of a competitor's lever on the left-hand side and your lever on the right. The levers both work in opposing synchrony, if you edge closer to the sale from any activity then a competitor's lever will edge further away from the sale. Vice versa applies too, if a competitor conducts an activity that influences the prospect then they will edge closer to the sale and you will move further away.

The point in this concept is to keep you hot on your toes with your activity. If your competitors are edging closer to a sale then you're moving further away. Bear in mind also that chances are you'll be competing with multiple competitors for one single opportunity. So your single lever may have five, ten or even more opposing levers to fight against in order to make the sale. So with this you should be asking yourself, what activities have my competition conducted? How many competitors am I against here? Does my prospect favour any or have a good relationship with any? How can I differentiate my proposition and hence activity from the crowd of competitors? All of these and more are great questions that come simply from picturing your opportunity as a SI Lever and multiple competitive levers fighting against yours.

Why I love the SI Lever?

Don't get me wrong, this is no exact science, but it's a fantastic way to measure our opportunities. Just the concept alone will make you think about activities, it will spark questions like what more could I add to my hourglass activity cradle? When was my last activity for this opportunity? What activity would add more weight? How can I add the most weight with the least effort? If we think like this and ask ourselves these types of questions then we'll close more sales and edge further towards our sales icon status.

Applying what we know:

In this section we're going to tie in everything that we've learnt in this book, I won't go into masses of detail as you can refer back to the specific parts of the book should you need a refresher.

Chapter One – Time

Everything in chapter one will help you in using your time effectively so that you can develop more opportunities and therefore more levers, there's isn't anything that directly applies, but indirectly it all applies.

Chapter Two – Planning

Reverse funnel-planning is your starting point, it'll tell you how many levers you need taking into account your conversion rates. Then all of the other topics in this chapter will increase your chances of closing the right business. For instance when you're identifying your prospect attack plan you'll be looking at the right size of business to attack, that sits in your sweet spot whether that be because of vertical, geographical location, seat size, turnover etc. If we do this right then we will have multiple levers which have a higher chance of closing as they're suited to our business offering. Moreover these prospects you identify are worthy of pursuing, for instance their value on the left-hand side of the lever is worth winning.

Chapter Three – Sniff Out What Sells

Alike chapter one, everything here applies to the lever principle but indirectly. If we can apply the right lead generation, plan it to a tee, utilise efficient channels and forecast our results then we're onto a winner. This chapter is what differentiates the average sales to the extraordinary. It's the difference between having ten mediocre levers to having one hundred levers all of a large value. This helps you to develop the levers but doesn't really help you in adding any weight to the hourglass activity cradle, that's where chapter four comes in.

Chapter Four – Preparation

Our preparation ties our pursuit to generate more levers with our focal point of adding weight to our proposition through activity. Things like our reference literature and basics of the sales process will aid us in building more and more levers. Then the showstoppers come in, those being the sales journey plan and transitioners. The two most profound concepts that will help you to add weight to your proposition in a timely, sequential and organised manner that all leads to one result, yet another sale!

Chapter Five – Motivation

Generating levers, adding weight to them and making sales can seem like an easy concept. But to battle through the daily struggle, the setbacks, the constant rejection, the stress, the targets, come to think it all of the negatives involved in selling is a challenging task, so maintaining our motivation is essential. This becomes even more integral when we become successful and regarded as a sales icon as this is where complacency often sets in. So, we must remind ourselves of our How, What, Why goals to keep us striving to the next visionary goal for our lives and prevent any plateau in our success.

Chapter Six – Success Formula

Like anything in life, there're a few hacks that you should be aware of, apply them and you'll be incredibly prosperous. Forward appointments, the staple makeup to any sales icon. Seldom do I find a high flyer in sales who doesn't pack their day with meetings, find me a poor performer and chances are their diary is empty. Forward appointments on their own will be strengthening our cause and adding to our activity cradle for an individual opportunity.

Basically the SI Lever concept ties in the whole book. Every sales opportunity is its own lever, use the tips in the book to:

- Develop more levers
- Add weight to levers
- Close our sales opportunities

From here on in think of every sale in terms of a lever. Visualise it, when and what activity have I conducted? How much weight does that activity hold? What more can I do? If you visualise each opportunity in this way you'll intrinsically ask yourself questions of this manner and start to close more and more opportunities as you develop the answers for yourself. Remember, it's not about the number of activities you conduct, it's how compelling that activity is and how much weight it adds.

6.9 – Calling Time of Death

Have you ever watched a soap opera or movie that had a scene in it where a person is being resuscitated? They'll be a doctor or nurse pumping away on a person's chest, pump after pump of arduous, tiresome work. Now with any person who passes, there will be a point in time where the doctor or nurse deems that their efforts to bring them back to life are futile and they call time of death.

Now apologies for the morbid scene but the concept works well for calling time of death with any opportunity. Think of the doctor scenario again, if they spent an hour attempting to resuscitate every person then most of their work would revolve around this. Whereas if they but tried all they could do to save the patient's life but called the time of death say after fifteen minutes of resuscitation then they'll have more time to save other lives.

Your sales opportunities, prospects and customers are no different. At some point you need to ask the question of when do I call time of death on this. This is so that we don't waste time on lost causes and instead use our time more effectively on other activities.

I understand completely that it's hard to let go of prospects, opportunities and customers, I've been there. You have a couple of who you have invested a significant amount of time into. Maybe you've called them many times, sent emails, had meetings, they've attended workshops etc. You get to a point where you feel like you've invested too much time to walk away now. Don't fret, it's not just you that feels this way.

It's down to something known as the sunken cost fallacy. Such sunken costs are payments that have been made that can never be recovered. It's easy to think of this first in monetary terms, but sunken costs work in the same way for effort or time invested. Hal Arkes and Catherine Blumer conducted a great experiment on this in 1985 which explained its effect perfectly[36]. They asked subjects of the experiment to assume they had spent one hundred dollars on a ski trip to Michigan. Then not long after they informed the subjects that they found a better ski trip to Wisconsin for fifty dollars and also bought that ticket. Shortly after it transpired that the two trips were at the same time, therefore they would need to pick only one and no refund could be provided. They could either pick the Wisconsin trip which was better suited to them, or the more expensive trip Michigan. You can guess where I'm going with this. The study found that despite the Wisconsin trip being better suited to them, more than half of the subjects opted for the Michigan trip as the loss felt greater if they had not attended this one.

Sunken cost fallacy will affect you in the same way, you'll want to hold on to the things that you've invested time and effort into. It's natural! The more time and effort you've put into something the harder it is to walk away. But we do need to call time of death in certain circumstances to increase our success, now let's look at some techniques to help us call time of death.

Before I go any further I just want you to note that when I say time of death I mean the time whereby we stop focusing on, and chasing a prospect, customer or opportunity in the short term. Calling time of death is never forever.

The point of this section is to help you with your balance. We've talked in depth about how the majority of salespeople don't persevere enough, they give up after the first call or don't follow up etc. Now you've read most of this book and I very much doubt that you'll be one of these people. Where you'll now fall foul is having so much to do but so little time. When you first start out in sales you're happy to chase any sniff of an opportunity as you have little else to attack. Even if you've got a tiny chance of winning a sale you'll often take it at this stage in your sales career or new job. As you become more successful this can't remain the same though, you'll have too many prospects, customers and opportunities to devote your time to that you'll have to be ruthless. You'll have to say when you've made enough calls and emails to a person or made too many reiterations of a proposal. If you don't become more ruthless then your day will be unachievable, you'll have too many calls to make, emails to send, meetings to have, presentations to prepare etc. and you'll be left feeling like a failure. This is where calling time of death comes in. It helps you decide whether that £1k opportunity is worth the tenth call this month or whether you should meet with that prospect again for the eighth time in two years who has never spent with you.

So how do I call time of death? Whether that's opportunities or prospects often the same things apply. But first things first we'll only call time of death on certain opportunities or prospects, for many I'm sure that you'll have a good feeling about them so I'm not talking about those. The ones I'm referring to are those that you're not so sure about. For me I focus on a few key things, those being:

- Value or potential
- Closing calculator
- Right fit
- Previous activity and interactions

Value or potential:

First things first I'll look at value or the potential of bringing the customer on board. If the value is low then it's easy for us to call time of death. However, for those opportunities we're uncertain about that hold a shiny price tag, those are the ones that are hard to let go. So first of all look at the value, if it falls below a threshold then call time of death. If it's above then keep it in. The size of threshold you use is down to you.

Closing calculator:

This is specifically for opportunities. I would use this in conjunction with an opportunities value, if I've got a tier one or two opportunity for a high value then chances are that I'll continue with this opportunity and not call time of death for some time if at all. Whereas if I've got a tier three or four opportunity then regardless of the value there's a higher chance I'll call time of death on these at some point.

Right fit:

As a salesperson you'll be ever the optimist, but honestly not every business is the right fit. So use what you discovered earlier in your sweet spot analysis. Is this business right for you? Do they fall within your sweet spot, if they don't then it may be worth calling time of death?

Previous activity and interactions:

What activity have you conducted? Have you exhausted everything you can? What's their interaction been thus far? These are the type of questions that will help you in calling time of death. If you have a prospect that is perfect in every way and you've explored every activity you can to encourage them to work with you, but you've had little to no interaction back then it may be best to call time of death on them.

Note – a word of caution with time of death, I reiterate what I mentioned earlier. This only applies to those opportunities or prospects that you're unsure about, not everyone in your prospect list or pipeline. You could have a cracking opportunity that falls outside of your sweet spot, you might be fully confident about it because of certain factors and so in such circumstance you definitely wouldn't call time of death on it. Only apply this to those you're unsure about. Be careful not to be overly ruthless too. I have countless examples of persevering past most salespeople and it paying off with making the sale. Be ruthless in a way that saves you time to repurpose elsewhere, the goal isn't to be less busy, it's to be more effective with our time.

6.10 – First Experience and Givers Gain

Now I don't condone the use or distribution of narcotics, however many drug dealers use a particular sales technique which can be a powerful approach. They poach new business customers by providing them with a fantastic first experience, two approaches they typically use are:

- Offering a freebie
    - As they're confident the user will become hooked and come back to them
- Offering their best grade drug to create a positive first experience
    - Then on later sales they drop the quality of their product

We have much to learn from such an approach. The key being, the art of the sale is in the first experience. Psychologists who have looked into human behaviour and psychology have found that first experiences dramatically effect an individual's future decision-making. Juliusson, Karlsson and Garling (2005)[37] found that when an individual experiences something positive from a decision they are more likely to decide in a similar way given a similar situation. The converse is true also, people tend to avoid repeating past mistakes.

If we know this then why aren't we using this to our advantage? First of all we should be using the drug dealer sales technique through either a freebie or trial of our product or solution. The plan is to give the prospect first-hand experience of how great you are so that they get a taste of what they're missing out on.

But securing a trial or offering a freebie isn't enough on its own, this is only half the battle. This first experience is essential, we've already talked about how a positive first experience will lead a person to opt the same way in the future. So we must make sure that the first experience is exceptional!

So how can you do this? What are the things that you can do to make the first experience exceptional for your prospects? Crack this and then just like a drug addict, they'll keep coming back for more!

Here are the core three tips I would recommend for an outstanding first experience:

- Communicate
  - Do this often, gain feedback and make sure the prospect is aware of everything that's going on and when
- Monitor
  - Monitor things your side. Make sure the things that are meant to happen do happen, and at the time they should
- Advise
  - Give the prospect advice as to how they can get the most out of the trial or freebie

If you've got to this stage in the sale then you're so close to being successful and making that sale. Don't make the mistake of letting things run their course without your influence. Do everything you can to build an exceptional first experience for the prospect.

So the take away is:

1. Come up with something you can offer on a trial or freebie that gives the prospect a taste
2. Develop a plan to ensure the first experience is exceptional

Before we move on I just want to accentuate the point about freebies and how imperative they can be. The point I want to make is that sometimes giving things away pays massive dividends. Often it can be the differentiator to your competitors, the gesture which gains you more air time, but most of all it's even more exposure. That exposure with the buyer, in whatever format builds familiarity, which dissipates the buyers' barriers and increases your chances of making the sale.

Sales icons call this the 'Givers Gain' approach, to demonstrate its power, let's start with an example. Many of you will know of or will have watched the Christmas classic 'It's A Wonderful Life'. If you haven't then just for your insight it is voted as one of the best Christmas films of all time. But why is this?

Well it maybe news to you that when it was first released in 1946, its reception from audiences and critics was poor. So much so that the film company that produced it, namely Liberty Films, went bust. It's what happened next which was astounding.

In 1974 the movie entered the public domain, meaning that TV stations across the land could play the film at no cost and air it as many times as they wanted. Naturally, this meant that the film was aired on many channels regularly every Christmas. So the exposure of the film was much more than any other Christmas movie. It was due to this that the film became a fan favourite, despite its poor results when it was originally released. Overtime people saw it regularly every Christmas, and that regular and consistent exposure turned it from a flop to a fan favourite!

So what's the point? Well if the film company hadn't gone bust, chances are that this film would have been yet another movie which would sit in the failed and forgotten list. But because they went bust, the film was given away for free so the broadcasting firms used it regularly.

It's the same in sales. Often the things that we give can lead to massive gains. So don't be reticent to offering trials or giving away freebies, this could be the step which enables you to make the sale.

Activity

Spend some now making a list of the things that you could give away to gain more exposure with a buyer. There are loads of things, from trials of products, to services such as consultancy. Every business out there has things it can give away.

6.11 – Reservations

When we get to the stage in a sale where we ask for an order, it's a rarity that your prospect or customer will just give you it straight away. Every so often we get a lay down sale, meaning that it all runs smoothly, you ask for the order they say yes and you go from there. However, commonly you're going to come across reservations, which we all know are usually a good thing, and often are buying signals in themselves.

I encourage all sales icons to ask two questions:

1. What reservations do you have if any?
2. What else is in the back of your mind?

First step is to ask the reservations question, or a reworded version that works for you. Then we need to counteract these reservations, whatever they might be, and face them head on. Now I can't tell you what to answer to them, as every reservation will focus on your business or offering. What I can help with is a sales icon tip, known as the reservation break down.

The Reservation Breakdown

The reservation breakdown revolves around negativity bias. We as human beings have some level of negativity bias; some have a stronger bias than others. What it means is that negative items will have a more powerful effect on our psychology than positive or neutral items, even if they're of equal intensity. So in simpler terms, if I'm gambling and win one hundred pounds one day, then the next day I lose one hundred pounds, the loss will have greater intensity psychologically despite the amount being the same.

Think about your own life. How many times have you had a great day, then one thing bad happens and it's all you can think about for the rest of the day. Well that's negativity bias in action.

Now that you understand negativity bias we can talk about the reservation breakdown. Now to overcome any reservation we must first understand what the reservation is, commonly a reservation will be dominated by negativity bias. For instance, if my offering had five main components, a prospect may like four of them but be unsure about one part, and because of negativity bias that part they're unsure of will overshadow everything. That's where the reservation breakdown comes in, we want to break down their reservations to find its true source and then attack it head on.

Keeping with my example of five main components, I'd break this down with the customer. I'd ask something like 'John, we've highlighted the key five components to our offering, which parts are you very confident in?'

They may answer something like component one to four, I'm paraphrasing obviously. Then my next question would be 'how do you feel about component five?'

Then I'd focus on overcoming whatever reservation they have. By breaking it down I know what I'm up against and what I need to overcome to get the sale. Conversely, if I don't break this down then I'm guessing, all I'll be doing is trying to overcome reservations that aren't there.

So start with the reservation breakdown as a first port of call, find out their true reservations and what you need to overcome.

Now in any case, when you're closing a sale whether there be none, a couple, or many strong reservations. I always encourage you use positive reinforcement.

Positive Reinforcement

So what is this? Well first off I don't mean give them a treat as you would a dog. What I mean here by positive reinforcement is the process of reverting back to things you have found and reinforcing their positivity. The key is to focus on getting them out of their pain situation and into a pleasure situation as well as reinforce the things they liked. So if they've given you feedback that they like certain parts then reinforce this again, if there is a major frustration that you can help fix then reiterate it. Paint the picture of all the positives from giving you the okay, this is a sure-fire way to overcome the strongest of reservations. All in all we want to take them from a pessimistic state of mind to an optimistic state of mind by focusing on the positives that matter most to them.

So when they say to you 'it's too expensive' or 'it's not the right time' or 'I'm not sure' then focus on positive reinforcement.

So when it comes to reservations, find the root cause of the reservation using the reservation breakdown technique. Once you know where their reservations lie then attack them head on, if you don't then the sale may be in jeopardy. Once you have done this, revert to positive reinforcement. Show them how you'll take them out of pain and into a state of pleasure and focus on the areas that will mean the most to them. Finally close with the question 'What else is in the back of your mind?' This is their final opportunity to give honest feedback regarding reservations. Whatever their answer is, attack that reservation head on again. Try to understand where they're coming from and explain how you can help overcome this. Finally, revert back to positive reinforcement once again and close that sale.

6.12 – Referrals

Referrals are always one of those untapped sources of business; it's a rarity when I see someone using referrals the way they should. It's as if as salespeople we have a mental block over asking for a referral, we're in some way scared to ask the question of our customer, when honestly, we have nothing to lose. Think about it, what's the worst that can happen when you ask for a referral? They say no, or a fancy phrase for no such as 'sorry no one springs to mind.' I can categorically say that asking for a referral won't mean you lose the customer.

My rule of thumb is that I ask every single customer for a referral in some form or another. How do I ask it? Well that's the key. Do I just blatantly ask, 'do you know of anyone else who might also be interested in working with us?' Well sometimes yes I do. But most of the time I like to refine my questioning first. I'll ask them for instance if they attend any networking groups. If so what for and who attends. Then I'll ask if they could refer me onto anyone in these groups.

Or I'll question about their family or friends. Do you have any friends or family who are business owners or X job title? Could I have a chat with them about the work we do together? If you plan it right you can use your customer base to open up hundreds of extra potential prospects for you, all of who you have a warmer in road with as you can mention the customer that you work with who referred you.

How about trying referral business from partner businesses of your customers? I can remember I worked with a construction firm and I noticed that their LinkedIn posts were regularly liked by people within other businesses who they worked with mutually on projects. What did I do? Well I asked my customer if they could broker a conversation with that person, and guess what, they did.

The Favour Referral

This is one of my favourite referral techniques. Think about it for a second, how many times a day or a week do you or your business offer a favour to your customers? When they set you outrageous deadlines which you meet for a favour. When they ask you to help with X or advise on Y for a favour. When they contact you in dire need and you make their life easier all through a favour. Well any favour is a massive opportunity for a referral, and when you fulfil that favour you should always ask for a referral. Will it always come off? Not every time no, but even if it only works 10% of the time that's 10% more than you had. So next time you're asked by a customer for a favour, fulfil it and then ask that magic question.

6.13 – Closing

I'm not going to go into too much depth on the subject of closing as it's a rather large topic. Though I do want to introduce to you a sales icon technique which can drastically increase your close rate. It all stems from a theory, we'll delve briefly into the psychology of that theory, its application in the real world and an example of how it can be applied.

Remember the common trait in sales that 'Time Kills All Deals.' The longer we give a buyer time to deliberate the worse our chances are. If they are given the luxury of time then they will scrutinise whether the solution is right? They will question whether they've evaluated the market sufficiently? They will ponder if the solution can be changed or amended in a certain way?

The longer that the deal hangs in the balance the unlikelier the close becomes. Now whilst we must give customers sufficient time to evaluate their options we should also be influencing and potentially incentivising them to speed up their decision making process.

So how do you do this at the moment? Are you simply proposing a solution and then leaving it to lady luck as to when it closes? Don't worry if you are, I've been there and done the same. The great thing is that your competitors probably do this too, but now after reading this you're going to have something in your arsenal to differentiate yourselves.

So to the point, how do we speed up the close? Well it all comes down to something known as the commodity theory also known as the scarcity effect. According to the theory, within human nature the instigation of scarcity enhances the perceived value or desirability of the item in question. This is why retail giants use such techniques as limited time offers or statement like "only while stocks last." It's one of the reasons why black Friday or cyber Monday are so prolific when it comes to sales. We think the offer is going to come to an end so we buy it and then we have the outlook that we've got a good deal.

Don't be under the misunderstanding though that the commodity theory only relates to price as it doesn't by any means, price however is often the route which people use the commodity theory for.

So how can we use this? Well we can use this theory to our advantage to influence a customer to buy from us in the short term. All we need to do is create some scarcity. So one way is the price route, something like we'll offer a percentage discount if the deal lands this month. But what about limited time offers that will benefit the customer if they buy in the timespan you desire.

Let me use an example. I worked with an IT provider who was pushing to sign more IT support contracts. We addressed their close rates and found that they weren't using commodity theory to their advantage. So we brainstormed a few items that could be used in a scarcity offer and we came up with the following:

If you opt for the IT support contract this month then we will offer:

- 1 day Cyber Security Training Session RRP £850
- 1 credit per month of a PC setup RRP £2,400

The result? Their close rate skyrocketed.

Activity

Spend ten minutes brainstorming how you can use commodity theory to your advantage. What items can you push to create scarcity? Remember that we want to create scarcity to influence the customer to buy in the short term.

Conclusion to Success Formula Chapter

This chapter has got to be one of my favourite chapters in this book as it applies so many lessons I've learnt from my own and other sales icons careers. Take forward appointments for instance, I've met seasoned veterans in sales who still don't do this, consequentially they have and always will have average results. They get to stages of the year when their pipeline is minimal, they have few if any meetings in the diary and the pressure starts to mount both personally and from their superiors. All that needs to be applied is to forward appoint, reappoint from the meeting you're in with the person or agree to meetings that are a couple of months away. The more people we meet with the more successful we will be, simple as that.

What about nurturing as a lesson learnt, such a simple and effective technique that is rarely applied. If I nurture effectively I'll always be in my prospects or customers mind, I'll look different than every other salesperson. Just reflect on the average salesperson again, they'll put in the odd call and maybe even send the odd erratic generic email. But they'll have no structure or nurturing in their approach, they'll be competing with hundreds of other salespeople who all do the same and get forgotten easily. Whereas he who nurtures will be different and get noticed for that reason. You'll use multiple mediums to nurture, content will be bespoke and interesting as well as the fact that contact time will happen at regular intervals. You won't ever be in the circumstance whereby four months or more go by without any contact taking place for a prospect. You'll set minimum contact periods for all prospects, aiming to nurture them in some way once or twice a month at minimum.

The sales icon lever concept is another thing I truly love in this chapter. When you've been applying this regularly you'll start to visualise every opportunity as a lever in your mind. Your brain will begin to fire into action and think of transitioners or other aspects which will add weight to the sales side of the lever. With that you'll also visualise the hourglass activity cradle to create some urgency in your proposition to ensure the sale goes ahead. It's a brilliant concept which when executed correctly can lead to the realms of success that only a sales icon experiences.

Every part of this chapter on the success formula is beneficial, so take it all in, apply it and adapt it to your approach. I only wish that I knew all of this earlier on in my career, then many of the mistakes I made would never have happened. I hope the items addressed help you too.

Key Takeaways – Discipline 6 – Success Formula

- Forward Appointments
  - The more people we meet with the more successful we will be
  - Always reappoint in meetings
  - Sell the benefit of meeting with you again
  - Focus on increasing your billables
- Initial Meeting Goals
  - On a first meeting don't
    - Expect a sale
    - Overly fact find
    - Push too much of your company or offering
  - Instead focus on
    - Getting a reappointment
    - Building rapport
    - Invoking interest
- Exercising Core Sales Icon Stages
  - Make sure that you continually exercise each stage including
    - Profiling
    - Prospecting
    - Selling
    - Account management
- Questions and Pitching
  - Find out what's important to them
  - Focus on pain and pleasure questioning
  - Always question in a logical and sequential manner
  - Use a benefit buffer to get the answers to more sensitive questions
  - Use leading questions to steer them down the sales path
  - When pitching opt for the sniper approach as opposed to the scatter gun approach
- Compound Work Rate
  - Be consistent in your work rate
  - Never become reluctant to make a cold call
  - Don't settle for the excuses of your peers
  - Hold yourself to a higher standard, set thresholds and goals for your work rate and meet or exceed them
- Communication
  - Quality of communication differentiates the sales icons from the average salespeople
  - Remember to

Acknowledge communication
Provide regular updates
Keep to your deadlines
Follow up

- Nurturing
    - Be purposeful when you make a phone call
    - Use nurturing campaigns as opposed to generic marketing content
    - Record and date stamp nurturing activity for each prospect or customer
- The SI Lever Concept
    - Every opportunity sits on its own individual lever
    - You add weight to the sales side of the lever through activity
    - Add enough weight to the sales side and you'll tip the scale and make that sale
    - Be conscious of time, the hourglass activity cradle will come into play, remember that time kills all deals
- Calling Time of Death
    - Trying to resuscitate someone who can't be brought back to life is pointless
    - Be conscious of the amount of effort you expel for an opportunity and how that is received and the progression rate of the opportunity
    - Endeavour with an opportunity as much as you can but be mindful to call time of death at a certain point
- First Experience and Givers Gain
    - Remember that when an individual experiences something positive from a decision they are more likely to decide in a similar way given a similar situation
    - To provide a great first experience use CMA
        - Communicate
        - Monitor
        - Advise
    - The 'Givers Gain' concept can be powerful, reflect back on the example with the film 'It's A Wonderful Life'
- Reservations
    - Use the reservation breakdown technique to get to the crux of any reservation
    - Use positive reinforcement, focus on getting them out of pain or into a state of pleasure or ideally both
- Referrals
    - Don't forget how powerful a referral can be
    - Always ask for referrals
    - Apply the favour referral technique wherever you can
- Closing
    - Remember that 'Time Kills All Deals' so the longer we give a buyer time to deliberate the worse our chances become
    - Apply the commodity theory/scarcity effect to incentivise the buyer to commit

References SI

1. *"Success is processional. It's the result of a series of small disciplines that lead us into habitual patterns of success that no longer require consistent will or effort"*
    a. Tony Robbins – awaken the giant within
    b. Page 15

2. *"Time waste is in some ways worse than material waste because there can be no salvage"* – Henry Ford
    a. Page 17

3. *Equity Theory*
    a. J. Stacy Adams
    b. Page 19

4. Hofstadter's Law
    a. reference Gödel, Escher, Bach: An Eternal Golden Braid
    b. page 45

5. Habit 2 – Start with the end in mind
    a. *Page 50*
    b. Taken from *The 7 Habits of Highly Effective People* by *Steven Covey*

6. *"Vision without action is a daydream. Action without vision is a nightmare."* – Japanese proverb
    a. Page 55

7. *"The probability of selling to an existing customer is 60–70%, the probability of selling to a new prospect is 5–20%"* – Marketing metrics
    a. Page 66
    b. https://www.forbes.com/sites/patrickhull/2013/12/06/tools-for-entrepreneurs-to-retain-clients/#111ef0672443
    c.
8. *"When you're green you grow, when you ripen you rot"*
    a. Page 77
    b. Ray Kroc

9. *"If you're not growing , you're dying"* – various
    a. Page 79

10. *"However beautiful the strategy, you should occasionally look at the results"*
    a. *Winston Churchill*
    b. *Page 94*

11. "*Become genuinely interested in other people, Smile, Remember that a man's name is to him the sweetest and most important sound in the English language, 'Be a good listener, Make the other person feel important and do it sincerely!'*"
    a. Page 121
    b. Taken from How to win friends and influence people by Dale Carnegie

12. Steven covey muses in his book the seven habits of highly effective people how one of the sweetest words to anyone is their own name
    a. *Page 121*
    b. Taken from *The 7 Habits of Highly Effective People* by *Steven Covey*

13. Malcolm Gladwells story on the Getty and the Kouros
    a. From the book Blink
    b. Page 125

14. *"Tony Robbins explains this beautifully in many of his books in that human behaviour all relates back to the principle of trying to gain pleasure or escape pain"*
    a. Page 127

15. *"70% of people make purchasing decisions to solve problems , 30% of people make purchasing decisions to gain something (Study from impact communications)"*
    a. Page 128
    b. https://www.impactcommunicationsinc.com/pdf/nwsltr_2001/ICINwsltrpr0108.pdf

16. The average tenure of a sales representative is 2.6 years (from a study created by the Bridge Group on Sales)
    a. Page 154

17. (Guy Winch Article – https://ideas.ted.com/why-rejection-hurts-so-much-and-what-to-do-about-it/) (University of Michigan studies – http://www.pnas.org/content/pnas/108/15/6270.full.pdf)
    a. Page 154

18. "Tony Robbins calls it CANI (constant and never ending improvement)"
    a. Page 165

19. *The oak sleeps in the acorn. The bird waits in the egg, and in the highest vision of the soul, a waking angel stirs. Dreams are the seedlings of reality.*
    a. Napoleon Hill
    b. Page 161

    Mans Search for Meaning' by Victor Frankl
    c. Page 162

20. *"You become 42% more likely to achieve your goals by writing them down on a regular basis"*
    a. Page 171
    b. study by a psychology professor called Dr Gail Matthews

21. The book was called 'Lead the field by Earl Nightingale'
    a. Page 174
    b. Lead the field by earl Nightingale

22. *"What the mind can conceive and believe, it can achieve"* – Napoleon Hill
    a. Page 175
    b. Think and Grow Rich – Napoleon Hill

23. Three Feet From Gold Story from think and Grow Rich book by Napoleon Hill
    a. Page 179
    b. Think and Grow Rich – Napoleon Hill

24. *"No thought, whether it be negative or positive, can enter the subconscious mind without the aid of the principle of autosuggestion."* – Napoleon Hill
    a. Page 181

25. *"If you don't provide your mind with the programming of the results you desire, someone else will provide that programming for you. If you don't have your own plan, someone else is going to make you fit into their plan."* – Tony Robbins
    a. Page 181
    b. Book called unlimited power

26. *"You can voluntarily plant in your subconscious mind any plan, thought, or purpose which you desire to translate into its physical or monetary equivalent."* – Napoleon Hill
    a. *Page 181*

27. Outliers book mentioned by Malcolm Gladwell
    a. Page 181

28. *"If you think you can, or think you can't, you're right!"* – Henry Ford
    a. Page 207

29. *"If you would win a man to your cause, first convince him that you are his sincere friend."* – Abraham Lincoln
    a. Page 213

30. Study on the Swedish International Adult Literacy Survey
    a. https://core.ac.uk/download/pdf/6559419.pdf
    b. Page 226

31. *Genius is 1 percent inspiration and 99 percent perspiration*
    a. Thomas Edison
    b. Page 226

32. Psychologist David G. Myers defined this as *"doing together what you would not do alone."*
    a. Page 227

33. 44% of salespeople give up after one follow up (the marketing donut)
    a. Page 239

34. The average salesperson only makes two attempts to reach a prospect (Sirius decisions)
    a. page 239

35. *"Give me a lever long enough and a fulcrum on which to place it, and I shall move the world"* – Archimedes
    a. Page 240

36. Studies by Hal Arkes and Catherine Blumer
    a. Page 248

37. First experiences dramatically effect an individual's future decision making
    a. Juliusson, Karlsson, and Garling (2005)
    b. Page 250